PRAISE *MARRIED SEX*

If the enemy can't take out your marriage on the battlefield, he'll do it in the bedroom. If you are struggling to see that God's plan for your sex life doesn't only involve pleasure but power, this book will hand you the keys to unleash God's rich blessing and strength on your marriage. Debra Fileta and Gary Thomas have a special way of combining science and truth in a powerful way. This book will help you become stronger and bring sexy back to your marriage.

Levi and Jennie Lusko, lead pastors of Fresh Life Church and bestselling authors

It's time for Christian couples to renormalize and reclaim God's vision for married sex. This book shines the bright light of God's truth into one of the most dimly lit and underexplored areas of Christian marriage. It's bound to be a treasure trove of wisdom and hope for all who read it!

Ryan and Selena Frederick, founders of Fierce Families and authors of *See-Through Marriage*

When you combine the wealth of knowledge that both Debra Fileta and Gary Thomas have about people, love, and relationships, you get this page-turner. Debra and Gary have skillfully provided a holistic guide to developing and maintaining a vibrant and satisfying sex life throughout the course of your marriage.

Chrystal Evans Hurst, bestselling author and speaker

When it comes to sex within marriage, the church has been awkward at best or silent at worst around the topic. That's why I'm thankful for the work of Gary Thomas and Debra Fileta to help married couples discover the good gifts God has given us through sexual intimacy. *Married Sex* is a practical guide for all married couples who want to know the sexual life God has created for you in every stage of your married life.

Kyle Idleman, bestselling author of *Not a Fan* and *One at a Time*

Gary Thomas and Debra Fileta will help your marriage get pretty hot and your bedroom even hotter. This is one of the most honest and descriptive books on married sex we've ever read. We honestly couldn't put it down. It will give you God's heart on married sex and get your heart pumping all at the same time! If you want to know what God dreamed for married sex, you just found it.

Dave and Ann Wilson, authors of *Vertical Marriage*
and cohosts of Family Life Today

Married Sex is a masterpiece, and it's one of the most practical, biblical, and helpful books on sex ever written. Apply its teachings into your own marriage, and your sex life (and many other aspects of your marriage) will see instant improvements.

Dave and Ashley Willis, authors of *The Naked Marriage*
and hosts of *The Naked Marriage* podcast

Gary Thomas and Debra Fileta have created a positive, balanced, and comprehensive resource that will guide you through the joys and challenges of sexual intimacy. Reading this book together and referring to it throughout your marriage will give you hope, encouragement, and practical help.

Juli Slattery, cofounder of Authentic Intimacy,
author of *Rethinking Sexuality*

Debra Fileta and Gary Thomas are both powerhouses in their own right. I'm thrilled that they have combined their wisdom to speak on this critical topic. Sex can be a source of great joy or great pain. I'm grateful for a resource that guides us into the enjoyment of God's gift according to his beautiful design.

Ben Stuart, pastor of Passion City Church D.C.,
author of *Single, Dating, Engaged, Married*

What a brilliant book! Written by two experts—different genders and different generations—sharing one faith and a common desire to help married couples enjoy God's gift of sex. This is a terrific blend of psychology and theology. Don't miss out on this grounded message, chock-full of practical suggestions.

Drs. Les and Leslie Parrott, #1 bestselling authors
of *Saving Your Marriage Before It Starts*

I devoured this book and was constantly reading paragraphs out loud to my husband. I also found myself taking mental notes of all the upcoming weddings I'm attending and reminding myself to gift these couples with this book. No matter how long you've been married or how awesome or difficult your sexual intimacy is, you will find something beneficial in *Married Sex*. Thank you, Debra and Gary, for this wonderful resource.

Jamie Ivey, bestselling author and host of
The Happy Hour with Jamie Ivey podcast

MARRIED
SEX

MARRIED SEX

A CHRISTIAN COUPLE'S GUIDE TO REIMAGINING YOUR LOVE LIFE

GARY THOMAS &
DEBRA FILETA M.A., LPC

ZONDERVAN BOOKS

Married Sex

Requests for information should be addressed to:
Zondervan, *3900 Sparks Dr. SE, Grand Rapids, Michigan 49546*

Zondervan titles may be purchased in bulk for educational, business, fundraising, or sales promotional use. For information, please email SpecialMarkets@Zondervan.com.

ISBN 978-0-310-36257-9 (international trade paper edition)
ISBN 978-0-310-36256-2 (audio)

Library of Congress Cataloging-in-Publication Data

Names: Thomas, Gary (Gary Lee), author. | Fileta, Debra K. author.
Title: Married sex : a Christian couple's guide to reimagining your love life / Gary Thomas, Debra Fileta.
Description: Grand Rapids : Zondervan, 2021. | Includes bibliographical references. | Summary: "Written by bestselling author Gary Thomas and licensed professional counselor Debra Fileta, Married Sex draws on fascinating research, real-life questions, and practical ideas to help you find greater spiritual and physical joy with your spouse than ever before"— Provided by publisher.
Identifiers: LCCN 2021009789 (print) | LCCN 2021009790 (ebook) | ISBN 9780310362548 (hardcover) | ISBN 9780310362555 (ebook)
Subjects: LCSH: Sex—Religious aspects—Christianity. | Marriage—Religious aspects—Christianity. | BISAC: RELIGION / Christian Living / Love & Marriage | RELIGION / Christian Ministry / Counseling & Recovery
Classification: LCC BT708 .T475 2021 (print) | LCC BT708 (ebook) | DDC 261.8/35—dc23
LC record available at https://lccn.loc.gov/2021009789
LC ebook record available at https://lccn.loc.gov/2021009790

Published in association with Yates & Yates, www.yates2.com.

Cover illustrations: Jasmin64 / vata / Shutterstock
Interior design: Kait Lamphere

Printed and bound by CPI Group (UK) Ltd, Croydon, CR0 4YY

---

22 23 24 25 26 27 28 29 30 31 32 /CPI/ 16 15 14 13 12 11 10 9 8 7 6 5 4

Gary

To Lisa, my "partner in passion"
for more than thirty-seven years now—
with all my love, always.

Debra

To my husband, John—
thank you for being so intentional to love me well
with your heart, mind, and body.
I love you more than words can say.
Here's to many more years of fun and adventure,
both above the sheets and under the sheets.

CONTENTS

INTRODUCTION

Debra

A godly couple I know is living their best sex life well into their sixties. They led a seminar at our church about how couples can keep their sex life hot as they grow in marriage, and their tips and tricks made the young newlywed couples in the room blush. Listening to them talk about how they pretend to be Adam and Eve and go out for a quickie in their backyard late at night, or how they secretly signal each other with veiled phrases when they're in a group, made me realize that sex can (and should) only get better as we grow older. Sadly, however, in my work as a licensed counselor, I see far too many couples whose sex life has never even started or whose sex life got going only for a short season before it collapsed.

One couple, let's call them the Martins, had been married for seventeen years. They had two children, were active members in their church, and had a decent marriage overall. But they also carried an embarrassing secret: their sex life was almost nonexistent. They had sex less than once a month, and the intervals between each time seemed to be getting longer and longer, and harder to keep track of.

Mrs. Martin loved her husband but was struggling to feel a desire for sex. Mr. Martin loved his wife but was struggling to understand *why* she didn't want to be intimate with him. They were coming to the table with completely different perspectives, needs, and desires—and it was starting to impact their relationship. They found themselves arguing more and feeling disconnected from one another. She felt misunderstood; he felt rejected. They felt like they had nowhere to turn. Counseling was their last-ditch effort to try to overcome this struggle.

This couple is not alone. Difference in sexual desire is one of the most common problems couples face in their sex lives. In fact, one survey reveals that more than 80 percent of married men and women report they are dealing with some form of sexual struggle in their marriage, whether it be a difference in sexual desire, a lack of sexual intimacy overall, or the effects of outside influences such as pornography, stress, or fatigue.[1] The truth is that many married couples are not enjoying sex the way God intended for it to be enjoyed. Far too many Christians (who, as we'll explain later, should be enjoying this gift more than anyone) are being robbed of the spiritual, relational, physical, and even neurological gift of a great sex life. Most of them don't even realize what they're missing.

We cannot "fix" a hurting marriage without addressing sexual intimacy, any more than we can sustain sexual intimacy without "fixing" the marriage.* One spouse may want to focus on one side, while the other spouse may be obsessed with the other side. But the solution is almost always both/and.

While sexual frustration is a *common* problem, it's an *uncommon* conversation in the church, because the topic of sex is something that often gets neglected within Christian culture (Gary has a cringeworthy story about this in chapter 1). We spend so much time teaching people to save sex for marriage but so little time teaching them to savor it after marriage. We hold in our hands one of God's greatest gifts yet are not fully appreciating it.

This sorry state of affairs reminds me of a couple from New York who bought a small white cereal bowl from a garage sale for three dollars. Unaware of its true value, they kept it on their fireplace mantel as a decoration for many years. Little did they know that this secondhand

---

* We're not talking about marriages where age, physiological issues, or illness make sexual intimacy problematic, if not impossible.

purchase was actually a thousand-year-old Chinese "Ding ware" bowl produced during the Northern Song Dynasty in the eleventh century. It ended up being sold at an auction for more than $2.2 million. Talk about a great garage sale find!

I wonder if we often approach sex in a similar way. We have it in our possession, yet because of our lack of knowledge and understanding, we underestimate the value it can add to our lives. We settle for the status quo and prop it on a back shelf rather than pursuing a sex life that could bring so much value and pleasure to our lives.

I made it my aim to help the "once-a-month Martins" realize that a satisfying sex life was something that was within their reach. Not only that, but it was something valuable they already possessed! They worked on getting to the root of their underlying expectations and beliefs about sex. We explored possible hormonal or chemical imbalances. We investigated the spiritual and theological foundations of a good sex life, and considered why it mattered to God just as much as it mattered to them. We talked about technique, mutual enjoyment, anatomy, and everything in between.

With time, energy, effort, and communication, they were able to see sex as an opportunity rather than an obligation. They learned that a good sex life is something we make, not something we find. But most importantly, they learned that making love is a process of becoming a better person as much as it is about becoming a better lover. As the Martins' marriage improved, so did their sex life. And as their sex life improved, so did their marriage. The two sustain and build each other up, and that's what this book is all about.

Sex Is a Process

Somewhere along the way, we may fall prey to the misconception that if we save ourselves for marriage, our sex life will be filled with hours and hours of amazing, hot sex. We imagine all the stars aligning, our bodies naturally taking over and knowing exactly what to do. But often our expectations are shattered by reality, and we're left disillusioned by the unexpected struggles of sex. Gary and I hear from so many couples whose sex lives are filled with frustration, fears, and many tears.

Not only do we bring false *expectations* about sex into marriage, but we're also carrying the baggage of unhealthy *experiences* regarding sex. Sexual experiences before marriage shape not only our expectations about sex but also our future experiences. I counseled a couple who struggled with sex because of trust issues and insecurities that continued to come up as a result of their unresolved sexual pasts.

It doesn't matter what side of the spectrum you find yourself on regarding your understanding and experiences of sex, because the truth is that none of us are immune to sexual struggles. But there is hope: a good sex life can be developed through committed work. It is within your reach!

Just like anything significant in life, good sex takes time, education, energy, and practice. I hear from older couples who are investing in their relationship and thriving in their marriage that their sex life always follows suit—getting healthier, happier, and more exciting along the way. The honeymoon night was simply the start—the beginning of the lifelong journey of communication, of intimacy, of getting to know each other, learning to please each other, and being vulnerable enough to give and receive from each other. When we align our expectations of sex with God's purpose for sex and realize that the phrase "making love" puts the emphasis on "making" as much as it does on "love," we can reach new levels of enjoyment, marital enrichment, and even worship. A proper perspective matters every bit as much as proper strategies if sex is to be the best it can possibly be and fulfill its purpose for the entire marriage relationship.

Married Sex

Gary and I are thrilled that you've picked up this book because it means you are ready to say no to the status quo of a bland and boring sex life in marriage and instead open yourself up to learning how to *really* make love. Or perhaps you already have a pretty good sex life but want to enrich it even more. We're excited to bring you this message, because we believe it's close to God's heart, as you'll discover in the coming chapters. When sex is fulfilling and mutually pleasurable, it enhances all of marriage. When it's subpar, it ironically becomes *too big* a part of the marriage. Frustrated spouses act as if "fixing sex" will fix the relationship when, in fact, it's usually the opposite. Unsatisfying sex may not be the problem; far more often, it's the symptom.

We know how hard it can be to find good resources to teach you how to make your sex life the best it can be, so we're teaming up to bring you the best resources we can find—resources built on the unchanging truth of God's Word paired with important psychological and scientific research. In the course of writing this book, we've also polled hundreds of married couples to gather data and interviewed many others to gather fascinating information about married sex. You can find more about our research in appendix 1.

Gary is a pastor who has written and spoken on marriage for more than two decades. He has been happily married to his wife, Lisa, for more than thirty-seven years. He'll help us explore the spiritual realities behind sexual intimacy and the biblical witness.

I'm a licensed professional counselor and relationship expert with well over a decade's worth of experience with clients. I've been married to my amazing husband, John, for fourteen years. I can offer practical strategies and psychological insights to help couples understand not just the purpose of sexual intimacy but how to get there.

The combined efforts of a fiftysomething male spiritual writer and a thirtysomething female licensed counselor will, we hope and pray, produce a unique work that will be beneficial to couples, individuals, and small groups.

Throughout the pages of this book, our aim is to give you the absolute best of both worlds—practical suggestions to increase your enjoyment and experience of sex along with foundational teaching to help you grow deeply rooted in God's truth. We believe with all our hearts that this will be your go-to handbook for married sex—for enjoying this beautiful gift of complete oneness the way God intends for it to be enjoyed. So what are you waiting for? Let's get started!

chapter
one

THE SONG OF ALL SONGS

Gary

Jocelyn and Danny come off as unusually integrated, connected, and intimate. They have the aura about them of knowing each other deeply, without facade, and delighting in who the other is.

"So what's your secret?" I asked them.

"We sleep naked," Jocelyn told me. "And Danny gets a full body-to-body naked hug every morning before he jumps in the shower."

Though they have a very large master bedroom, they sleep in a relatively small, full-sized bed. "It looks like a postage stamp in that room," Jocelyn said. "But we want to be close all night long."

Jocelyn and Danny are living embodiments of the power of physical touch and sight to foster marital connection. This desire to connect and enjoy each other helps them avoid one of the most common marital arguments—yes, the nighttime thermostat setting.

"I've learned not to care what the temperature is," Danny told me. "Guys usually think their wives want the temperature set too high and they complain about it being too hot to sleep and then fight to make it colder. But I'd rather Jocelyn feel warm enough not to want to wear any clothes, so I've trained myself not to care how hot it is."

Jocelyn and Danny aren't newlyweds, by the way. They've been married for a decade and a half, and in Jocelyn's words, "The sex keeps getting better and better and better."

That's not the message we're getting fed, is it? We live in a culture today that wants to fool us into believing that marriage is where sex goes to die.

The common lie that it's "all downhill" after the honeymoon, sexually speaking, allows far too many Christian couples to settle for mediocre or even pathetic sex lives. I'm astonished when Debra tells me how common it is for her to counsel couples who haven't been sexually intimate *in years*. And she's not talking about couples in their fifties, sixties, or seventies—she's talking about couples in their twenties and thirties.

Dr. David Schnarch, a clinical psychologist and certified sex therapist, points out that while our genitals reach peak performance before the age of thirty, "genital prime and sexual prime are entirely different, each occurring at opposite ends of your life span. People don't reach their sexual prime until their forties, fifties, or beyond."[1] A flourishing sexual relationship takes emotional maturity, relational maturity, and spiritual health, all of which can take decades to achieve. He captures the intent of *Married Sex* perfectly: "If you depend on horniness to carry you through a century of marriage,"[2] you're going to be sorely disappointed. If you're willing to build the kind of life, relationship, and spiritual vitality that energize sexual intimacy, your best, most satisfying years, sexually speaking, may very well lie ahead of you.

This evil, stupid lie that sex is most enjoyable and active only at the start of a relationship has stolen more marital pleasure than perhaps any other lie that Satan has concocted. The enemy's plan is always to subvert God's plan, which in this case means encouraging people to have as much sex as they can before marriage and as little sex as possible after marriage. And if sex is one of God's greatest gifts to us, you can be sure it is one of Satan's favorite targets to shoot at to ruin a marriage.

Thankfully, some couples fight back against this false view of sex, people who believe that God's plan for sex is better than anything we could have thought up on our own. These couples are "marriage explorers," determined to map out, traverse, experience, and sightsee in this wondrous "land" called sexual intimacy in marriage.

Christians should lead the way in this endeavor. We worship God when we enjoy his creation, and sex is part of his creation. *But marriage is the necessary context in which sex reaches its supreme beauty.* A woman presenting her naked body to her husband in the privacy of their bedroom is a thing of beauty, intimacy, and loveliness. A woman walking naked through an airport makes us shudder and assume something is wrong with her mentally. Context is everything. Take sex out of its intended context, and a beautiful thing can become an agent of destruction.

The biblical context for a flourishing sex life is *marriage* and *love.* Since God is a God of love, we know that every healthy act of sex must be rooted in love, must be governed by love, and must be an expression of love.

The fact that God created sex tells us quite a bit about him, not the least of which is that he is the kind of God who approves of pleasure that feels transcendent. When we clearly know and love God, we can accurately see and understand sex. When we accurately see and understand sex, we can freely enjoy it.

As we will discover in God's Word, *God loves sex, and therefore we should too.* Scripture affirms time and time again that sex in marriage is not only God's plan but also a splendid gift that is ours for the taking, and one to be enjoyed throughout our married lives.

The Song of Songs

God is a giver, and his gift-giving ability and creativity are stupendous. As I get a bit older, I value the gift of friendship. I treasure the wisdom that pours from the pages of Scripture. I marvel at a grandparent's infatuation with a grandchild and would have laughed at myself years ago if I had known that a photo of our precious little Anna would become my screen saver. My wife and family relish the savor and smell of exotic foods. Adrenaline-soaked pursuits, creative endeavors, musical delights, the exercise of the spiritual gifts—it's amazing how many good things God gives us to enjoy.

And yet none of these good gifts receive a title like the distinctive one given to a long poem explicitly celebrating sexual intimacy between a man and a woman: the Song of Songs.

While some translations prefer "the Song of Solomon," the Hebrew title for this book of the Bible is translated Song of Songs, and that's significant because "something of something" is a powerful and poetic ancient Near Eastern phrasing that leads to an astonishing conclusion.

Let's consider the phrase that describes God as "King of kings." What does "King of kings" mean? It *doesn't* just mean that God is the strongest of kings, the wisest of kings, or the mightiest of kings. It goes beyond that to mean that if you put all the kings of the universe together, God would still be King of those kings. There is no equal; there is not even a close rival. He's different *in kind*, infinitely beyond comparison.

So when describing the sexual relationship between a man and a woman as the "song of songs," the Bible doesn't call this physical union merely the most powerful human experience, the most pleasurable human experience, or the most celebrated human experience—it's called the experience beyond all others. In this book we will discuss everything this sexual intimacy entails—the spiritual analogies behind sex, sex's ability to create human life, the pleasure two bodies can make each other feel in a fallen world, the spiritual connection that is fostered, the way our brains are rewired during sex to desire and celebrate the one we're having sex with—and we will see that no other human experience could hope to rival the "song of songs."

Think about all the songs in the Old Testament that could have assumed this name: the song of Israel celebrating deliverance after the crossing of the Red Sea (Exodus 15); the song of Deborah celebrating victory after God delivered the Israelites from the Canaanites (Judges 5); the song of Samuel's mother celebrating parenthood after the dedication of her promised son (1 Samuel 2); the song of David celebrating success after he defeated Goliath (1 Samuel 18:7). A nation delivered, enemies defeated, a child conceived, a victory won—none of these songs are called the *song of songs*. None of them receive the title given to sexual intimacy in marriage.

Before the writer of this celebrated poem uttered a single point of instruction, his title alone preached a powerful sermon about God's view of sex.

And what an explicit song it is!

Modern readers may not understand *how* explicit this Song of Songs is because it's an "idyll"—a stylized, romantic form of poetry that brilliantly conveys clear erotic truth to any adult who picks it up and can "read between the lines," while not scandalizing any ten-year-old who comes across it and who will be clueless about what those pomegranates, grape clusters, and henna blossoms are really all about. In fact, the ability of Song of Songs to be *so* explicit to the married and *so* innocent to the uninitiated may make it one of the most brilliant acts of authorship ever produced.

A Woman's Pleasure

Jocelyn started attending a women's Bible study, only to be shocked at how regularly some of these Christian women bashed their husbands.

"And the worst," one woman said, "is when I come to bed with my robe on and am reading my book, and he actually thinks I might be interested in sex! Honey, this robe is your clue that the store is closed for the night!"

Most of the women laughed, but Jocelyn grieved. "Danny and I have a strict 'no clothes in bed' policy," she said out loud—and the laughter stopped. "And sex is *always* on the table."

The women looked at Jocelyn like they had heard the most bizarre thing in the world, like she had uttered something profoundly offensive.

"Sex isn't a chore," she explained. "It feels so wonderful. Why wouldn't you want to have good sex? If it's not great, work at it and make it better. I'd much rather come to bed naked and enjoy a good climax at night and then wake up feeling close and connected to my husband in the morning. I'll put on a robe to make breakfast for my kids in the morning, but I would never put on a robe to tell my husband to keep his hands off me at night."

The very next day, Jocelyn received a phone call from one of the leaders. "Jocelyn," she said, "we've been thinking that maybe it's time for you to start your own Bible study. You're so honest and open—maybe that's what God is calling you to do."

You read that right: talking positively about her sex life got Jocelyn thrown out of her first married women's Bible study.

Though it may have been uncomfortable for the Bible study women, Jocelyn was acting and talking very "biblically." The second verse in Song of Songs offers God's fundamental statement about sexual satisfaction for a woman, essentially saying that there's nothing else like it: "Let him kiss me with the kisses of his mouth—for your love is more delightful than wine."

In spoken Hebrew, the words for "kiss" and "kissing" sound like someone kissing (like the word *moo* tries to imitate the actual sound of a cow). The Song isn't a technical treatise; it's a sensual retelling of bedroom antics. And the repetitive "let him kiss me with the kisses *of his mouth*" may sound redundant (what else is he going to kiss her with?), until you realize that the kissing may involve *his* mouth but not always *hers* (meaning he's also kissing elsewhere). She wants his mouth all over her.

Why does she want this?

She wants her husband to keep kissing her because it is one of the supreme pleasures in her life. The Hebrew word describing the husband's "love" is *dod* and refers to acts of lovemaking, not to the emotional feelings. She is explicitly saying that his oral and physical caresses are "more delightful than wine."

To explain the astonishing power and revelation behind this

assertion, let me ask you to go back three thousand years and try to imagine what life was like for an ordinary Middle Eastern woman. There was no cup of coffee and certainly no caramel macchiato in the morning. There was no air-conditioning in the desert at noon. There was no dark chocolate in the afternoon (it hadn't been invented yet). And there was no bed to lie on at night—she slept on a mat or blanket.

She didn't get to wear cashmere. Silk had been invented in China, but it wouldn't have been found in the desert. Virtually every luxury that modern women enjoy today was denied to a woman living back then, except for one:

Wine.

To an ancient woman who enjoyed precious little entertainment, there was no more celebrated pleasure than wine, except, apparently, for sex with a generous, creative, and thoughtful husband.

A modern reader comes across the phrase "your kisses are better than wine" and isn't stopped in her tracks because she has catalogs of pleasure to compare wine to. She might not even like wine! But three thousand years ago, this was a shocking comparison.

So the Bible's book on marital sex *begins* with a woman confessing that one of her highest pleasures in life is being kissed all over by her husband. If it were pictured in a movie, it would go like this: the husband approaches his wife with a full glass of wine and she purrs, "Put that wine down and get busy." The Song says sex isn't just for the husband or even primarily for the husband. The first person to be pleased is *the wife*. The Bible celebrates and sanctifies the pleasure women get from sex.

When Jocelyn was first married, she enjoyed sexual intimacy, "but," she says, "I didn't realize it could keep getting *better*." What helped her value Danny's kisses "more than wine" was growing in understanding.

"Fifteen years ago, I didn't know what I didn't know. I never imagined it would take me a decade and a half to enjoy the best sex in my life. In fact, early on I thought it was great and would have asked myself, *How can it get any better?*—but it does! It's like learning a new sport or playing a new instrument: you hone your craft."

Jocelyn was truly surprised by what she discovered. "When I was a teenager, you'd hear boys talking about masturbation and porn and wanting sexual stuff from girls, but my friends and I never talked about sex like that; it was a whole different level of interest, so I grew up thinking sex was for boys, not girls."

Fifteen years of marriage have radically changed her mind. "When wives push away their husbands, what amazes me is how much *the wives* are missing out. How do you not want to have that release? It feels so good. You sleep better, and the way it brings you closer to your husband that night and the very next day—well, I suspect they're just not having an orgasm, because I don't know why a woman would turn that down."

What helped Jocelyn get to this place? "It wasn't just becoming more knowledgeable about sex. Most importantly, I learned *me* better. I have to turn off the rest of the world and focus on the moment, refusing to think about children and work and the house. At the start I'd remind myself, *This is good. This is what the Lord wants for Danny and me.*"

NOTE FROM DEBRA

I love Jocelyn's attitude about sex with her husband. But as a licensed counselor, I also know that reaching orgasm and engaging in a fulfilling sex life often take much more understanding for a woman than for a man. I've worked with many women who struggle to enjoy the act of sex because their bodies aren't letting them enjoy it. If you find yourself regularly experiencing pain during sex, facing an ongoing lack of sexual desire, or coping with an inability to reach orgasm, there are often both physiological and psychological issues that need to be understood and addressed. I don't want you to read this chapter and think you're not being a "biblical wife." I want you to soak in the pages of this chapter as an invitation to hope, to see that it is possible for you to work toward a fulfilling sex life that is just as enjoyable for you as it is for your husband. I want to pause here and promise you that we will address both the physiological and psychological barriers together in later chapters of this book. You don't have to figure this out alone. We're here to help you get there.

Turbocharge

Song of Songs 1:2 presents quite a picture for wives, but let's venture just a few verses further into the Song of Songs until we hit verse 9 of chapter 1 and find the fundamental statement the Bible makes about the pleasure *a husband* gets from sex: "I liken you, my darling, to a mare among Pharaoh's chariot horses."

When these words were written more than three thousand years ago, the hearers knew Pharaoh's chariots weren't pulled by mares. Only stallions fulfilled that function. Back then, the pharaoh was like the king in a game of chess—if the king went down, the battle was over. Stallions were the strongest, fastest horses in the kingdom, so they were the preferred animals to empower the leader's chariot.

Enterprising Egyptian horse handlers discovered a way to make a stallion go even faster, however. Put a mare among the stallions, and her very presence and even scent could whip the stallions into a sexual frenzy. Sexually excited stallions are stronger and faster than nonexcited stallions. This was how you literally boosted the "horsepower" thousands of years before we could inject additives into combustion engines!

Song of Songs 1:9 presents the picture of a man who glories in his wife's sensuality and who assures her that their lovemaking is an energizing force for good in his life. Remember how Jocelyn described what sexual intimacy did for her? She has seen this same benefit for her husband, Danny. "His personality bends him toward being connected to people. He tends to feel rejected and not loved. When he is loved by me sexually, it's like he blossoms into this other person."

Danny concurs. "Being sexually desired means I'm accepted and appreciated and that someone wants me. The way my brain works, if my wife doesn't want me sexually, then she doesn't want me *period*—and that makes me feel alone and rejected. It affects my identity."

It's worth pointing out that Danny goes out of his way to make sure their sexual relationship isn't primarily about him. He glories in the times he brings Jocelyn to climax and then they both slip off to sleep without him "finishing" or even being inside her, something he thinks every husband should do from time to time.

"It's really not just sex that Danny wants and needs," Jocelyn explains. "It's me being interested in and enjoying sex. Danny certainly doesn't want it to come across like it's a chore. If that's my attitude, I may as well not bother."

They both laughed about a recent morning when Danny literally skipped in the hallway as he walked into work (they work together) after a morning of making love.

"You can see he holds his head a little higher," Jocelyn says, "and his whole day is different."

"Starting out the day like that gives you a sense of confidence about yourself," Danny explains. "I bring a new force and confidence and even creativity to the office when I know Jocelyn and I are connecting."

Intoxicated

One of the things that scared Jocelyn the most about sex early on is also one of the most surprising admonitions in Scripture about sexual intimacy: its *intensity*. For instance, Song of Songs 5:1 (ESV) reads, "Eat, friends, drink, and be drunk with love!"

This is biblical encouragement to let ourselves be carried away by our passion and desire for each other, even to be "intoxicated" with each other. It's God's way of saying, "Feast on your desire; let your passion carry you away." *Within marriage*, this is a safe and holy journey, a divine celebration of the power of sexual passion to make us forget everything else.

As her and Danny's sex kept getting better, Jocelyn was actually getting a bit worried because she didn't like the "out of control" feeling.

"I don't like to lose control because I'm so used to controlling everything: our money, schedules, homework, the kids' meals, their closets, you name it. It's not comfortable for me to be out of control. But to reach orgasm, a woman has to let go. It's scary at first, but the reward is so overwhelming that once you learn to do it, it gets a lot easier."

God apparently designed sex on this earth to give us otherworldly experiences through our bodies (metaphorically speaking, of course). Take Proverbs 5:18b–19: "May you rejoice in the wife of your youth. A loving doe, a graceful deer—may her breasts satisfy you always, may you ever be intoxicated with her love."

The Hebrew word for "rejoice" is a fascinating choice. It's used elsewhere in the Bible to describe how joy is manifested "in joyful frolicking (Jer. 50:11), in stamping the feet and clapping the hands (Isa. 55:12; Ezek. 25:6), and in dancing, music, and shouts of joy (e.g., 1 Sam. 18:6; 2 Sam. 6:12, 14; 1 K. 1:40, 45; Neh. 12:27). The joy is so effusive that one is beside oneself."[3]

The sensual delight a man takes in the beauty of his wife's body leads him to dance! Imagine what that must make a woman feel like—to be so celebrated and cherished. And then Proverbs gets downright sensual, referring to a husband's being *enthralled* by his wife's breasts. This strong attraction is presented as a blessing. The Teacher hopes the husband will continually, throughout his days, be "intoxicated" by his wife's naked body and that the wife will enjoy having this magnetic allure over her husband.

Another couple with whom Lisa and I have become great friends, Darrell and Joanne, use Proverbs 5:18b–19 as they work with married couples. Darrell and Joanne have been married for more than twenty years, but Darrell will quickly say, "I am more captivated today by Joanne's body than I was even on our wedding night, and it's not that my eyesight is getting worse as I get older."

At this point Joanne jumps in and says, "It's true. I'm twenty pounds heavier; my body has aged; and I've got some gray hair now, which Darrell calls highlights, but he is even more enthralled with my body than ever. And now to see Darrell continue to be captivated by my body above all others gives me absolute confidence that this will be true for the rest of our lives.

"When we got married, it felt a little awkward that Darrell loved my body so much. I mentioned it to my mother, who asked me if I would want it any other way—and of course, I wouldn't. She went on to say that I should enjoy enthralling him. Not just that he was enthralled, but that I should actively enthrall him."

"I will always be captivated by her body," Darrell continues. "Fast-forward another two or three decades from now, and I'm certain that her body will continue to excite and intoxicate me. God truly knew what he was doing when he created her body and then wired my mind."

When Darrell and Joanne work with couples, they challenge the newlyweds to try activities such as naked night (no clothes after 6:00, except maybe an apron while cooking). Darrell reports, "It's surprising that this is outside many couples' comfort zones. We encourage the couples to appreciate each other's body and to be 100 percent unashamed and uninhibited. We point out that this is God's design. We recite Proverbs 5:18–19 and parts of Song of Songs. Eventually, they start to understand."

By creational design and divine revelation, God clearly wants a wife's beauty to enthrall her husband. In Song of Songs 7:5, the king says he is "held captive" by his wife's *hair*. In 6:5, it's her *eyes:* "Turn your eyes from me; they overwhelm me." "Captivated" and "overwhelmed" are beautiful and true poetic descriptions of a wife's beauty that arrests her husband's attention.

We are emphatically *not* reducing a woman's power over her husband to her sexual appeal alone. That would be grossly inaccurate. But to deny this power entirely and not seek to understand its creational design is to choose ignorance about the way marriage is designed to work and thus to miss a significant aspect of sexual intimacy between husband and wife. It is a good thing, a holy thing, and a divinely ordained reality for a man to be smitten by the wonder of his wife's body.

The Hebrew word for "intoxicated" (*tisgeh*) is explained by a classic Old Testament commentary as a "morally permissible love-ecstasy."[4] Dr. Michael Fox, an American biblical scholar, comments, "The term connotes no disapproval here, but perhaps it bears a slightly 'naughty' overtone by suggestions of 'straying' deliciously dazed in the ecstasies of lovemaking."[5] Dr. Bruce Waltke points out that the father here "*admonishes* that inhibitions be left behind in the marriage bed."[6]

Have you ever given yourself over to sexual enjoyment and desire to such an extent that you feel intoxicated?* Doing so may sound scandalous (and would be outside of marriage), but within marriage it's *biblically commanded as a blessing.*

We pastors have spent thousands of years warning young people to say no to sex outside of marriage; the biblical record is just as strong that married couples need to ramp up the intensity of their "yeses." It's okay to let yourself go in each other's arms, to experience the dimensions of pleasure and enthrallment with each other that God designed us to feel.

We will never understand sex in marriage if we ignore the scriptural truth that it is good, holy, and sacred for us to be captivated by each other's bodies. God wants husbands and wives to have this power over each other, to intoxicate and to be intoxicated.

The biblical record presents a God who reveals to us the sacred power behind sexual passion in marriage and who urges us to explore

---

* We realize that not all marriages are healthy, and the thought of "losing control" in a potentially abusive situation is (and should be) terrifying. This advice isn't absolute—it's specific to a healthy marriage with both spouses committed to the truth of 1 Corinthians 13:4–7.

it to the very depths. God is letting us know with explicit language: "I've created something wonderful, powerful, and delightful for wives and husbands to enjoy together. Take advantage of it, use it, and honor me by honoring it."

Making Up for Lost Time

A pastor called me after I had led a Sacred Marriage seminar at his church. "Thanks for giving me the most awkward pastoral counseling conversation of my life," he said.

"What happened?" I asked.

"After your talk on sex, a seventy-one-year-old woman in our church said it was like God flipped a switch in her brain. She said no one had ever told her in church that it was okay for women to enjoy sex, that in fact God *created* them to enjoy sex. Her very tired-looking husband who was standing next to her got a big smile on his face. 'She's been making up for lost time,' he said, 'and I'm not sure I can keep up.'"

The pastor finished with these words: "She was actually quite angry about all the years that had been stolen from them as a couple because they had never heard the biblical basis for sexual pleasure."

Our prayer is that couples will hear and take to heart this instruction long before they turn seventy. We've seen many couples blessed by the sexual intimacy that flows from their union. Their fulfillment in the bedroom colors every aspect of their marriage and relationship. It brings joy, peace, contentment, and a special shared intimacy because they regularly do something together that they share and talk about with no one else. Many have affectionate "code language" that creates a unique bond. They can say something seemingly innocuous in public, like "stapler," and nobody realizes they're using a sexual innuendo unique to them (I can't figure it out either). This code language gives them a secret, shared intimacy that nothing else can match.

NOTE FROM DEBRA

I love the idea of having a unique phrase that signals our intimacy. It's a lighthearted way of sharing something special and communicating desire. My husband, John, and I have defaulted to a certain phrase, but if I shared it with you, it wouldn't be our special code word anymore! Over the course of time, I've asked married couples to tell me the code word they use with one another to communicate that they want to have sex.* Here are some of the unique and hilarious phrases couples shared:

- *One of us will say, "Do you want a back rub?"* *Disclaimer: He found out that sometimes she actually *does* just want a back rub!
- *We say, "Let's have some grown-up fun!"*
- *"Stuff." As in, "What do you want to do tonight? Stuff."*
- *One of us says, "Do you want a night out in Funkytown?"*
- *We say, "We need to pay the bills."*
- *One of us will say, "Wanna wrestle?"*
- *One of us says, "Do you want some Skittles?"*
- *We call it "magic mornings"!*
- *My husband tells me he wants to go to Disneyland, where we ride all the fun rides!*
- *One of us asks, "Is it Wednesday?" Because Wednesday is usually the day we end up having sex, so that's our term!*
- *We say, "Salsa time!"*
- *We refer to it as "time for us" or just good old "let's have sex." No need for code when we know what's coming!*
- *One of us says, "Can I interest you in having sexual relations?" We are both big nerds!*

---

* See appendix 1 for research information.

- *One of us says, "Rubby!"*
- *One of us says, "Bow chicka bow wow."*
- *We simply found ourselves saying, "I've missed you," to mean we want to have sex!*

It's fun to hear the different ways couples refer to their sex life. But the key to remember is that it's less important what you call it and more important that you learn to communicate about it. Because, as Gary mentions, depending on how you approach it, sex can become the greatest blessing in your life, or it can be the biggest burden.

We have also witnessed how sexual intimacy, created to be a blessing, has become a heavy burden for many couples. Few pains are felt more intensely than sexual pain, and few rejections are felt more personally than sexual rejection. Perhaps no offense stings quite like sexual betrayal. It's as if one or both of the spouses know they're missing out on something profound, and so they grieve it all the more.

The reason Debra and I chose to begin this book with the biblical record is that too many books and discussions about sex begin with what the couple wants, enjoys, and "needs" from each other. For Christians, sexual intimacy should begin with what *God* wants us to enjoy from sex. He designed it, after all, and it's clear from his Word and his creation that sexual pleasure is a good thing. Our bodies are designed to experience sexual climax.

Since that's the case, let's move forward, committed to being sexual explorers, people eager to search out this amazing "land" that God has created. We don't need to separate our faith in God from our desire to be sexually intimate. Quite the opposite is true: our marriages will be best served when we care about sex as much as God does.

chapter
two

SEXPECTATIONS

Debra

I never imagined I wouldn't be having sex on my wedding night.

That I would fall asleep that night *still* a virgin was so far off my radar of expectations that I didn't even see it coming.

Like most Christian couples moving toward marriage, my husband, John, and I came into our honeymoon with a set of unspoken expectations—beliefs about sex and sexuality that had been formed over time—that influenced what we assumed sex should be like, including the activities of our wedding night. If you would have asked me to describe what I expected my wedding night to be like, I would have said, "A romantic evening, with rose petals scattered all around and the lights dimmed low. It will be a night of passionately exploring one another's bodies and then fitting together easily as we have sex for the first time." If you would have asked John to describe what he expected that night, he would have said, "Amazing lovemaking sessions lasting for hours in an exotic, secluded location."

But the reality of our wedding night was much less exotic and much more awkward than we ever could have imagined. No one told us how difficult it would be to actually "make love" and that as virgins, getting part A into part B would require a whole lot more than just desire. After quite some time of trial and error, hoping to make the process a little easier, we tried slathering on some lubricant. But within a few seconds we found out that it was an "ice-hot" version that went from freezing cold to blazing hot in a matter of a few seconds until we literally felt like our genitals were on fire! "I need to get this stuff off of me, now!" John said as he leaped out of bed to find a towel. At this point, we were both slightly disappointed yet also laughing hysterically at the absurdity of it all. "This isn't working," John said. "Yeah, let's go eat some leftovers and try again tomorrow," I suggested. We ended the evening snuggled up together in bed, eating leftover steak and chocolate-covered strawberries and talking the night away. Needless to say, we've never used that kind of lubricant again. Talk about getting our expectations wrong in every single way.

Sexual expectations shape the entirety of our marriage and influence what we assume and expect throughout every season of our relationship. Each one of us approaches sex with a set of beliefs that have been shaped and influenced over time—influenced by things like the entertainment industry, church culture, our past experiences, and our families of origin. All of these factors play a role in shaping our expectations and beliefs. But if we're not aware of our *sexpectations* or not willing to adjust them, we'll find that these expectations can cause serious damage and disappointment to our sex life. Thankfully, John and I were able to reset our expectations of our honeymoon night and enjoy our time together while we practiced instead of letting our unrealistic expectations drive us apart (and let me assure you, we eventually got it right!). But if we're not careful, unrealistic expectations of sex will quickly lead to an unfulfilling sex life. Let's take a look at some common sexpectations that can influence our sexual experience in negative ways all throughout our marriage.

Sex Will Always Be Amazing

Tom and Melody both grew up in conservative Christian households, where the concept of saving sex for marriage was drilled into their heads. They had waited all their lives to have sex. They committed to waiting for sex, with the expectation that when they got there, it would be great! They assumed that if they held out, God would bless them with an incredible sex life in marriage. Their expectations came crashing down when just months into marriage, sex wasn't all they thought it would be. Intercourse was painful and uncomfortable. Their lack of education about sex, coupled with their high expectations, created disappointment and discouragement. Their evenings were filled with tears, fears, and frustrations until they ended up avoiding sex altogether. They felt ashamed, incompetent, and alone. They felt a growing bitterness toward God because they had been obedient to wait for sex, only to end up struggling. It seemed as though God wasn't holding up his end of the bargain. Therein lies one of the first false assumptions we bring into our sex life: just because we've waited, sex will be great.

In my book *Choosing Marriage*, I explain:

> The problem with this entire belief system is that it's rooted in a false claim. We don't wait so we can have an evening of ecstasy on our honeymoon night . . . We wait because through the process of waiting our relationship is built, our trust is strengthened, and our commitment to each other is tried, tested, and refined. We wait because through the process of waiting, we learn discipline, self-control, loyalty, and reverence for the sacred. We wait because it's an act of worship and obedience to a God who knows exactly how we're wired, what we need, and what is best for our lives. We wait, not because of what it will do for us, but because of what it will do within us. Because you can't establish a good sex life until you've established good character first.[1]

The truth of the matter is that just like anything else in life, sex takes practice. It may never get perfected. It may never be perfect. But it can always be godly.[2] That is the reality we need to hold on to no matter what season of marriage we may be in.

I Will Always Feel Sexy

"I assumed I would automatically feel sexy, confident, and knowledgeable about sex and that it would be equally pleasurable for me and for him," one woman said as we were unpacking her sexual expectations. "In reality, I've struggled terribly with confidence, shame, lack of knowledge, and pain." Another false expectation we can unknowingly bring into sex is the underlying belief that we're always going to *feel* all the right kinds of feelings about sex and during sex. We don't expect to feel shame, guilt, or even pain during sex—and it can become a real point of contention when our feelings don't cooperate.

In trying to motivate young people to save sex for marriage, well-intentioned leadership may use methods of fear, shame, and guilt. The problem with these methods is that for so many people, they leave a residue. Feelings of deep shame and overwhelming guilt cloud their emotional experience of sex. People struggle to switch their mental gears from seeing sex before marriage as "bad" to all of a sudden feeling sexy, competent, and secure in their sexuality. We can feel positive about sex only when we begin to understand the factors that have shaped our beliefs and expectations along the way and then learn to replace false beliefs with God's truth about sex.

Sex Will Be Easy and Happen Often

Have you ever noticed how unrealistic the portrayal of sex is in the entertainment industry? It is pictured as passionate, quick, easy, and—might I add—mess-free. No matter what time of day it is, characters are portrayed as feeling turned on, looking their absolute best, and instantly aroused and ready to go anytime and anywhere. No foreplay,* no emotional connection—just "on your mark, get set, go!" No need

---

* *Foreplay* refers here to the arousing physical and sexual touch that preludes the experience of sexual intercourse. We'll dive much deeper into this in the coming chapters.

to even brush those teeth before morning sex, and definitely no need to clean up afterward. Couples reach an exhilarating climax together, moaning and groaning, and then fall asleep entangled in each other's arms. Talk about unrealistic sexpectations.

One couple shared a funny story of what sex looked like shortly after the birth of their first son: "We hadn't had sex for eight weeks, so we were really excited to connect. But within just a few moments, my breast milk started leaking everywhere, including all over my husband's face. Needless to say, we ultimately accomplished the deed—and it was meaningful and fulfilling. It just looked *way* messier than in the movies."

For most of us, the romanticized but unrealistic portrayal that Hollywood gives us is one of the primary sources from which we download our views and expectations of sex. What we see becomes what we expect. But what Hollywood tells us is nowhere near reality. Not only that, but add the effects of the pornography industry to the unrealistic messages we get from the entertainment industry, and our ideas and expectations of sex become completely skewed.

As one couple shares, "Modern-day TV and media display couples like animals with massive sex drives. We both have a sex drive, but it wasn't something we wanted 24/7, which made us feel embarrassed when we didn't fit into that mold." Another couple shares, "We thought achieving orgasm would always be easy, but in reality, it didn't play out that way, and we even went an entire year without her being able to orgasm."

Let me pause to say something really important here: it's not our underlying expectations of sex that can harm our sex life; it's our inability to change those expectations and align them with reality. When we're faced with reality—the reality that sex isn't always easy, that we won't always want sex, or that sex takes a lot more work than we thought it would—either we can hold on to our false expectations and grow in resentment, or we can accept reality and grow in experience, education, and intimacy as we learn to make love together.

Sex Is Primarily for the Man

I worked with a husband who had to work through the false sexpectation that sex was for his own pleasure. Having been regularly exposed to the hypersexuality of the entertainment industry, as well as frequent pornography use before marriage, he was conditioned to feel that sex was about his own personal pleasure. When he had sex with his wife, he actually felt let down by the experience of real sex in marriage.

Because of the influence of pornography in his past, he thought sex in marriage was going to happen every day, multiple times a day. He thought his wife would be excited and ready to go far more often than she was in reality. Simply put, he didn't realize sex would take so much "work," that there was so much "giving" on the journey to receiving. He had spent so much time in the realm of false sexpectations that he lost touch with how real sex in a real marriage looks and feels. He needed to recalibrate his expectations and get his heart and mind aligned with reality. The reality is that movies might portray chemistry, but they don't portray true intimacy. The reality is that great sex takes time, energy, and work. The reality is that sex is about two imperfect people engaging in an act of love that is much more about relating than it is about releasing. He had to get his sexpectations right, and it started with getting his heart right.

On the flip side, one woman shared, "I was always taught that sex was primarily about the man, and he would want it more. So when I was the one who wanted it more in our relationship, it really messed with my head. I thought there was something wrong with me for wanting it more—or even that there was something wrong with him." Another woman says, "I thought sex was something I would simply do for my husband just to please him. I didn't realize how much I would enjoy it myself, and we both had to work together and communicate in order to make the experience about both of us."

Sex Will Eventually Fizzle Out

By the age of sixty-three, Seth and Rachel were pretty much done having sex. Neither of them discussed the fact that their sex life was slowly dwindling until one day, it had totally disappeared. When I met them, they hadn't had sex for at least two years and had come to counseling to discuss what they assumed was an unrelated issue: the unrelenting grief they had experienced after the loss of their adult son a few years earlier.

Somewhere along the way in our conversations, their sex life came up in one of our sessions. They both admitted that after the loss of their son, it was hard to bounce back into intimacy. Their sex life had been on the decline even before that, and it seemed perfectly reasonable to assume that this was just what happened once you reached a certain age. "To be honest, I just assumed that once you're done having kids, sex eventually fizzles out," Seth said in one of our sessions. He recalled how when his parents hit their sixties, they eventually started to sleep in different rooms. "I think we just assumed that sex ends up being a means to an end, and then once you're done having kids and you hit a certain age, well, that's that."

"I'd agree with that," Rachel chimed in. "I always assumed that sex only got more complicated as you aged, and when Seth stopped asking for it, I just followed his cues."

The sexpectations that Seth had adopted from his family of origin, paired with the trauma of losing their son, created a perfect storm for the false assumption that their sex life had run its course. But little did they realize that so many couples report experiencing sex at its *best* in their sixties! They were missing out on so much because of a set of false expectations that they had carried into their marriage, expectations that neither of them had ever confronted or addressed.

I'll Always Be in the Mood for Sex

Erin had been married for almost five years and was struggling to desire sex. "I just assumed I'd always want it, but I almost never do." She had grown up in a home where her mother was very open about her low appreciation of sex: "Sex is such a chore! Is that all you men ever want?" are phrases she would commonly hear as she was growing up. Erin knew her mother had been through some past abuse, but what she didn't realize is that her mother's view of sex had slowly seeped into conversations and comments and ultimately shaped her own view of and attitude toward sex.

"I've always known my mom struggled with relationships in general, but I guess I never realized that it actually influenced my own view of sex," she said in one of our sessions. When Erin began to identify and then take ownership of her own negative beliefs about sex, she found that her desire for sex increased. The more she learned to understand and appreciate sex as the gift it is, the more she desired it.

The script for how we understand sex is written for us at an early age. All the messages we hear, relationships we experience, and exchanges we witness in our family of origin write the script of our sexpectations without our permission. Perhaps you relate to some of the expectations listed above, or you may even have a list of your own.

Maybe you grew up in a home where intimacy was hypersexualized. You learned to see people as objects, and sex was just another appetite that needed to be filled. Or maybe you grew up in a home where sex was overspiritualized. You learned that sex was just every man's (and woman's) battle and that there was nothing you could do to control your sexual urges and no way to appease your sex drive but ignore it and pray. Or maybe you grew up in a home where sex was demonized or never even mentioned or discussed; it was the forbidden fruit that was evil and wrong, and the more you avoided it, the better life would be. Or maybe you grew up in a home where sex was glorified. It was the reward at the end of a journey of faithfulness to God, and you never imagined it could be an area of stress or struggle. Before we can adopt a healthy view of sex, we must take inventory of the familial sexpectations that have been passed down so we can begin to understand the things that might be holding us back.

This is not to say that a lack of desire for sex is always rooted in familial sexpectations. In fact, many times, lack of desire can point to relationship problems, medical issues, exhaustion and fatigue, misordered priorities, or a host of other issues that may be impeding your libido. But the point I'm making is this: we need to recognize that the expectation that we'll always want to be intimate with our spouse is profoundly unrealistic. It's normal to struggle with sexual desire, but what we do with that struggle is what will set our marriage apart. We'll address this topic in much greater detail later in the book.

Sex Will Be Explosive

"I'm having a really hard time not comparing him to the guys I've slept with in the past," she said with frustration. Maci and Dan had been married for seven years when they hit a slump in their sex life. Dan entered their marriage as a virgin, but Maci had been with a number of sexual partners in the past. When things got slow in their sex life, she found herself flashing back to the passion and excitement of her past. She knew it wasn't healthy or right, but she couldn't help the fact that she expected more in their sex life. Her current sexual satisfaction was being influenced by her sexpectations, and the things she had experienced before were holding her back now.

Part of helping Maci was getting her to understand that her sexpectations had been impacted by her experiences. She had a set of preconceived notions of what sex was "supposed to look like," and Dan wasn't measuring up. But he couldn't measure up, because the standard Maci was using was based on her experiences with others—not on her experience with him. She was measuring him against an unfair standard and coming away frustrated rather than starting fresh within the context of their relationship. Her experiences had become her standard.

In order for Maci to begin healing, she had to realize it wasn't Dan who was holding her back; it was her unrealistic sexpectations. She was putting the responsibility on him to "make their sex life hot," when in reality she was accountable for taking ownership of her expectations and aligning them with the truth. The truth is that sometimes sex will be explosive, and other times it takes effort. Maci had to let go of her past expectations and begin to create new ones with her husband by her side by being honest with him about what she needed and what she liked. She had to rewrite the false expectations that were rooted in the experiences of her past and create something new together.

NOTE FROM GARY

Ordinary Sex

I *hate* ordinary. I happen to be a preacher, so I hate ordinary sermons too. I want every sermon to be the best ever.

When I'm writing a sermon, there are predictable stages. I love the research—getting deep into the Scriptures and exploring the meaning of the words. In the excitement of this new discovery phase, I become convinced that "this is going to be the best sermon I've ever preached." God's words are rich and powerful, and they pack such liberating force that I can't wait to get in front of people and talk about them.

But then I have to organize the research into a coherent whole, and that one act of corralling seems to deplete the power of the sermon by 25 percent. And then, horror of horrors, I have to fit all of this majestic, life-changing, divinely inspired truth into the tiny box of *thirty minutes*. "Out goes that point." "No time for that illustration." "Shorten the opening." "Kill that thought." It feels like pouring a bottle of death onto the tapestry of life.

And then there's that dreadful, discouraging moment when I think, *This is just another* ordinary *sermon.*

As I said, I *hate* ordinary. I want the best. But wanting every sermon to be the best is absurd. When a close, thoughtful, and intelligent friend told me, "Gary, that sermon was among your very best," my first thought was, *What was wrong with last week's?* It's a curse. By definition, every sermon can't be the best. If I can't live with ordinary, I'll drive myself crazy.

I used to do the same with sex. *How do we top the last time?* It's hard to appreciate *what is* when you're constantly comparing what is with *what could be.*

The danger of a message that promises to "improve" your sex life is that real life and real marriage work against that. We can't, by definition, continue to improve our sex life if that means every time we have sex is "better" than the last time we had sex.

God has created a good world with many ordinary moments. Some sunsets look like portals to heaven; some overcast days suck the life out of us. Some meals make our taste buds come alive; some make us hate the fact that we have to eat.

In your pursuit of excellent sex, don't eschew the delight of ordinary sex. There's a place for both.

Sex Will Be Problem-Free

Sometimes it's the wife who struggles to enjoy sex; sometimes it's the husband. Take Benjamin, for example, who found it difficult to enjoy sex with his wife. In fact, he would have much rather avoided sex altogether. He had experienced sexual abuse at the hands of his father—painful memories he had worked hard to forget. But more often than not, he found himself dealing with feelings of guilt and shame after reaching climax. He didn't mentally make the connection at first, but it was as though his body remembered and carried that guilt.

His sexpectations were being influenced by the pain of his past. He was struggling to enjoy sex the way God intended for it to be enjoyed because the idea of sex had been completely tarnished for him. He never expected sex could come with so many problems. When Benjamin and his wife came to see me, they were at a point in their marriage where sex was becoming less and less frequent. Ben wanted to connect with his wife, but deep down he would have preferred to avoid sex rather than engage in it, which made him feel even worse, given that he had been taught that men were supposed to have a high sex drive. He felt like he was letting down both his wife and himself, and he didn't know where to begin to deal with the problem. In order to move forward, Ben had to let go of the assumption that this was *his* problem and start seeing it as *their* problem to work through together.

Past abuse is only one of the many problems that can come up in sex. At some point in marriage, every couple struggles with something, whether it's premature ejaculation, the influence of pornography or infidelity, pain during sex, lack of desire, feelings of rejection—you name it, someone is experiencing it. Ben had to understand that every combination of two people leads to a specific set of sexual problems. His difficulty was really *their* difficulty. This new awareness set him free to share this challenge with his wife and allow her to become part of the solution. They were able to work together in counseling and come out stronger on the other side.

Our sexpectations have a significant impact on our sex life, yet they often go ignored and unaddressed. People typically want to dive right into the "good stuff" and skip right over the prelude. But establishing a good sex life is like building a skyscraper. We can't begin to work on the many levels of techniques or sexual positions or the art of orgasm until we lay the foundation by putting into words how our thoughts, beliefs, and expectations shape our understanding of sex. If we don't get this part right, every other level of the skyscraper will be incomplete. But even more troubling, a skyscraper built on a flawed foundation could end up crumbling.

Let's take a look at other sexpectations that couples said they brought into marriage. See if you can relate to any of the following.

Unrealistic Sexpectations

- *I thought sex would only happen at night, but my husband actually prefers it in the morning.*
- *I expected sex to always be passionate, but sometimes it's just practical.*
- *I expected to always have a high sex drive, but I really struggled during menopause.*
- *I expected sex to last for hours, but in reality, it doesn't last very long.*
- *I was sexually assaulted as a child, but I expected to immediately feel safe with my husband during sex, while in reality it took me fifteen years before I truly believed he wouldn't harm me.*
- *I thought we would have sex every day, but we're lucky to squeeze it in two times a week!*
- *I thought orgasms for women were as common as for men, but in reality it's been much harder for me to reach climax.*
- *I thought a successful experience had to include my husband reaching his climax. It doesn't.*

So far, we've talked through some of the unrealistic expectations we can bring into sex from our past religious experiences, cultural experiences, family of origin, and our past sexual experiences. But just as important as understanding those expectations is embracing truths about sex. From both personal experience and experience in working and interacting with thousands of couples, I want to share a few crucial things you need to understand and believe about sex.

Sex Must Be Mastered

Before any healing can begin, we have to get real about the fact that we can't let our sexpectations rule us. We have to learn to take charge of our sex life by *creating* the sex life we want to have instead of just reacting to our unrealistic or unhealthy expectations. Making love really comes down to what you make of it. Mastering sex takes time, effort, understanding, and awareness. In all the stories and situations above, one thing that set apart the couples who thrived from the couples who didn't was their ability to recognize that their expectations did not have to inhibit their reality. Even though sex didn't play out the way they *expected*, they could still make the most of the sexual relationship they did have. The couples who were willing to step back, adapt, recalibrate, and learn and grow together were the ones who were able to come out sexually stronger on the other side.

Good sex isn't ready-made. It's not fast, nor is it easy. In fact, often it's not even convenient. Sometimes we expect sex to be like fast food. Just like the popular slogans say, we want to "have it our way" and get it "hot and ready" whenever we want it. But what we have to realize is that good sex isn't a quick fix; good sex is a process. Much like cooking an amazing meal from scratch, good sex takes time, energy, quality ingredients, and the patience to master the craft. We'll learn later that when it comes to sex, the ingredient list includes things like character, communication, compassion, and a deep connection. Those things take time to cultivate, but in the end, great sex is always worth it.

There Will Be Problems

Another important thing to understand about sex is that at some point along the way, you will have problems. *Problems are to be expected.* The sooner you set that expectation, the easier it will be to come up with a plan and move forward. As Gary said during one of the many conversations we had as we worked on this book, "Couples shouldn't be surprised when a problem arises any more than a basketball player is surprised when they miss a shot or a football player is shocked when they drop a pass. When this happens, you review the game film and assess why it happened rather than act like it's something unique."

Not only should we not be surprised by problems, but we also don't need to fear them, because problems in our sex life offer us the opportunity to take our relationship to the next level. They pave the way for greater understanding, more meaningful connection, and deeper vulnerability. We'll dive into specific problem areas and how to overcome them together later in this book, but for now, hold on to the understanding that you are not alone.

Sex Is Powerful, but So Are You

Sex is a powerful force, and it's something we must learn to take ownership of with a commitment of time and communication. The reality is that anything powerful can be used for good or evil. So many analogies about sex exist, some far more useful than others, but the one that has always spoken to my heart is seeing sex as a fire. It has the power to bring warmth, sustenance, and enjoyment, but it also has the power to bring death and destruction. We have to understand that although sex is powerful, it does not have power over us; *we* have power over sex. We are the ones who have been given this powerful gift, and *we* get to decide how we will wield this power and what we will allow it to do to our relationship. We can choose, from this point on, to use it to bring about good or to spread evil. By God's grace and in his strength, we have the power to make the fire of sex burn for the good of our marriage.

God created sex to bring about unity (Genesis 2:24), purity (Hebrews 13:4), pleasure (Song of Songs 7:6), love and comfort (Genesis 24:67), and deep joy (Proverbs 5:18). When we begin to align our expectations of sex with God's expectations of sex, we claim sex for good. When we find freedom from past abuse, when we're released from the guilt and shame of past sexual experiences, we declare that by God's grace we are the ones who hold the power and will use this powerful gift for good. For the good of our marriages and relationships and for the glory of God.

If you've had painful experiences in your past or find yourself struggling to believe that sex is worth the work, I challenge you to consider seeking the help of a professional counselor. Some beliefs about sex have deep and painful roots, and in order to begin to heal from the past, we often have to go backward before we can go forward (see chapter 13). God longs for us to see sex the way he sees it and to take back the power of this precious gift.

Sex Is Not *Just* about Sex

If sex was just about sex, my job as a licensed counselor would be easy. When people come in with sexual struggles, I'd give them a diagram of the human body along with a handbook of instructions about which body parts go where—and that would be the end of it. But establishing a good sex life isn't as easy as studying a simple diagram, because at the end of the day, it's not really about the physical act of sex. Most sexual struggles have less to do with sex and more to do with something else. Here are some of the underlying issues I've seen come up over and over, disguised as sexual struggles, that prove to me that sex isn't really about the sex:

- The underlying problem has to do with a lack of emotional connection.
- One or both people in the marriage are fighting off feelings of guilt and shame.
- One or both are struggling with insecurities about weight, physical appearance, or body image.

- One or both are feeling misunderstood or unappreciated.
- Underlying depression and anxiety are affecting sex drive.
- An addiction issue is buried underneath the surface.
- Conflict and a lack of communication in the marriage are causing an emotional rift.
- One or both in the marriage are feeling depleted and emotionally or physically exhausted.
- An underlying hormone imbalance is impacting the physical aspects of sex.

These are just a few examples, but the bottom line is that *sex is often not about sex at all.*

In fact, sexual frustration and problems are almost always symptoms of something going on beneath the surface—and more often than not, they are symptoms of a lack of connection with our spouse, with ourselves, and, believe it or not, with God. Sex is almost always about something more.

We have to get this expectation right as we prepare to talk through this subject in detail, because if we make sex just about the physical act of sex, we're going to find ourselves disappointed, confused, and in the end really missing out. If your sex life is struggling right now or if you find yourself wondering how to make it better, the first thing to be attuned to is the fact that sex is probably just one part of the equation.

As we walk through the following chapters one by one, I invite you to open your heart and mind to taking inventory of your relationship and getting to the bottom of the well-being of your spirit, the condition of your heart, the state of your physical health, the depth of your emotional connection, and, ultimately, the accuracy of the beliefs and expectations you're bringing to bed with you. Good sex is about becoming a better person just as much as it is about becoming a better lover. And more often than not, this process begins from the inside out.

chapter
three

YOUR BODY IS A WONDERLAND

Debra

It's hard to enjoy something when you don't quite know how it works.

Years ago, Wham-O, the company that makes Frisbees, shipped seven thousand plastic disks to an Angolan orphanage. John Bowes, who was chairman of Wham-O at the time, received the following reply: "The dishes you sent are wonderful. We eat all our meals off them. And the most amazing thing has happened. Some of the children are throwing them as sort of a game. This may be an idea for you."

When it comes to sex, particularly sex within Christian marriages, too many people go into it without really understanding how to make the most of it. We're often taught that sex is a gift from God, that it's the avenue to procreation, and if we're lucky, we're even told that it's intended for pleasure. But while we may understand the basic mechanics of sex (i.e., put part A into part B), we're missing out on the thrill of sex, the enjoyment of sex, and the fun of sex. It's like eating off a Frisbee without realizing it's made to be played with and enjoyed. We're engaging in sex without understanding how to make it the best it can be. Only the lucky ones happen to "get it right." So many others are missing out on the fun because of a simple lack of knowledge and awareness. In other words, they don't have good instructions.

I know this to be true because I was working with a married couple recently who was having trouble with their sex life. After I mentioned the word *clitoris*, the husband looked at me sheepishly and said, "What's a clitoris?" Maybe you're reading this and wondering the very same thing. If so, fear not, because this is the chapter where you're going to learn that the clitoris is the main sexual organ in the female body and the spot of the most enjoyment and pleasure when handled with care. You're going to learn a whole lot more than that too.

The way God made the human body is truly miraculous, and especially as it relates to sex. Our body is a wonderland of sensory inputs that create overwhelming feelings that lead to thrilling physical reactions and ultimately to an explosion of pleasure called an orgasm. This is what is referred to as a "climax" in sexual terminology, because it's the height of the experience. But far too many couples are struggling with orgasm because it's an experience that requires knowledge, understanding, connection, and communication. In fact, nearly 40 percent of the women we surveyed for this project reported that they reach climax less than half of the time during sex, and a whopping 10 percent of women reported experiencing orgasm *one or fewer times* out of every ten sexual encounters!* Clearly we have a lot of room to grow in this area.

Reaching the Top

When it comes to understanding how to make our sexual organs respond properly, it's helpful to imagine that reaching orgasm is sort of like climbing to the top of a mountain. Before I go on, let me make something clear: achieving orgasm is not the ultimate be-all and end-all goal of sex. No, the ultimate goal of sex is to connect intimately with

* See appendix 1 for research information.

your spouse, regardless of whether you achieve orgasm. In fact, many women report having a satisfying sex life even while struggling to achieve orgasm.[1]

But with that being said, *physically* speaking, the climax is the feeling we get when we've made it to the peak of the sexual experience. It's the physical height of the experience, the tipping point when our body has received such a pleasurable amount of stimulation that it begins to contract. For men and women, this looks a little different but works much the same. Both men and women experience orgasm as an intense, pleasurable feeling accompanied by involuntary contractions of their genital muscles and a tightening of their abdominal muscles. Men typically ejaculate during an orgasm (releasing sperm from their penis upon contraction). An orgasm typically lasts a few seconds, but its benefits last much longer. In fact, the act of orgasm is known to release hormones in the body, such as oxytocin and endorphins, that create a rush of intense relaxation.

The aftermath of sex has the potential to be another enjoyable part of sex in the sense that both partners are completely relaxed in each other's arms after having experienced a moment of intense pleasure together. "My favorite part of sex is definitely the end," one woman said, "when both of us are naked and entangled in each other's bodies, feeling relaxed, vulnerable, and so completely connected physically and emotionally."

"If you're going to get to the top of the mountain, make sure to enjoy it once you get there." I often give this advice to couples I counsel, and it's my own view of the after-sex phase. We live in such a go-go-go world, and too many people rush through sex to get to the end goal of orgasm and then quickly climb off each other and move on with the rest of their day as if the job has been completed. But sex isn't just about the climax; it's about being present, communicating love, and giving and receiving affection. When we rush through the act, not only do we skip over many of the physical benefits of the "afterward," but we miss out on the deep emotional connection as well.

Now that we've made the analogy that reaching orgasm is like climbing to the top of a mountain, we have to remember that as with climbing a mountain, getting to the peak doesn't "just happen." Many small steps occur along the way. Some of these steps are skipped or misunderstood altogether, which is why people often struggle to get to the peak of their sexual experience.

Before we go on, we should note that men and women share a lot of similarities when it comes to reaching climax. They have differences too, and we'll cover those in the coming chapters for men and women, but for now it's important to understand the similarities, because these are what create deeper connection in marriage. Too many books spend too much time on the differences and thus make men and women feel like they come from different planets. The problem is that this mentality leaves us feeling disconnected from our spouse. If men really are from Mars and women from Venus, then our efforts to connect and communicate are doomed. But the beautiful truth is that we're all created in the image of God, and we have many similarities that bind us together. Following are several basic truths to understand about reaching orgasm for both men and women.

Reaching the Top Requires Physical Awareness

When it comes to understanding how our physical bodies work, and specifically how our sexual organs work, far too many people have never taken the time to do the research. As a Christian, I do understand the struggle. It's not easy to pick up a random sex manual in a bookstore for fear of looking like a pervert, and if you try to google the subject, you never know what kind of inappropriate content you'll get or how reliable it will be. So for many couples, it's often easier to take the do-it-yourself approach and try to learn along the way. We asked couples where they get most of their information on sex, and a startling 25 percent of them answered, "Nowhere." They just try to figure it out themselves.*

But the problem with the DIY mentality is that too many couples get stuck in a sexual rut, doing the same things over and over because they don't know there's another way—a better way. It's not like you can compare notes on sexual positions and experiences when you're on a double date with your friends or during the Q and A time at Bible study. Getting information can be challenging, so we default to the "this is the way we've always done it, so this is the way we'll continue to do it" line—whether it's working or not.

One couple I counseled used humping (rubbing their genitalia against each other's bodies) as their primary method of getting aroused for many, many years without realizing there's much to gain from using their fingers and hands and even their tongues and lips (we'll talk details about oral sex a little later). They just never thought to do it that way. They got stuck in a sexual rut.

One way men and women are similar physically is that when they get aroused, a rush of blood flows to their respective sexual organs. For a man, it's his penis (often called "getting hard"), while for a woman, it's her clitoris (often accompanied by a release of vaginal discharge or mucus referred to as "getting wet"). Arousal causes their sexual organs to become enlarged, to "plump up" and become even more sensitive. This is a necessary step to reaching orgasm for both men and women.

The differences appear in how each person gets to the point of arousal. Men typically get aroused by *direct* touch to the penis, while women initially get aroused by *indirect* touch before they're ready for direct touch. I always tell men and women to picture arousal like a target. For men, you can go right to the bull's-eye. But women need to ease into it from the outer rings, slowly moving toward the bull's-eye. This starts with gentle touch to other parts of the body, including the back, shoulders, buttocks, breasts, nipples, and so forth, then slowly

* See appendix 1 for research information.

moving to the thighs, then to the outer lips of the vagina (the labia), and eventually to the extremely sensitive inner part of the vagina (the clitoris is the firm nub that rests between the top folds of the vagina).

For a woman, the slower and steadier the approach, the more intense the feelings. You both eventually get to reach the top, but getting there requires a different approach. Both men and women have millions of nerve receptors surrounding their sexual organs. It's important to remember that sex is not just about putting part A into part B and thrusting; it's about learning to activate all of those different sensations along the way, seeing each step as gaining momentum for the climax we'll reach at the top. We'll talk through the sexy details of how to get each partner aroused in the next chapters, where we examine the physical differences between a man and a woman and how to activate all of the different sensations.

In addition to the anatomy of the body, we need to understand the role of hormones during sex. Both men and women have changing hormone levels in their bodies, and those hormones lead to changes in sexual desire and drive. It's much easier for women to get an idea of changes in hormones, since they often correlate with changes in a woman's menstrual cycle. You may notice that during certain times of the month (usually during ovulation or close to menstruation, or both), a woman can begin to feel more aroused than usual. Studies show that the changes in hormones cause an increase in sexual energy, usually right at the time of ovulation, as well as after menstruation.[2] These hormonal changes can have significant impacts on a couple's sexual experience. Understanding these physical changes not only helps spouses have grace and empathy for each other but also helps couples make the most of the seasons of natural arousal.

There are two other components to keep in mind when it comes to physical awareness: the roles of physical health and medication in achieving orgasm. The first important area to watch carefully is your *physical health*. Understanding the implications of physical health and well-being and their impact on sexual function plays a major role in the process of sexual satisfaction. If we struggle with a physical condition or illness or a lack of general health, we need to take inventory of how it affects our sex life and make sure we're doing what we can to keep it under control and managed in the best way possible so that we give ourselves the best chance to make the most of our sex life.

The second component to consider is *medication.* Many medications are known to decrease the frequency of orgasm and sexual desire altogether, such as antidepressants (SSRIs and SNRIs*), heart medications, blood pressure medications, and heartburn medications, among others. If you recently had a change in your medication or dosage and are experiencing a decrease in sex drive or an inability to reach orgasm, be sure to check with your doctor about side effects and options with regard to medication. Sometimes all it takes is a simple shift in dosage or brand to start climbing back to the top of that mountain!

We'll address some of these factors in detail in chapter 11. Understanding how your body works makes all the difference.

Reaching the Top Requires Sexual Stimulation

Most couples don't realize that reaching orgasm together is not always easy or realistic to achieve 100 percent of the time. In fact, fewer than 1 percent of couples we surveyed said they reach climax together every single time. A majority of respondents (50 percent) said they were lucky to climax together *once* every ten times, and the rest (49 percent) said it varied.† The reason is that for a person to reach orgasm, consistent sexual stimulation must occur from beginning to end. Let's talk about some of the ins and outs (pun intended) of sexual stimulation and how to maintain it consistently so both parties will have the best chance of achieving sexual satisfaction and orgasm.

---

* SSRI stands for selective serotonin reuptake inhibitor, while SNRI refers to serotonin-norepinephrine reuptake inhibitor.

† See appendix 1 for research information.

Erogenous Zones

As discussed earlier, the female body often needs a little time to warm up, starting with the gentle touch of nonsexual organs. This isn't always the case; some days she may be revved up and ready for you to go for the gold! But for the most part, it's good to assume that helping her get ready will take a little time and effort, unless she suggests otherwise. For many women, going straight for the clitoris can actually be painful and uncomfortable if she's not properly aroused. The body is loaded with sexual sensors, and touching those broader areas (listed below) can often be the key to the greatest orgasmic success in the end. All of those little touches and sensations add to the buildup of sexual stimulation, helping her get to the point of climax. We call sensitive areas of the body the "erogenous zones," from the Greek word *eros*, which means "love," and the suffix *gen* + *ous*, which means "producing." These areas can assist you in the process of making love and can be amazing sources of sexual arousal for men and women both during foreplay and all throughout the sexual experience. Some examples of erogenous touch include the following:

- **Neck:** Gently kiss up and down the neck or try using your tongue or fingertips to stimulate all of those sensitive areas. Doing so can send a tingle down your partner's body and add to the buildup of sexual energy.
- **Ears:** Nibbling or licking the ears can often be a point of arousal for both men and women because ears are so sensitive. You can also try using your fingers to gently trace around the outer parts of the ear. Some people may find this touch a little too ticklish or intense for their liking, but for others it can send them straight to paradise.
- **Buttocks:** The buttocks can be one of the most pleasurable parts of the body because of its proximity to the genitalia. A lot of sensitive nerve endings reside in this area! Try gently caressing and even allowing your fingers to slowly find their way to the

middle of the buttocks, gently inserting your fingers into the fold or tracing up and down to really get those nerve endings going!

- **Lower back:** This part of your body is so sensitive that just a gentle touch can send pleasurable shivers up your spine.
- **Inside the elbow/Behind the knees/Inner wrist:** Try reaching up and down, gently caressing the arms and legs, slowly making your way to the sensitive spot just inside the elbow or behind the knee, or tracing circles on the inner wrist.
- **Hair/Scalp:** Many people enjoy having their hair played with. It relaxes them and fills them with pleasure. That's because the scalp is full of nerve endings that can add to sexual stimulation. Try gently massaging your spouse's scalp or running your fingers gently through their hair.
- **Armpits:** Another nerve-ending arousal spot is found in the armpits. You might not think of the armpit as a point of sexual pleasure, but a gentle touch or circular massage can bring heightened arousal.
- **Stomach:** The stomach (especially the lower stomach below the belly button) is often an arousal favorite because it's so close to the genitalia, yet not too close. It's the perfect spot to build up sexual energy by teasing, pretending like you're reaching down to touch the genitalia but then gently bringing your touch back up. Try starting at the chest and making your way down to the belly button, then a little lower, and then a little lower. Women often enjoy teasing as a way to build the sexual tension. The more you wait it out, the more the sexual tension builds and the easier it is to get to orgasm when it's finally time. Try using your fingers or gently licking and kissing down the stomach, getting as close as you can to the genitalia. You can even give a quick lick, caress, gentle touch, or kiss down there and then quickly come back up.

An important point to remember about erogenous zones is that not everyone likes the same thing. What works for you may not work for your spouse. In fact, caressing some spots can trigger a negative reaction from your spouse. I know a woman who hated having her stomach touched during sex. Rather than turn her on, it brought the opposite reaction. It's important not to assume but rather to ask, "Does this feel good for you?" as you're making love, or better yet, to make time for these conversations when you're not in the heat of the moment. Conversation and communication pave the way for greater intimacy (see conversation cues in chapter 7).

You may find a spot we haven't mentioned that gets your partner going. The process of discovery can be exciting when you go into it selflessly, with an attitude of serving and a desire to give pleasure to your spouse. Some people like to experiment with different sensations, such as using a feather or a very gentle touch, a stronger or firmer touch along the way, or a heated lubricant or an ice cube. The key is finding what works for you and your partner and learning to communicate both during and after the experience. You can't read the other's mind, and it's okay and important to gently say, "Honey, that doesn't feel very comfortable—why don't you try this instead." I use the word *gently* because you want to make sure you're communicating with kindness, since kindness and sweetness are the two collaborators that move sex in the right direction, whereas irritation and frustration are known to totally kill the mood.

Primary Sexual Zones

Now that we've talked about some of the best erogenous zones, let's keep the sexual stimulation going by getting to the sexual hot spots. Hopefully you're already getting a little warmer as you read this chapter, and later tonight you can take it to the next level by exploring some of these spots with your spouse.

- **Chest and nipples:** In both men and women, the chest and particularly the nipples are chock-full of sensitive nerve endings. Not only that, but the more stimulation to different parts of the body at one time (for example, her vagina plus her nipples), the more excitement and arousal your spouse will feel. When it comes to these hot spots, men often prefer a direct and firm touch, while women often prefer to ease into the experience with a softer touch and gain momentum from there.

You'll know you're doing the right thing when the nipples begin to get firm and erect, often referred to as "getting hard" (essentially, arousal causes blood to make its way to the area that's getting stimulated, which you can physically see happening in parts of the body like the penis, nipples, and clitoris). The harder the nipples, the more sensitive they are to touch—and for most people, the better it feels. A gentle touch or rub of the chest and nipples or a firm warm lick or kiss can really help to keep sexual arousal going. Tell your spouse what feels good and how much (or little) pressure to apply to make it feel the best.

***Special note to nursing moms:** Sadly, many women know how sensitive their nipples are because they equate the sensitivity of their nipples with the pain of breastfeeding a child! I've talked to some women who have a hard time disconnecting this part of their body from its function with their children and giving themselves permission to see their breasts and nipples as a means to their own sexual pleasure. For a certain season of life, your breasts are used as a method of feeding and sustaining your infants, and then all of a sudden a few hours later, you have to make the shift from milk machine to sexy woman.

For some women it can be a difficult mental shift—understandably so! If you're currently in that season where you struggle to allow yourself to enjoy foreplay or even sex altogether, remember that giving yourself permission to enjoy intimacy is important for your personal and relational health! It's one way to allow yourself to be filled up and satisfied. It's natural to struggle for a season, but be careful not to allow infrequent intimacy to become a pattern and rob yourself of the joy of being sexually satisfied. You deserve it!

- **Vagina:** Now we're getting to the main spots everyone associates with sex. But if you don't work on foreplay by making use of all the other erogenous zones, you'll miss out on how incredible it can feel to touch these parts when your body is already in arousal mode. The vagina is an often misunderstood part of the female body. The truth is that most women have never even actually seen their vagina. It's not like a penis, where you can just look down, and boom, it's there. You'd really have to contort your body to get a full glimpse of it, and unless you're a Cirque du Soleil acrobat, there's a good chance you couldn't even do that.

  You and your husband should have a good understanding of the female vagina and specifically *your* vagina. Women, do yourself a huge favor and grab a handheld mirror. See what things look like down there. Understand the different folds and crevices, the lips and curves. For beginners, what we call the vagina is anatomically called the "vulva." It consists of two sets of lips—the larger set is called the labia majora, and the smaller set the labia minora. These two sets of lips are home to thousands of nerve endings that can stir up arousal and sexual energy when gently stroked and caressed. Understanding what each part is and how to identify each one by touch can help you communicate to your spouse what feels good.

  Nestled at the very top of the labia minora is the clitoris, which we'll talk about next, and a little lower down is the vaginal opening. Most women enjoy being gently stroked using finger(s) or tongue in a back-and-forth or circular motion, and some women even enjoy having finger(s) or tongue inserted into their vaginal opening during foreplay. The key is being willing to try different things at different times and finding what feels good!
- **Clitoris:** The clitoris is essentially the female equivalent of the penis. It's a round piece of hard flesh at the very top of your labia minora that gets erect upon arousal, just as a man's penis does. It's covered with a thin piece of flesh called the clitoral hood, and

both the clitoris and clitoral hood can cause tremendous arousal when touched just right.

Men, take note: getting the clitoris ready for action can happen in a few different ways. It usually helps to start with some kind of lubricant or oil (or even saliva) to increase the sensation of pleasure. Once a woman feels aroused and ready for clitoral touch, you can try sliding your fingers on or around it in a circular motion, gently tapping it, caressing in a back-and-forth, up-and-down motion, or even softly pinching it between two fingers and gently rubbing up and down. Some women enjoy indirect clitoral touch, which means you'll mostly be caressing the labia and the area around the clitoris, with a little direct clitoral stimulation here and there.

There's no specific formula for sexual stimulation, and different methods can bring arousal in different seasons or even on different days. One night she may want you to rub her in a circular motion, and another night she may not want that same thing. Good communication will be your biggest asset. Also, don't forget to include a little teasing in the process by stopping intermittently to take a short break to work on other erogenous zones, but don't break for too long or you may risk losing arousal altogether. The goal is to build up just enough sexual stimulation to prepare your wife to reach orgasm but not so much that she reaches climax before she wants to. There's a balance that comes with this touch that takes practice, conversation, and experience. If you're open and expressive with one another, you'll get better with time!

- **A-spot and G-spot:** Oh, the famous G-spot (and its not-so-famous A-spot)! Some women swear by this little round piece of flesh located right inside the wall of the vagina (facing the belly button). Another way to think about reaching the G-spot is to insert your finger into the vagina and make a soft and gentle "come here" motion along the inside of the vaginal wall. The G-spot is not a body part in and of itself but is an extension of the clitoris, which is much larger than most people imagine. If the clitoris that is visible is the top of the arousal spot, then the G-spot is sort of like the root. If that's the G-spot, what is the A-spot? The A-spot is the cousin of the G-spot, located two to four inches above it, also on the vaginal wall. It can be harder to reach, but it has been known to provide a similarly deep feeling of arousal.

What matters isn't that you find either of these spots, but that you find spots that work for you and get you aroused! Knowing that God created *so* many different spots for female arousal and pleasure reminds us that sexual stimulation is a scavenger hunt of discovery that is meant to be enjoyed and explored together!

- **Penis:** A man's penis becomes more sensitive as it increases in blood flow and becomes "hard" or erect. There are many ways to stimulate your husband's penis, but remember that, as with the female vagina, there are many parts to a male penis. The glans of the penis (also known as the "head") is the very tip, and it is one of the most sensitive areas, comparable to a woman's clitoris. The edges around the head are the most sensitive portion and will give a boost of pleasure when stimulated.

  Try starting at the base of the penis closest to the testicles and working your way up the shaft (the main trunk of the penis), with your hand gently closed around it. The shaft is the biggest portion of the penis anatomically, but it actually holds the fewest nerve endings. That's not to say it should be ignored—in fact, you'll want to touch it frequently—but don't forget the surrounding sensory areas. Once you've worked your way up the shaft, spend some time stimulating the head, clasping your fingers around it and gently holding it in your palm while you slide your hand up and down. A little lubricant (or saliva) can go a long way to make this experience extra pleasurable. Make a special effort to touch the rim of the head, and feel free to use your other hand to stimulate the lower portion of the shaft or another erogenous zone at the same time. If you're feeling frisky, bring your head down and wrap your lips around the head of the penis, using your tongue and lips to gently—I say *gently*, because, well, teeth can cause pain—caress up and down along that sensitive area.

- **Scrotum:** The scrotum (the sack that holds the testicles) is often the forgotten zone when it comes to pleasuring a man. The scrotum is so sensitive that it has to be handled with care, but proper stimulation of this area can bring intense sexual pleasure. When your husband is sufficiently aroused, make your way down to the scrotum, cupping it in your hands, blowing on it, or gently caressing or massaging it while simultaneously caressing the shaft and head. Just remember to be gentle and to respond to your husband's cues!
- **Perineum:** This area between the testicles and the anus looks like a webbed piece of skin that connects them together. Gently tracing your fingers up and down this area can cause great pleasure for your husband. In fact, try gently reaching back to caress this area during intercourse to take his orgasm to the next level.

When it comes to sexual touch, stimulation, and technique, it's important to understand that there is no one-size-fits-all approach to reaching orgasm. I mentioned earlier that couples often find it difficult to reach orgasm together during intercourse, and some couples never get there at all. And that's okay! Whether you take turns pleasuring one another or find ways to reach climax together, the main gauge of the vitality of your sex life is how connected and satisfied you both feel in your marriage.

After making love, do you feel closer together or further apart? Are you focused on your spouse's sexual pleasure and not just your own? Your closeness and connection are more important than anything else. Your intimacy and communication matter far more than your orgasms. That's why you'll want to be sure your sex life makes its way into your conversations. Ask your partner if they are enjoying this area of your relationship (including frequency of orgasms), and be open to suggestions of ways to make it even better. Both of you should feel comfortable sharing your needs and desires and various approaches you'd like to try. The goal of sex isn't *just* orgasm—but closeness.

NOTE FROM GARY

Women's Bodies Are Different

I typically ask soon-to-be husbands prior to the honeymoon to imagine what would happen if they had never played tennis before and then began to play it every day.

"Blisters," many of them say in response.

"Exactly," I say.

This analogy is intended to help men see that sex is different for women than it is for men in that women feel (and frankly, physiologically speaking, *are*) far more vulnerable to problems resulting from increased sexual activity. Many guys can go from never having sex to having sex three times a day and never wipe the smile off their faces. Most women can't.

Men, be aware that women can face issues of soreness, pain, and discomfort during sex that most of us don't know about because our wives are trying to hide it. Our unshaven faces may feel like sandpaper against their cheeks (or other body parts). Trying to enter them when they are not sufficiently lubricated may mean that while we go, "Aaah," she's going, "Aaack!" We're so into our "aaah" that we completely miss her "aaack!" The *same act* that feels immensely pleasurable to us can elicit immense pain in our wives.

So, men, be present to your wife's vulnerability and pain. You're letting your wife get close to you, but you're not letting her *inside* you. The best sex will happen when your wife is convinced that you are far more concerned about her comfort and pleasure than you are about your own release. A little sensitivity here can go a long way toward making your wife feel cherished.

Reaching the Top Requires Emotional Connection

Perhaps you'll be surprised to see this section in a chapter about your body. But the truth is, our emotional connection always affects the quality of our physical connection.

Mike and Anne hadn't felt close in quite some time. They lived a hectic life. They had been married for twenty-five years, but as they looked back, it all seemed like a blur because their lives were so full. Mike was the CEO of a small company that required him to work long hours and be available on weekends. Anne was involved in every organization, charity, and volunteer program imaginable. On top of that, their three boys were involved in sports, and most of their free time was spent shuffling teen boys from practices to games to more practices. They hardly had time for one another, and sadly, that had become the norm.

I met them shortly after their youngest son had graduated from high school, as they officially entered the empty nest stage. With so many of their distractions gone, the tension in their marriage came to the surface. Mike was frustrated with the lack of intimacy in their marriage and finally convinced Anne that they needed to see a counselor to find out if this was normal. "We have a good marriage," they both said. "We hardly ever have sex, though, and when we do, it often ends in frustration and disappointment for one or both of us."

Let me invite you to hear a counselor's perspective: never take the phrase "good marriage" too seriously, because the word *good* means different things to different people, based on numerous factors, including the way people were raised and the home life they experienced, as well as their presuppositions of what a good marriage looks like. At any rate, as my conversations with Mike and Anne went deeper, it became clear that even though they didn't argue much, they didn't have an emotionally intimate relationship.

They were *very good* at cohabitating—they took turns with housework, communicated about their work schedules, and managed their finances with ease. But if truth be told, they were better at managing their household than at nurturing their marriage. Because sex is such an intimate connection, when something is off with a couple's emotional connection, it will always end up affecting the physical connection as well. If Mike and Anne were going to learn to connect again, we couldn't start with sexual techniques or methods of stimulation; we had to back up and begin with the most important building block of a satisfying sex life—namely, a deep and meaningful emotional connection. Without even realizing it, they had lost that deep connection somewhere along the way, and they needed to take ownership of nurturing their marriage if they had any hope of bringing back their sex life.

Because our emotional connection always impacts the quality of our physical connection, a problem in a person's sex life is often symptomatic of a problem in another area in their relationship with their spouse. This isn't always the case, of course, and as we'll see in chapter 11, sometimes a sexual struggle can be traced to an underlying physical illness or issue. But the majority of the time, the emotional and physical are interconnected.

Unlike animals that can have at it because their carnal instinct just calls them to it, human beings are much more complex in the ways our physical, sexual, and emotional worlds come together. We've all felt this at some point. You've probably experienced a time when you were both ready for sex, and then your spouse made an off-putting comment just moments before you crawled into bed. All of a sudden, the entire mood was shot. Your sex drive can go from 100 to 0 as a result of a poorly timed conversation. After hearing from the many couples I've spoken with, I've come to believe this scenario is probably more common than any of us could imagine. This physical, sexual, and emotional reaction happens for men just as much as it does for women.

When we've been struggling with long-term problems in our sex life, we need to start looking for long-term patterns in our emotional life as well. This was the case for Mike and Anne, and this issue of emotional connection is such an important concept that I'm going to be spending an entire chapter (chapter 14) giving guidance on how to take inventory of our emotional and spiritual connection. The closer we feel emotionally, the better we'll feel sexually. The two go hand in hand.

From our physical anatomies, to our sexual desires, to our emotional connections—God made our bodies so amazingly complex, elaborate, and wondrous. Our bodies truly are a wonderland, and as is true in exploring any new territory, understanding and enjoying our bodies to the full capacity that God created requires an attitude of discovery, collaboration, humility, and perseverance. Thankfully, we've been given a lifetime to explore.

chapter
four

WHAT GETS HIM GOING

Gary

Many women we talked to as we wrote this book laughed openly about how difficult it is to understand them and, in a sense, to please them sexually. "We women change our minds all the time," Jocelyn told me. "Danny might have understood me yesterday, but that doesn't mean he understands me today."

A woman's sexual interest tends to fluctuate according to the time of the month or according to her mood. In contrast, most of the men we talked to had quite similar and predictable preferences. As the language of the wisdom literature discussed in chapter 1 pointed out, many husbands are motivated by sight in a way the Bible describes as "captivated" and "overwhelmed." A quick glimpse of her breasts or the beauty of her bare back as she gets dressed can make many husbands swoon, even if they know their wives are in a rush and sex is off the table. Husbands also said how much they desire their wives, how much it means to them when their wives pursue them, and even more, how big of a thrill it is—not just physically, but emotionally—when their wives enjoy themselves during sex.

We're going to address each of these issues, with this caveat: while men tend to be similar to each other in this regard, please talk this chapter over with your spouse. Not every man is alike in all the same ways, so please talk about the issues addressed here. Your marriage could suffer all kinds of harm if you start treating your husband like most men want to be treated if that's not how *he* wants to be treated.

The very act of sex speaks of profound differences in gender: forcefulness that requires gentleness, initiation that requires receiving, control met with surrender. The complementary acts of sex reflect the divine truth of two becoming one, each partner adding something the other lacks in a gorgeous physical symphony. Learning to understand and appreciate each other will allow those differences to draw you together and give you a fresh appreciation of the wonder of marital sex between a man and a woman.

Beauty to Behold

Good news, wives! In our private Facebook group in which dozens of couples shared their stories, all of the husbands who responded said they are not looking for the "supermodel" standard of beauty but instead are drawn to their wives as they are. If you want to get your husband excited, you don't have to become someone else; you just have to let him see you naked.

Braden says, "For me, the supermodel look isn't beautiful. It isn't realistic. I love the fact that my wife weighs a bit more and has stretch marks and scars. I truly appreciate that about her. And seeing her naked is amazing. There is an intimacy to it because I'm the only one who gets to see that—and that excites me. Even when it's not a sexual thing, it's exciting to see my wife naked because this is my wife. I wish she could get it out of her head that she does not measure up to the cultural standards of beauty. In my eyes she is the hottest lady ever."

Craig agrees with Braden. "My wife is short and curvy and just plain beautiful. I don't have a toned body at all, and I think it's a severe double standard for me to expect her to focus on being a supermodel when I'm mushy around the midsection. She loves me and has dedicated her body to our marriage, and I find that very sexy."

That phrase, "dedicated her body to our marriage," is particularly powerful. Craig goes on to say, "When she is able to put aside our society's physical expectations and simply let go, it is the epitome of a Garden of Eden encounter! Simply unashamed. When she allows me to see her naked, it is a physical manifestation of telling me she trusts me, accepts me, loves me, and likes me in one fell swoop. There is absolutely no critiquing in that moment, but simply the first stages of the mingling of our souls."

Camille notices the same reaction in her husband. She says that undressing in front of him lights up his face "like a child waking up on Christmas morning! I know that grin."

When a wife embraces her feminine beauty, she becomes even more beautiful to her husband. Marco explains, "To me my wife is at her most attractive when she thinks she is beautiful. Like most women, my wife has struggled at times with her looks. No matter how much I told her I thought she was the most beautiful woman in the world, she struggled. After we had been married about five years, she started diving into understanding color palettes and how clothes are cut. She wanted to learn what worked best for her skin tone and her figure. After seventeen-plus years, she is still learning. But now when she feels like she looks beautiful, it's like her beauty is magnified to something I would not have thought possible."

Notice what Marco said: "When she feels like she looks beautiful, it's like her beauty is magnified to something I would not have thought possible." I've heard husband after husband echo this sentiment. Seeing his wife show confidence in her beauty is pretty much the biggest turn-on a husband can experience.

Listen to Luke's enthusiasm for his wife: "We dated for six and a half years before getting married and stayed virgins the whole time. Undressing her on our wedding night was like unwrapping the greatest gift I could ever receive. After seven years of marriage and one child, I still feel that same way, maybe even more so. Her general body shape and curves drive me wild and keep my head turning! I'm constantly finding features of her that distract me and keep me captured by her beauty. Some days I'm infatuated by her breasts, other days it's the way her hips meet her butt, other days it's the way she looks from behind, but I'm always turned on by the way her gorgeous eyes look at me. I love every inch of my wife's body and find it sexy. She is wonderfully made, and I feel so lucky to be able to enjoy her entirely."

Luke joins the club of men who don't prefer the supermodel look. "It feels superficial, and I've always been most attracted to reality. When my wife is at her most uninhibited and free while we are having sex are the times when she is the most beautiful. Not because she has a perfect body or because the lingerie fits her like a Victoria's Secret angel, but because she is choosing to trust me and engage fully in the moment of intimacy."

Notice that Luke is saying he is more attracted by his wife's *trust* (letting him see her naked) than he is by *lust*. Wives, please understand your husband's passion to be lost in your beauty. He wants to see you. All of you. There's a reason your husband is drawn to *look*. God created him to find the female form fascinating and even enthralling. Just listen to Anthony: "Most beautiful to me physically are her curves—all the curves. Her cleavage, her hips, her graceful neck, that magical spot at the small of her back—everything that makes her feminine. I appreciate that she keeps fit and healthy, but even the impact of three kids on her body has made some of those curves more curvy and beautiful to me."

Just because you may feel something is lacking in your body doesn't mean your husband agrees—not at all! Mickel writes, "My wife hates her body, but she knows I love it. Thankfully, she's not afraid to be naked around me. I love her breasts. Even after breastfeeding two kids, her breasts are just amazing to me. I could stare at them for hours. I also love her short little legs. She's not tall, and she thinks her legs are fat, but every time she wears a dress or shorts, it turns me on."

It may be difficult for you to believe your husband appreciates your body when all you can see are the things you wish were different, but it's likely true. If you allow yourself to lay aside your concerns and fears of not measuring up, you'll give yourself the gift of being adored as a unique creation of God who can "captivate" and "overwhelm" her husband. You will also give your husband a particular kind of thrill that God designed a man to enjoy—celebrating his wife's nude body. It's not that you aren't drawn to your husband's physical form, but usually the experience is much more intense for your husband.

So to get your husband going, look for ways to show off your beauty. And for the husbands reading this chapter, you can help your wife leave her inhibitions behind by saying out loud what you're thinking internally. Let her know how much you delight in her, celebrate her, and cherish her. She has spent her entire life comparing her body to friends, models, and actresses. Let her know the "competition" is over. You chose *her*. You want to see *her*. You look at *her* in a way you will never look at another woman.

Feeling free to be naked and unashamed together is a picture of life as it was in the Garden of Eden. As a couple, you were made to enjoy this freedom in the private intimacy of marriage.

NOTE FROM DEBRA

As a woman, I understand the inhibitions that can come with being "totally naked" in front of our husbands. Sometimes even when we know our husbands love and enjoy our bodies, we can struggle to really love our own bodies. I once met a woman whose husband had never seen her totally naked in their twenty-three years of marriage! She was so filled with insecurity and shame about her body that she wouldn't allow him to take even a peek unless all the lights were off.

If you find yourself struggling with insecurity on any level, you're definitely not alone. Having birthed a few children myself, I'm seeing the processes of aging, stretching, and gaining weight starting to take a real toll on my body.

But I've discovered two little secrets I want to share with you:

1. *I can be grateful for my body*, and doing so tends to increase my confidence and decrease my insecurity. I'm grateful for this body that God has given me, complete with its flaws, failures, and extra pounds. I'm grateful for this body that has been able to give birth to children, work hard, and live the life God has called me to. I remind myself often of the importance of gratitude, and it especially became a reality a few years ago when an emergency medical complication brought me very close to not having a body to appreciate. That moment was a wake-up call, affirming that this body is a miracle for which I need to be actively grateful.
2. *I don't need to try to measure up to the supermodel standard.* That's not what my husband wants anyway. I can build up confidence and security by blocking out the noise that's telling me otherwise. I've had to examine the things I allow myself to watch on TV, the magazines I allow myself to browse, and the people I allow myself to follow on social media. If I'm not careful, I'll find myself comparing my body to other women's bodies—airbrushed, photoshopped bodies that don't even exist. I can be my greatest enemy when it comes to my confidence because there's no way to win with that kind of unrealistic comparison. Real women have wrinkles, cellulite, extra pounds, stretch marks, and everything in between. And if we're honest, so do real men! When we take away the competition, we can begin to love the body God has given us,

which increases our willingness to share our body with our spouse. What steps can you take to increase your gratitude and block out the noise?

Quantity

Throughout this book you'll notice that we are working diligently to improve the quality of the sexual experience. But take note, wives: when it comes to men, many desire a certain *quantity* of sexual experiences as well. One delightful episode a month won't be enough for most husbands, no matter how good the experience may be. Many wives have a higher libido than their husbands, so quantity may matter more to you than it does to your husband, but if your husband seems to be the higher-drive spouse, it may be helpful to remember that he has a different brain than you do.

Dr. Louann Brizendine, a neuropsychiatrist and researcher who studied at UC Berkeley, Yale, and Harvard, points out that "men have two and a half times the brain space devoted to sex drive in their hypothalamus."[1] For those of you who are married to men with a higher libido, the quantity of sexual activity has the potential to create either long-term gratitude or slow-simmering resentment. Let's not discount Dr. Brizendine's surprising scientific truth: *your husband has two and a half times more brain space devoted to sex drive than you do*. So, yes, your husband is likely to think about sex more than you do.

We want to avoid implying that a man's higher sex drive will require his wife to engage in "marital duty" sex, which doesn't satisfy and as a long-term strategy is doomed to failure. The best sex is mutual; but even when it is mutual, there may be seasons when your husband's brain cries out for sex *physically* in a way that yours doesn't. I urge you to be empathetic toward your husband's wiring, yet my intention is not to guilt you or put you under obligation, but rather to inform you of the way God designed your husband's brain.

Let's talk a bit about how to make this aspect of your husband's brain work in your favor. I remember the fear I had early on in my marriage when I realized that in a real marriage, sexual "deserts" will occur—seasons when because of health, schedule, or kids, sexual relations just weren't going to happen very often. These seasons didn't affect my sex drive, however—it was as strong as ever—so I even asked God to tamp down my desires, as if the desires themselves were the problem.

Here's why I now think that prayer was sick rather than healthy. I was looking at my sex drive and hormones—which God created—*through the lens of the fall*, as if they had been engineered by Satan for my downfall. But Satan didn't create my body, my sex hormones, or the influence my sex drive has on my brain. *God* did. I had to begin looking at strong sexual desire for my wife *through the lens of creation*, and that's when I discovered how brilliant God is. Why did God choose to make me and other husbands so vulnerable to our wives that we feel like we *need* to be intimate with them?

Most men are captivated by, and solicitous to, their wives before the wedding, but after the wedding, we often find ourselves thinking, *Okay, I got the girl. What's the next challenge?* If she had told us before the wedding, "There's a flower I need for my bridal bouquet, and it only grows on the top of Mount Everest," our response would have been, "Give me six weeks, babe. You're going to get that flower!" Now she asks us to put a coaster under our drink or pick up our socks from the floor, and we act like she's requesting twelve hours of hard labor.

God isn't unaware of this tendency, so he has given us men a physiological compulsion to keep our wives near and dear in our affections. If it has been a while since we've had sex, those hormones start to boil, and the "drive" slowly begins to captivate our minds. If we grow in love and understanding, we'll learn that for our wives to be sexually available to us, they need to be relationally and even spiritually connected with us. When I saw this as God's creational design, I realized that my sex drive was God's way of keeping me aware of my wife's *relational* needs. I'm not saying the only reason men pursue their wives nonsexually is to get them into bed. I treasure my wife's friendship, her companionship in Christ, her intellect, and her conversation. But the fact that male brains tend to have more space devoted to the sex drive can motivate us men to pursue our wives on all those levels—with loyalty, empathy, and love. God's design is for men to be so sexually vulnerable to their wives that they don't neglect them in other aspects of the relationship. It's as if God made a "creational check" against letting our vocation, hobbies, or even children eclipse our passion to cherish our wives. Our sex drive simply makes the relational needs at times feel a little more urgent. It's a *means* to a more intentional relationship, not an end.

Let's draw this out a little further, in a way that I believe gives even more glory to God's brilliance. Wives, when your husband's vulnerability is met with your generosity, he will be drawn to you in a particularly powerful way. A woman has significantly higher levels of oxytocin going through her brain than a male does.[2] Oxytocin has been called the "cuddle chemical" because it releases feelings of affection, warmth, and bonding. When a man has sex with his wife, his low levels of oxytocin rise to flood stage. A woman's level of oxytocin rises as well, but because her "resting rate" is higher than a man's, she doesn't notice quite the same bump.

During sex, oxytocin combines "with the hormone vasopressin, which helps create vivid, emotional, sensory memories, which in turn deepens feelings for the love object. This little bonding hormone instantly works like superglue to the heart and makes you feel happy, even euphoric, when you . . . hear the soft sound of her voice. It makes you prefer the shape, sound, smell and look of your mate above all others."[3]

So by God's design, the husband's generally stronger desire (we know there are exceptions) moves him to be sexually intimate with his wife, which requires him to be relationally and even spiritually intimate, so that the couple's passion is renewed, strengthened, and focused and the husband's view of his wife's beauty above all others is confirmed and even enhanced.

It's a brilliant process designed by a master Creator who truly knew what he was doing—strong sexual hormones in the male brain can strengthen the entire marital relationship when both husband and wife are faithful, generous, and active.

After fifteen years of being married to Danny, Jocelyn has learned firsthand how understanding this process can serve her marriage. She concluded, "They say men need respect, but men also need sex." (Of course, women need respect and sex to the same degree.)

Some women understandably cry foul when we say, in this regard, that your husband "needs" you. *Needs* is a strong word that can carry dangerous connotations. And the concept falls apart completely when we admit that your husband will not die and does not need to fall into sin if the two of you don't engage in sex. The fear that your husband will sin against you if you don't have sex with him every so often is a great way to turn a mutual delight into an abusive obligation that feels like relational terrorism. So I'm somewhat wary of using the word *needs* in an absolute sense, the way Jocelyn does, because every man is responsible for his own pursuit of purity. But I can tell you this: sex *feels* like a need when you are young. When a wife understands this and responds accordingly, her husband's gratitude is immense. When she acts as if she just doesn't care about something that matters so much to him, she risks bringing alienation into the relationship.

Some women have protested, "Well, what does that say about single men? How do they maintain sexual purity if sex is such a 'need'?" A single man following the will of God isn't sleeping next to a scantily clad woman every night. A single man isn't seeing a woman his brain believes is the most beautiful woman in the world get dressed and undressed a couple times a day, and sometimes even stepping naked out of the shower. A married man's brain is being awakened by visual sexual cues all day long, while a single man isn't.

More than your husband wants your *willingness*, however, he likely craves your *desire*, which is why "unexpected" initiations can be a powerful component of marital intimacy. When you surprise your husband with unexpected sexual desire, you renew the mystery that keeps sexual interest alive and exciting. Unexpected initiations are the spice of monogamy. Whether you find a place to pull over and "park," stop to kiss him in the middle of the woods on a long and isolated hike, or surprise him in the morning with a special wake-up, small acts like these create a fascination that serves romantic love and cherishing. When your husband never knows what you're going to do next, you're re-creating the spark of discovery that animated your season of early love and infatuation. If you have young children, you may not be able to surprise your husband this way every week (maybe not even every month), but just a few times a year will keep that spark alive. If you truly want to know what gets him going, occasionally shock him with your unexpected sexual desire.

I want to point out that when we're talking about frequency, we're not talking about a situation where a husband is insisting on sex several times a day (long past the honeymoon) or even every day. Something else other than sexual desire for your mate is going on in that case, and whatever it is will have to be dealt with by seeing a counselor, not by putting unreasonable demands on your spouse. Since every wife's desire is different, every couple's frequency will be different, but when a husband of a few years tells me three times a week just isn't enough, I'm likely going to focus on his expectations, not on his wife's willingness.

A Turndown That Turns Your Husband On

For the vast majority of men, being turned down sexually doesn't feel like you're avoiding an act; it feels like you're saying no to *him*, saying that *he's* not desirable. I know you want to say, "I'm just not into sex tonight," but he'll still hear (unless you're very careful in the way you express it), "I'm just not into *you* tonight."

Your husband longs to hear, "He is altogether desirable. This is my beloved and this is my friend" (Song of Songs 5:16 ESV).

Does this mean you should never say no? Of course not. Saying "I do" to your husband on your wedding day is not saying yes to twenty-four hours-a-day, seven-days-a-week, 365-days a year sexual availability. Sex as a marital duty more than a mutual delight falls far short of the standard couples should be striving for. A husband who expects his wife to be in the mood just because he is in the mood doesn't understand psychology, physiology, or sex in marriage. If he keeps pushing, it can even turn into abuse.

Which means, of course, there are legitimate moments when physically or emotionally you just *can't* "get there." If these "moments" last for weeks instead of days or become too common, we hope the two of you will seek professional care (medically or psychologically) to deal with the underlying issue (recognizing that part of the problem may be your husband's attitude or his pattern of lovemaking).

That's why learning *how* to turn down your husband is so important. Many wives have learned how to turn down their husbands in a way that turns them on!

Let's begin with this. Instead of saying either yes or no, recognize there's a place in marriage for "maybe." Cassine likes to suggest a middle ground. "Hmm. Let's start kissing and see where it goes." She's not saying intercourse is on or off the table. She's just saying she's willing to kiss for a few moments as she decides.

Corrine takes a slightly different approach. "Why don't you try to convince me I want to have sex?" Her husband can try to talk her into it. He can try to touch her into it. He can give her a back rub, and often (but not always) she may decide sex sounds like a good idea after all. But she and her husband have a healthy marriage, and he can take a "no" without pouting, even if he gives her a back rub and she realizes that tonight just isn't going to be the night.

What I want every wife to understand is how vulnerable your husband feels when he approaches you for sex. This is true even in long marriages, even in marriages where the wife has seen him naked every day since their wedding. Shaunti Feldhahn writes, "Many men in my research told me there is no time more insecure, scary and vulnerable than when they approach their wives in that way. They are essentially laying their 'desirability' and their heart out in front of you and asking, 'what do you think of me?' Without realizing it, when we are tired or just not in the mood, it is easy to brush him off in a way that cuts that vulnerable heart deeply."[4]

Jenna has learned to replace "no" with "why don't we try tomorrow?" But then she has to make sure she's physically ready and mentally prepared twenty-four hours later, or that answer will start to mean the same thing as "no."

Another woman I interviewed, Camille, said the following: "I want your [insert a few explicit words], but I'm not feeling well right now. You know I'm a sure thing, though, and I promise I will make up for it and rock your world tomorrow night!" Camille tries not to use this response very often, because she's determined to be as available as possible. But a response like this brilliantly creates *anticipation* instead of *frustration.* Camille's response makes it clear that her refusal is not about a lack of desire; it's about the moment, and then she sets up the anticipation so that her "no" actually becomes creative "foreplay."

Rebekah never wants her husband to feel rejected, so she usually offers something besides full-on intercourse if she doesn't feel ready for an entire session of sex. The healthy dynamics in her marriage (her husband wouldn't even approach her or ask her to have sex if he thought she was hurting or tired) help make that attitude possible.

Diane and her husband heard Dr. Juli Slattery offer a suggestion that has worked wonders for them. Dr. Slattery urges the higher-drive spouse to put in a formal request, a "requisition for intimacy," in advance—say, that morning or afternoon, or even the night before. That gives the other spouse the opportunity to get there mentally and plan their day accordingly. For some couples, what works best is for the wife to simply say, "Hey, babe, it's really helpful to get some kind of advance notice. Then I can be at my best for you."

Chloe is an amazing wife in that she anticipates Christopher's sexual interest. "If I know I have a busy day tomorrow, I'll often initiate sex the day before." She foresees any circumstance that might make having sex unlikely for the next several days and decides to be the one to suggest "taking care of each other" before the necessary "fasting" starts.

In general, "Not tonight, honey" will be received well when offered in the context of a caring relationship, as well as one where such a response isn't the norm. And lest there be any doubt, "no" means "no," and every wife (or husband, for that matter) should feel free to say no without enduring abusive pouting, shouting, or chilling silence.

The Power of Your Enjoyment

A podcast host asked how as a wife she could "spice things up" for a special fifteen-year-anniversary lovemaking session. My answer may surprise some because it seems counterintuitive. "Ask yourself what would get *you* most excited and tell your husband you want him to do that." The host was thinking, *What could I do to him?* I wanted her to think about what she'd like him to do to her, because a sexually excited wife gets a husband's engine revving faster than just about anything else. If a husband is in a healthy place, nothing will get him going more than when his wife thoroughly enjoys the act of making love. Some women may have to "school" their husband a little bit in the early days, helping him understand her body, but her moans, squeals, and orgasms will get him more excited than any sexual trick, move, or position performed on him ever could.

Psychologically, most men desire to be great lovers. I did a completely unscientific Twitter poll and asked men if they'd rather be known as a great lover or a prominent CEO. Nearly 75 percent of the responders chose "great lover." Miguel told me, "I feel like Superman when I'm pleasing my wife sexually. I also feel like a failure when I can't." When a man can leave his wife panting, spent, and smiling after a particularly satisfying orgasm and then say to himself, *I brought her to that mountaintop, thank you very much*, you both win!

A friend of mine named Laura, married for more than forty years, explains the beautiful spiritual underpinning for a wife's enjoyment of sex with her husband: "By receiving her husband in the sex act, the wife is receiving him as a gift from God, saying yes to God, thanking God for her husband and appreciating him as God's gift to her. That blesses and builds up both of them."

Your ultimate gift of enjoyment, of course, is your orgasm. As you learn to orgasm (which can mean helping your husband grow as a lover), you achieve more than your own pleasure, significant as that is; you also give your husband one of the best gifts a man could ever receive. This is the amazing power of a mutually enjoyable sexual relationship. If you have to read up on how to orgasm or if you have to practice, you're not being selfish in pursuing enhanced pleasure. You're serving your husband. You give much to your husband by learning to receive yourself.

How do you let him know you're into it? Use your voice. If something feels good, let an "ohhh" slip out, or if it fits who you are, find a creative way to describe how much you like it.

Second, use your hands. Not on him, but on you. If you want him to touch your breast, grab his hand and put it there. If you want his fingers placed in a particular spot, put them there. Guiding your husband this way isn't selfish, and it isn't shameful. Taking charge and helping your husband excite you can be the most arousing thing you can do. To keep a healthy balance, make sure you comment on what he has already done right, not just what you want him to do.

Third, find ways to move and use your body. Instead of just thinking about him, think about moving yourself (a leg, your torso, etc.) here or there, this way or that way, a little faster or a little slower. Your movement to pursue pleasure is an exciting move for him.

Just keep this in mind: if your husband is spiritually and relationally healthy, he gets more pleasure from your pleasure than he does from his own, so strive for a sex life that sends you into orbit more often than not.

We've written many times throughout this book that sex is not just for the husband, so perhaps it's appropriate that we end this chapter that focuses on the husband by saying that the wife's enjoyment remains paramount. Sex isn't just physical; it's emotional and even spiritual. What I have seen is that when a husband is dedicated to his wife's pleasure and the wife is dedicated to her husband's, sex can be a supremely powerful tool to make each spouse feel loved, cherished, adored, desired, and respected. A spouse who feels loved, cherished, adored, desired, and respected is apt to be a very happy spouse indeed.

It's not just about the orgasm; not even close. It's about those wonderful smiles later in the day when the husband remembers his wife's loving care and the wife thinks about the pleasure her husband has given her, in a way that makes them grateful to God for each other and eager to get back into each other's arms.

chapter
five

WHAT GETS HER GOING

(Women, Don't Skip This Chapter!)

Debra

Men, I did you quite the favor.

I got to the bottom of what really gets your wife going. In fact, I've had intimate conversations with women in our research group, sharing their deepest, sexiest fantasies and the things that bring them to the point of complete and total arousal. And I'm about to share those things with you. But as always, be sure to bring your wife into the conversation. Ask her how she feels about these things and which ones really work for her. When it comes to learning how to please your wife, you need to be the student and allow her to be your teacher.

What I find most fascinating about sexual arousal for a woman is that it's a holistic experience—every facet of her being is involved. The word *arousal* in and of itself means "an awakening," a moving from a place of rest and slumber to a place of vigilance and excitement. Learning to awaken your wife, to draw out her appetite for sex, and to bring her to a place of wanting to let go and give it all away requires that you have an attitude of patience, a heart of humility, and a desire to learn. Awakening your wife to the place of sexual pleasure involves the arousal of her heart just as much as the arousal of her body. The two are so intertwined that it's impossible to separate one from the other. Every single woman I spoke with affirmed that in order to arouse her body, you need to begin by arousing her heart.

Arousing Her Heart

If you want to have sex tonight, gentlemen, you have to remember one thing: *foreplay starts in the morning*. Every single interaction you have with your wife throughout the day is either facilitating foreplay or extinguishing it. Every glance, every conversation, every act of service (or lack thereof), is either building emotional connection, and therefore fueling sexual connection, or hindering it. We can't start this chapter with the physical techniques, because without understanding the power of emotional arousal, you'll never be able to master the art of sexual arousal. Take a moment to read through these honest desires from the women we interviewed across the country:

- *The more intimate connection we have in our relationship, the more often I'm turned on and ready for sex. When he initiates meaningful conversation with me or even participates in meaningful conversation, it makes me want to further that connection through sex.*
- *The way he speaks to me both in and out of the bed matters to me. When he doesn't communicate verbally that he loves and desires me, I kind of crumble and forget. I have to hear it. That is especially true in bed.*
- *One of the biggest turn-ons for me is when he gives me his full and total attention and sets apart specific time for our sex life, especially when he has initiated it. Knowing that his attention*

is fully engaged helps me feel secure and important and excited for our time together. Once we're connected emotionally and mentally, I get turned on by physical touch and sexual contact, but usually everything else needs to come first for me to be the most excited for sex.

- *When he leaves little notes for me, empties the dishwasher, or sends me a text during the day, I know he cherishes me, and that makes me feel emotionally closer to him. That in turn will either lead to my initiating because I feel more cherished, which in turn makes me want to cherish him, or to my being receptive to any sexual advancements.*
- *A thoughtful compliment text in the day, coming home to find him getting housework done or him freshly showered, and him taking the time to hug me and really listen as he asks me about my day all contribute to me wanting to connect with him more through sex. Without my husband taking the time to care about me emotionally and practically, I know I wouldn't be ready to connect with him sexually.*
- *Physical touch is my number one love language, but if he doesn't touch me except for sex and spends no time with me, it's hard to be turned on. If my love tank is empty, there's no gas to be turned on.*

I could go on for pages, but the responses all convey the same message: *To arouse me sexually, you have to start by arousing me emotionally. In order for me to want to give my body to you, I need you to give your heart to me. I want to be seen, valued, loved, appreciated, supported, and cherished.*

That list might sound daunting, men, but a little goes a long way. In a few chapters, we're going to take time to dive deep into how to foster a strong emotional and spiritual connection in marriage "above the sheets," but for now, here's a list of practical suggestions to help get you thinking of what you can do and what you can do better:

- Send a text message during the day telling your wife you're thinking about her, sharing something you love about her, or letting her know how you feel about her.
- When you see each other for the first time after a long day of work, be deliberate about walking in the door and going straight to her, using the first five to ten minutes to embrace her, look her in the eyes, and ask her about her day.
- Ask, "What can I do to help?" when you see her rushing around to get things done around the house.
- Before you both start your day, give her a kiss and ask her, "What's one practical way I can show you love today?" She will let you know!
- Bring her an unexpected small gift, something you know she would love—just because.
- Ask her to tell you about the best part and the hardest part of her day, and take the time to really listen.
- Take initiative by tending to something around the house (a chore, a project that needs to be done, and so forth) in a way you normally wouldn't think to do.
- Leave a sweet note by the coffeepot in the morning or somewhere you know she'll see it that tells her you love her.

Be aware that arousing your wife's heart isn't a pay-to-play type of exchange. Not only is that approach disrespectful, but it's dangerous to assume, *Well, I did the dishes after dinner, so I guess that means sex tonight.* Arousing her heart is a reflection of your love and your commitment to her, which is most accurately displayed through sustained effort, time, and intent. It's how you live your life. For those of you who don't regularly have these types of emotional exchanges and are entering this process for the first time in your marriage, you have to understand that you need to lay the framework of emotional connection long before you can build a thriving sexual connection.

Arousing Her Body

If foreplay starts in the morning, it goes without saying that everything in between counts. Every touch, glance, cuddle, and caress throughout the day plays a significant role in turning up the heat in your sex life. As one woman put it, "I want hand-holding, moments of shoulder rubbing, a kiss on the cheek, or quick hugs throughout the day." Trying to be sexually intimate without having been physically intimate throughout the day or week is like trying to start a fire with no fuel. It can happen—but it takes a lot longer. One woman said it this way: "I prefer physical touch on a daily basis. If we haven't been physically affectionate for a couple weeks and then try to have sex, it takes me quite a while to relax and enjoy myself."

Sex experts and therapists refer to this kind of touch as "nonsexual" touch, meaning you're initiating touch simply because you want to be near your spouse, not necessarily because you want sex. But the truth is, in marriage even nonsexual touch has the power to become sexual touch because it's adding to the fuel that will eventually light the fire of an amazing experience of feeling sexually satisfied in each other's arms.

Here are some practical ways to practice physical touch throughout the day. Read through the list and ask yourself how regularly these types of affectionate touches make their way into your marriage (and women, remember that these are important for men too):

- **Holding hands:** Unfortunately, too many couples phase out of this simple gesture of affection. Holding hands produces a chemical in our bodies called oxytocin, the same chemical released during sex, which means it sends a powerful signal to our bodies that this is a person we're deeply connected to. The interlocking of fingers, the soft stroking of your partner's hand, is all part of the process of communicating affection and desire. It makes sense that this deeply meaningful touch paves the way for sexual arousal. How often do you hold hands, and what gets in the way of this simple act of touch?

- **Kissing:** One thing I know to be true as I've worked with thousands of couples is that the average marriage needs better kissing. Early in a relationship, it's common for a couple to engage in make-out sessions for hours on end. Somewhere along the way, this romantic kissing fizzles out in exchange for friendly pecks on the cheeks or lips. But there is so much power in romantic, long drawn-out kisses. In fact, one study showed that just by increasing the amount of kissing in their relationship, couples increased their level of relational satisfaction as well. Interestingly enough, they also reduced their stress and cholesterol levels.[1] That's some powerful lip activity! Kissing is an amazing aphrodisiac, and pressing your lips together and tasting each other's mouth and tongue send powerful messages of desire to every part of your body and brain. Consider how much (or how little) you kiss your spouse on any given day, and think through how you can be more deliberate about taking your kissing life to the next level.
- **Massage:** Nothing is more relaxing than the deliberate, pressure-releasing touch of a massage. Whether shoulders, back, feet, or something in between—the release of stress and pressure through massage is a powerful force of emotional connection and increased sexual energy. Many couples associate massage only with sexual activity, but taking the time to pleasure your spouse through a massage any time of day only adds to a couple's emotional connection and sexual fuel. Any touch is good touch, but you can take a massage to the next level by using scented oils or lotions and even by learning a thing or two about pressure points and methods to make the massage as pleasurable as possible.
- **Hugs and cuddles:** Study after study has shown that both men and women have higher marital satisfaction when physical touch is part of their everyday life.[2] Integrating touch into your daily routine means snuggling on the couch together to watch a TV show before bedtime (instead of sitting at opposite ends of the room); being deliberate to give long, lingering hugs when you

greet one another after a long day; cuddling in bed before you go to sleep or after the alarm goes off in the morning; and keeping track of how much your bodies physically touch throughout the day when you're *not* having sex. Nonsexual touch is one of the most important ways you can increase affection and security in your marriage.

- **Gentle strokes:** Lightly touching the lower part of your wife's back; wrapping your arms around her from behind and gently nuzzling your chin on her neck; stroking her arms, thighs, or back while you're sitting close—these are the gentle strokes that communicate strong and loving affection to your spouse. Do this on a long drive in the car with your spouse, even with kids in the back seat, and you'll turn something boring into something that makes her want to be alone with you. Ask your spouse to let you know the kinds of touch that speak the most to them in terms of affection and love, and then make those touches a regular part of your marriage.

Adding Fuel to the Fire

If you've taken the time and effort to make affectionate touch a regular part of your relationship, it's time to add fuel to that fire. In chapter 3, we covered the importance of understanding and identifying erogenous zones as a primary way of getting your wife aroused. I want to emphasize again something that most women want their husbands to know: *getting her turned on doesn't always look the same every day.* Different parts of her body are going to increase in sensitivity at different times of the month, week, or even day! One day, rubbing her nipples a certain way might really get her going, and the next day, you may as well be rubbing your belly and patting yourself on the head because it's doing absolutely nothing for her (or worse, it's causing pain).

This is where your attention, effort, and affection are more of a turn-on than anything else you could do to her physically. When she knows you're primarily interested in getting her to enjoy the experience, she'll be more inclined to relax. Because most women tend to need more time to get turned on than men, many women can feel like foreplay is a "chore" for the husband—and they're afraid to complicate it more than they have to. The more they feel this way, the harder it is for them to get turned on. Your wife needs to know she has the freedom to take as long as she wants and that your ultimate desire is to pleasure her. You'll be amazed how simply communicating your desire to please her can help your wife relax and get her going. You can take the initiative in creating this environment by saying things like this:

- I want you to take your time and enjoy this.
- I just want to pleasure you right now.
- Does this feel good to you?
- What would feel the best for you right now?
- What turns you on?
- How do you want me to touch you?
- Don't feel rushed. Just enjoy it.

One woman told me the best orgasm she ever had happened when her husband was able to assure her that she was his priority. Sometimes after he climaxed, if she had yet to, he would roll over and ask her if she wanted him to bring her to orgasm by using his fingers. She always wanted it but felt self-conscious about the mess and felt like she needed to go wash up first. But by the time she did and got back into bed, the mood was gone. When she finally explained her dilemma to her husband, he told her that the only thing that mattered was that she felt good, and that he didn't mind the mess. After that, she was able to let go and enjoy. All it had taken was his reassurance that her pleasure was his priority. He played a primary role in taking the pressure off her, and in turn, she was able to enjoy sex more than she ever had before.

Men, if you really want to get your wife going, be sure to remind her continually that you are available and willing to give her what she needs, when she needs it, no matter how long it takes her to get there. Don't give up, don't doze off, and don't lose interest. Practically speaking (unless you choose to get her to climax first), you're likely going to orgasm first, and after you do, you'll then want to turn all your attention toward your wife. Let her know that you are there for her, and adjust your attitude to remember that you're in this together. Because you are. Her pleasure influences your pleasure. Wives who always or almost always have an orgasm are naturally going to be more interested in sex more often. It's just human nature.

Remember that helping your wife reach orgasm will require consistent physical touch. As a man, you may not need to be touched consistently to climax; in fact, you may even need a break so you don't climax too quickly. But most women need consistent and prolonged sexual touch to help them get to the top of that mountain.

In chapter 2, we explained that a woman's sexual arousal involves working from the outside in, starting with peripheral touch of the erogenous zones (neck, back, legs, thighs, and so forth) and slowly moving toward the primary sexual zones. The key to a climax is getting her ready to receive direct stimulation. With every tender touch and gentle stroke of her body, her clitoris becomes more and more engorged, and her nipples become more and more sensitive and ready to be touched.

Once her body is ready to receive it, the top two areas for maximum sexual pleasure are steady and consistent vaginal and nipple stimulation. I asked women of different ages and stages to tell me what really gets them to climax, and the answers were consistent: *Don't stop touching, and don't give up!* Read through the following statements about what really gets a woman going, and remember that your availability and willingness are the best gifts you can give your wife in bed.

- *I like a* lot *of nipple action, most of the time. There is about a 1 percent chance I wouldn't want nipple action. The rest of the time I like pinching and licking, and even gentle biting can do the trick.*

- *At the start of sex, my husband caresses and licks my breasts while using his fingers to stimulate my clitoris. I've found that this combination makes me reach climax faster. If he ignores my breasts, it usually takes me much longer to climax.*
- *We don't give up! At the beginning of our marriage, he would finish and just roll over, which would hurt my feelings. But we worked through that, and now he always makes sure I finish! We keep at it until it happens each time.*
- *If we're in a position where he can pinch or suck my nipples or stimulate my clitoris (either by leaning forward or using his fingers), that helps me, as well as words of affirmation—but excellent foreplay is what works the best.*
- *I really enjoy both nipple and clitoris stimulation, but if he starts too quickly, I can begin to feel overstimulated, so I love a good make-out session beforehand.*

NOTE FROM GARY

You're Not Done Yet

Husbands, if you look at sex as a marathon of 26.2 miles, your climax occurs at about mile 22. If your wife hasn't had an orgasm yet, you may only be at mile 18 or 20. You're near the end, but don't stop running.

One wife mentioned how painful it was early in her marriage to see how easily her husband finished and how difficult it was for her. Another wife said, "I remember fighting back tears when my husband would collapse into pleasure while I still had no idea how to get there."[3]

Even if your wife has orgasmed, she usually experiences a plateau during which she wants to remain close, maybe talking a bit or just being held. Orgasming and then falling off her like a beached whale (one of my friend's favorite phrases to describe this) can turn a meaningful sexual experience into a hurtful encounter. I know you probably know this, but consider it a helpful reminder: sex isn't about your orgasm; it's about connecting as a couple. Having a great orgasm and then acting like the show is over is like an Olympic diver nailing all the acrobatic twists and turns of a dive, only to belly flop at the end. Run all the way to the finish line.

Men, the most sacred thing about sex in marriage is that the only person who has permission to get your wife going is you. You are the only one who holds the key to her pleasure and passion. It's a vulnerable and sacred position. It's a great privilege and a great responsibility. Your attitude of sacrifice and heart of service will arouse her heart and her body. Within the walls of this holy commitment, you have everything you need to pleasure your wife more than anyone else on this earth can. All you need to awaken your wife's desire are ears that are willing to listen, hands that are willing to learn, and a heart that is willing to serve.

chapter
six

WHAT GETS *YOU* GOING

Debra and Gary

What if we told you that the main contributor to your sexual satisfaction is *you*? You are ultimately responsible for making your sex life the best it can be.* You have the power to either take your sex life to the next level or let it stay stagnant.

Let's make this very, very practical. For some of you, this may be the most freeing thing you'll read in this book:

Men, it's not "your job" to make your wife wet.

Women, it's not "your job" to make your husband hard.

Blaming our sexual atrophy on our spouse can be so easy: "He just doesn't know how to turn me on." "She's just never in the mood for sex." But as a professional counselor, I (Debra) know one thing to be true: when you have no role in the situation, you also have no control. The moment you start blaming your spouse for your sexual struggles is the moment you begin to fracture the foundation of your marriage. But when you see *your* role in the situation, you can begin to take back

* A disclaimer about taking ownership of and responsibility for your sex life: we're referring to the average healthy married couple and the importance of seeing your role in your personal arousal; we're *not* referring to broken or abusive relationships, and in no way are we implying that one spouse is responsible for another spouse's sins and struggles. In cases of addictions, adultery, pornography use, deceit, and the like, your personal responsibility is *not* to make your sex life better but to set clear boundaries and limits and take care of your emotional, physical, and mental health.

control. When each of you takes responsibility for your own sexual pleasure, you can both breathe a sigh of relief.

Because physical bodies are so finicky and ever-changing, none of us can so master our spouse's body or memorize enough all-star tricks that whatever we do is guaranteed to work 99 percent of the time. Human bodies don't work that way, and if you're expecting your spouse to accomplish that, you're asking them to work miracles.

Your brain knows how your body is responding second by second. It's *your* job to adjust, verbalize, and move around to accommodate, increase, and ride that pleasure.

With so much discussion in the last few chapters about how to get your spouse going, we can't proceed without taking a little time to remind you that there are things you can do to aid and facilitate the process of your personal sexual arousal and response. You can get *yourself* going, but it starts by understanding that you have a role to play, and with that role comes a beautiful, powerful, God-given sense of ownership and responsibility for your own sex life.

Let's start this chapter by turning our attention toward the women. Later in the chapter we'll focus our attention on the men.

Debra

Women, we have so much more power over our personal arousal than we often realize, because, to put it bluntly, a significant part of "what gets her going" is *her*. You have a vitally important role to play in preparing your heart, mind, and body for sex. Let me offer some suggestions for how to get there.

Block Out the Distractions

We had just started making out in bed, which is usually the prelude to sex for me and John.

"Oh, I forgot to tell you something the kids said today that was *so* funny," I said, interrupting the lovemaking. We stopped for a moment to chuckle and then got right back to it.

"Hey, tomorrow, what time do you think you'll be home?" I stopped again to ask.

"The usual," he answered briefly as he pulled me a little closer, a subtle way of clearing the "space" between us, and we started back up.

"And—" I was about to comment on one last thing that had popped into my head until he stopped me.

"Less talky, more kissy," he said.

I've heard that phrase in our marriage during sex more often than I'd like to admit! It's amazing how easily my mind can wander during sex, and I know I'm not alone in this because I've heard from many women (as well as some men) who struggle to keep their mind in the right place during sex. Now, they may not verbalize their mental meanderings like I did, but the struggle to keep the mind focused is real! One of the most important sexual organs that people (and by people, I mostly mean women) fail to take advantage of in their sex lives is the brain.

If you're anything like me, you're a spouse, a parent, a daughter, a friend, a coworker, a sibling, and perhaps a lot of other roles as well. You manage the house and finances, raise the children, and accomplish your work somewhere in between all of that. You're having to multitask constantly, and your brain is filled with the million different things you're responsible for. It can be difficult to shut off that part of you, and it may be especially difficult during the quiet moments of sex.

In helping men and women improve their sex lives, I've come to realize the underestimated power of our brains. In fact, I'd go so far as to call the brain our number one sexual organ because it's responsible for every other part of our body. It's the control center, and the signals it sends out pave the way for our sexual experience. If the control center is occupied by lists, schedules, and responsibilities, it will send a rush of stress hormones and adrenaline to our body and move it into "work mode," which is the exact opposite mode we want to foster for an environment of arousal. In order for our body to move into arousal, we need to be in "relaxed mode." We need to clear our minds and focus in on what's happening. We have to deliberately put aside the to-do lists and zero in on our spouse. This applies to both men and women, but I've found that women generally have a harder time tuning out the distractions.

How do you tune out the distractions? In counseling, we call this "thought stopping," and it means exactly what it sounds like. As soon as a thought pops into your mind that doesn't belong there, you tell it to *stop*. Mentally speaking, you take that thought and file it away for another time. You take control of your thoughts rather than letting your thoughts take control of you. During sex, you don't allow yourself to dwell on any random things bouncing around in your mind; instead you "thought stop" and then turn your focus toward your husband and the sexual experience—who he is and what he means to you, how he's touching you and what feels good, where you want him to touch you and how, what you want to do to make him feel good, things you love about his character, his body, and his heart. Your thoughts pave the way for your body. You may not feel aroused at the start of sex, but your thoughts are what help you get there! Take control of your thoughts during sex and focus them on your spouse, and be aware of what feels good and what you want, and I guarantee your arousal and sexual response will follow.

Reserve Your Energy

One of the most common things I hear from women (especially women with young children) is that even when they want to have sex, they just don't have the energy to do it. After a long day of taking care of the kids, working at their jobs, and doing countless household duties, they're feeling worn-out and empty. They've been touched, needed, and clung to all day by little people, and the last thing they want is to be touched, needed, and clung to by a big person—namely, their husband.

As a mother of young children, I totally empathize with that perspective. If you find yourself preferring to avoid sex and feeling empty and depleted at the end of the day, I want to challenge you in two areas.

Make Sure You're Taking Care of Yourself

Regularly feeling empty at day's end may be a sign that you've neglected the discipline of self-care. You won't be able to take care of those closest to you if you don't take care of yourself. Self-care includes setting boundaries, making time for activities that fill you up, and setting limits on the things you can (or should) do. Another component is learning to communicate what you need. Tell your spouse what you need to help you feel filled up so that you can have the capacity to give sexually and emotionally. Don't assume he can read your mind, and don't just "do it all" because it's easier, or you risk ending the day feeling bitter and resentful. Communicate what you need and how you'd like to receive from your spouse, and then give yourself permission to enjoy being on the receiving end.

Learn to See Sex as an Act of Receiving, Not Simply an Act of Giving

Keep in mind that sex is for *you* too. I understand the perspective of the tired wife and mom who has no energy left for sex. But I believe this outlook can rob you of the joy, pleasure, and intimacy of sex by putting sex in the category of "more giving" without seeing sex as an opportunity for receiving. Going into the experience with the thought, *This is for me because I want to feel good at the end of the day*, changes your perspective about sex. Sex is just as much for you as it is for your spouse. You get the chance to take a moment to feel the pleasure of arousal.

Sex is God's gift to you at the end (or beginning) of a long, demanding day as a way to fill you with pleasure, connection, and emotional intimacy. Not only that, but the chemicals that are released in your body during sex help you fight off negative emotions and offer significant benefits to your physical body as well. When you can connect with your spouse and reach orgasm, your body and mind benefit in so many ways, including decreased stress levels, increased oxytocin (the bonding chemical), decreased blood pressure, and an increased sense of intimacy between you and your spouse. Dr. Daniel Amen has even found that sexual enjoyment and frequency prolong life![1] You can go to bed feeling fulfilled and relaxed.

Sex is an opportunity to replenish and recharge, but only if you shift your perspective and view it as an opportunity to receive just as much as to give.

Men, one way you can help your wives reserve their energy is by sharing the burden when it comes to tending to household duties and taking care of the children. One husband took on the task of cleaning up after dinner and then getting the kids bathed and put to bed while his wife had a few moments to herself to shower, read, and unwind and prepare herself mentally and emotionally for the evening. That little stretch of time away from the kids and household duties helped her unplug, clear some mental space, and reserve her physical and mental energy for later in the evening with her husband. Some women describe this buffer from parenting as necessary to get out of "mother who makes all the decisions mode" into "hot wife who wants to make passionate love to her husband" mode. It's amazing how much better your sex life can become when you've planned ahead and are deliberate about sharing the load. You can help your wife tremendously just by being attuned to how you can give to her throughout the day, freeing her up to be able to enjoy sex at the end of the day.

Invite the Mood

Once you've blocked out the distractions, put your mind in the right place, and set boundaries for your energy, the next step is to get in the mood. So much of this happens mentally—in how you think and what you allow yourself to feel about sex. Your thoughts and actions in regard to sex contribute to your ability to get in the mood, so choosing to think the right things and preparing yourself physically for sex often bring you a lot more enjoyment in the end. Here are some suggestions to help you get in the mood:

- **Invest in sexy lingerie:** Some women have an aversion to lingerie. For many women, the idea of wearing lingerie makes them feel objectified; for others, it makes them feel silly. I know a woman who decided to push herself out of her comfort zone and came downstairs wearing skimpy lingerie and high heels to impress her husband, who was in the kitchen making a sandwich for lunch. Unfortunately, not being used to high heels, she ended up tripping on the way into the kitchen and nearly smashing her face on the floor. Needless to say, the experience didn't arouse sexy feelings, but it did make for a good laugh.

When it comes to sexy lingerie, first and foremost, find something you feel comfortable in. It's important to remember that inviting the mood includes seeing sexual intimacy as something for *you*, not just something for your husband. Truth be told, your husband will likely want to remove that lingerie in less than ten seconds flat, but the key is that it gets *you* in the mood and ready for sex. Almost every woman will tell you that when she feels sexy, it's easier to act sexy and ultimately to enjoy sex! Consider investing in a few body-accentuating or revealing outfits (focus on your best features!), a couple little thongs, or a nightie or two that make you feel your best, and see how it impacts the mood!

Husband tip: Try picking out some lingerie you would love to see your wife wear, tuck it in a place where she'll see it, and leave next to it a little love note letting her know what you love about her body.

- **Prep your body:** Another way to get yourself in the mood is to shower and shave before sex. Whether a full-out Brazilian wax gets you feeling sexy or just a practical trim of the vaginal area and shaved legs—when your body is fresh and ready to go, your mood feels fresh and ready to go, sexually speaking! Put on your favorite lotion or perfume, and even try some flavored lip balm. Not only will your physical preparation help you get in the mood, but it will signal to your husband that you want to be an active participant in prioritizing sex.

Husband tip: Fresh husbands are just as helpful as fresh wives. Run a hot bath for your wife, with scented bath soaps, and then join her in the tub for an evening of soaking and . . . well, you'll have to wait and see!

- **Prep your mind:** One of the best things to do to get your mood ready for sex is to be intentional about dwelling on the things you love about your husband. Fill your mind with pleasant thoughts of who he is, how he loves you, and what he has done for you and your family. Every positive thought toward your husband is another way to prepare your heart and body for sex. Make a detailed mental list throughout the day, and then watch how this exercise has fueled your sexual mood later on that evening—if you can get yourself to wait that long after all those incredible thoughts, that is!

  Husband tip: Think of ways you can add to your wife's mental list of what she means to you and how much you love her. Be specific about showing her love and showering her with affirming words and acts of service throughout the day.
- **Put sexy time in the calendar:** Sometimes all it takes to help get yourself in the mood is to know that sex is right around the corner. Consider marking "sexy time" (you can call it ST for short or use a little heart symbol) on your weekly calendar, and use that day to get your thoughts in the right place as you anticipate and mentally prepare for being close to your husband. Think ahead about what you want to do for your husband, and what you want him to do for you. Send him a sexy text or voice mail to let him know you're thinking about it and preparing for it. The buildup will help get you ready when the time comes.

  Husband tip: Ask your wife what days and times she tends to prefer for making love. Taking her wishes into consideration, grab the calendar, mark down these spots, and call it a date!

Get in the Mood

Here's a list of additional mood-inviting actions women have shared with me. Be creative. Let loose. Give yourself permission to get in the mood. Try something new, and see what it does for your sex life!

- *Getting a Brazilian wax helps get me in the mood. I think it turns me on to know he's turned on by it. I hate getting them, but the reward outweighs the pain!*
- *Going without panties when we're on a date sparks something for me and makes me anticipate what's to come.*
- *For me, sleeping naked guarantees that it will almost always happen in the morning, if not the night of!*
- *Listening to "our music" from when we got married brings back such good memories and gets me going.*
- *Wearing crotchless panties and a skirt puts me in the mood!*
- *I make it a point not to discuss anything touchy or controversial when Sexy Time is on the calendar!*
- *Soaking in the bath helps me unwind and gets my body and mind ready for sex.*
- *Fun, flirty texts and exchanges throughout the day get me fired up!*
- *Tracking my menstrual cycle, I find myself in the mood much more during ovulation and right before my period. Knowing that helps me use my cycle to our advantage by being extra intentional around those times of the month.*
- *I have him put the kids to bed and then wait for him nude in our bedroom. That's a clear green light for him and gets me in a good mindset before he arrives!*

Gary

As Christians we rightly talk about unselfishness, humility, service, and sacrifice. Those are all good things, and in the right context, they all serve the goal of sexual satisfaction.

But I've learned something curious about sex. It took me a long time to get used to this idea, and to be honest, it confused me spiritually. I want to be a generous lover. I want to be a skilled lover. I want to focus on my wife. But I get most turned on by my wife when she is desperate to get her own needs met, which could seem selfish on her part, but it works.

Assertiveness Is Sexy

If Lisa were to meet me in a hotel room and say, "How can I please you?" the turn-on factor would be maybe a three out of ten. If she were to walk up to me and say, "I need you inside me *right now*, so get naked," the turn-on factor would be a ten out of ten.

Why does her *need* create more interest than her *offer*? Here's my guess: more than I want to be pleased, I want to be wanted. I know the same is true for my wife. If she says, "Would you like to have sex tonight?" and I respond, "I'm really into this novel right now, but if you need me to take care of you, I'm happy to do that," I may as well be splashing cold water in her face. That's exactly how my "offer" will feel.

Ironically, focusing on our own pleasure is a great way to give pleasure to our spouse. Of course, we can take this idea too far. We're not talking about being selfish and ignoring our spouse. We're not talking about an unhealthy dynamic where sex has become about "serving" one spouse almost at the expense of the other. What we mean is this: if we're a healthy Christian, we get pleasure from our spouse's pleasure, so when they focus on their own pleasure, they're pleasuring *us*. If we *both* do that, we have a wonderful recipe for a Song of Songs wedding bed.

If I could go back and talk to my well-meaning younger self, I'd tell him that "piety" can assault our passion if we think it's selfish to want to be pleasured sexually by our spouse. True to my codependent nature, I became at times too focused on Lisa to the exclusion of myself. If either of you has the attitude, even 90 percent of the time, "Just tell me what to do; I want to please you," there will come a time when the turn-on factor may feel like a "three out of ten" experience for your spouse—a nice occasional treat, but a miserable foundation for lifelong sexual enjoyment.

If all this is true, to get your spouse excited, *you* have to get excited.

Some of you have to get comfortable with how to feel, receive, and sustain pleasure. There will be seasons in your marriage when the wife may need to focus on what feels good to her, and move accordingly or even ask for more of the same, or she'll never reach orgasm. There may come a time in the husband's life when he has to think about what feels good or fall prey to erectile dysfunction. Selfishness can be a big problem in the bedroom, but going to the other extreme by not taking responsibility for your own pleasure creates problems of its own. In other words, if you are *only* thinking about getting your wife wet and she is *only* thinking about making you hard, sex may become dry and soft, and it won't entirely be your spouse's fault.

Of course, in an unbalanced or unhealthy marriage where one spouse has been acting selfishly, always making the bedroom about their own pleasure and never thinking about their spouse, this bit about focusing on and relishing your own pleasure doesn't apply. This is for the men and women who are genuinely prisoners of "too nice syndrome." In a generally healthy marriage where two people sincerely want to please each other and believe sex is for mutual enjoyment, a little bit of assertiveness can create a lot of sexiness.

Setting the Menu

To build on this principle that your marriage will benefit when you both take responsibility for your own pleasure, strive to create a menu of "mutual enjoyment." There may be times in a marriage when one partner does something that isn't their favorite, but they know their spouse really enjoys it, and they want to offer something special. But for the lion's share of your sexual relationship, seek to find mutually enjoyable pleasures. You can do great damage to your sexual relationship when you insist on doing one particular thing, especially if you know it's a sacrifice for your spouse. There are more roads to orgasm than there are to Beijing. Demanding that you travel one precise road at the expense of your partner's pleasure is a good way to make sure neither of you ever arrive.

Here's an analogy: We all know that exercise is important, but there are many ways to exercise. We can run, bowl, play volleyball, swim, or hike. If we choose a form of exercise we enjoy, we're more likely to do it more often and for longer. If we choose a form of exercise we can barely endure, eventually we'll stop exercising or at least resent exercising.

Don't fault yourself or your spouse if they simply don't enjoy one particular sexual act. I love to run, and I've run my entire life, having completed fourteen marathons to date. Lisa doesn't like to run at all; she has never completed a 10K. But we walk together. We bike together. We paddleboard together. Many times, Lisa will paddleboard while I watch, but I'll participate on some vacations just to be with Lisa. If Lisa wanted me to paddleboard twice a week, I'd probably start to hate it, but I'm happy to do it now and then. We believe in exercising together, but there are some forms of exercise we'll never share.

Likewise, in the bedroom, my job is to find things I enjoy and then find out how those things intersect with what Lisa enjoys. We can build our sexual menu from there. Don't be a dictator, but don't be a doormat either! Speak up: "I'm willing to snowshoe a couple times a year, but you need to know I enjoy cross-country skiing a lot more." As a pastor, I see couples err on both sides of this equation. Some spouses think only of their spouse's pleasure and never of their own, and so eventually they lose their desire for regular sexual connection. Other spouses demand one particular kind of sexual activity and make sure their spouse knows how dissatisfied they are if that one desire can't be met. Be more creative than this. If you can't find a way to become sexually excited that also sexually excites your spouse, keep reading. We offer a lot of suggestions in the later chapters of this book.

Both attitudes—thinking only about your spouse or only about yourself—will eventually crater your sexual passion for each other. So explore freely what gets *you* excited, but know that there are many ways to be pleasured. Wives, if your husband finishes before you do, and you know that continued intercourse isn't going to happen, you have a few options. His hand. Grinding on his leg or even on his lower back. His mouth. I don't think any healthy husband is going to mind his wife "using" him to get sexually excited and then fulfilled. Hopefully he won't stop—but maybe you'll have to help him help you.

When each partner takes responsibility for their own pleasure, so much pressure is lifted, and sex becomes a lot more fun. This is true early in marriage when the wife may have a difficult time reaching orgasm, or later in marriage when the husband may begin to experience erectile dysfunction issues. Since pressure to perform is one of the biggest turnoffs in marital sex, we can't stress enough how important it is to take responsibility for your own pleasure. When both of you know what gets you going, you're likely to find fulfillment far more often. When you feel responsible to guess what gets your spouse going, you may have better luck playing the stock market.

Staying in the Moment

To discover and explore what gets you going, try to be more present mentally. My wife continually works on getting me to be more mindful when I'm eating or even walking because I'm often lost in reverie, thinking about a talk, a book, or something else. I'm not always present with her. I might qualify for having attention deficit disorder, so maybe it's just me. But if you lean at all in this direction, work on your focus.

The next time you're in bed with your spouse, without judgment, think about what works *for you*. Think about what feels good and what doesn't. Move toward the good, and don't berate yourself if something doesn't feel good. In a healthy marriage, if a wife stops and says, "Hey, let's try this," excitement increases for the husband because he knows his wife wants to feel good.

Sometimes music can help enhance mindfulness as it blocks out background noise and makes you feel more comfortable that you won't be overheard by someone else. You may find it easier to be more mindful in a hotel room. Just try to focus on being where you are and feeling what you're feeling. Think about your pleasure. Enjoy the pleasure. Breathe deeply and thank God for the pleasure. And then thank your spouse for the pleasure. Rest in what it feels like so that you'll look forward to returning to it again and again and again . . .

Upholding Radical Exclusivity

Guys, one thing is clear: the best way to ruin your desire for your wife is to look at pornography. If I need to think about what gets me going, I first need to rid myself of anything that *stops me* from getting going. And if statistics are to be believed, more than half of today's husbands are sabotaging their marital bed by viewing pornography.[2]

Here's how porn works: The dopamine hit that makes porn use so enticing for some men comes from seeing a naked woman you've never seen before. This has been called the "Coolidge effect." It's the "something new" that gets you excited. If you come across a picture or video that's familiar, your brain doesn't get the same pop. That's why, for seriously addicted men, porn sessions can last for hours. There's always one more click to make, one more "new" woman to see.

This is the exact opposite of marital sexuality, where sexual satisfaction comes from desiring a woman you've seen naked hundreds or thousands of times through all stages of life. *Porn actually trains your brain to find less satisfaction and interest in your wife.*

If we preserve a faithful and loyal mind, however, the exact opposite happens. When we make love to our wives, we get a huge hit of oxytocin. When the oxytocin is released, our wives become more attractive to us, while other women become less attractive in comparison. By remaining mentally faithful and regularly making love to our wife, we are training our brain to view our wife as the most beautiful woman in the world. And we are cementing our sexual satisfaction in the way God intended.

Some men may say, "But watching porn gets me excited to have sex with my wife." Two things to think about here. First, is it your wife you're excited about, or is it the thought of sex? Those are two very different things. Second, as time goes on, many wives who agree to watch porn come to resent it and start to ask, "Why can't he get excited about having sex with me without seeing other naked women first?" Just because something worked once or twice doesn't mean it's an intelligent or healthy long-term strategy. Similarly, getting drunk may make you *momentarily* forget your pain, but it opens the door to all kinds of long-term problems.

We husbands should strive for the testimony of Song of Songs 6:9 (ESV): "My dove, my perfect one, is the only one." Our wife becomes our standard of beauty. There's no competition. The Song of Songs leads men to a place of asking, "Why would I want to look at anyone else when I can fill my eyes, mind, and heart with the beauty of my wife?" While we may still find the feminine form attractive and still notice the beauty of other women, our sexual desire is reserved exclusively for our wife. Embracing that truth leads to a satisfaction that porn will never match. Learn the difference between gratification and satisfaction. Porn may leave you momentarily gratified but never satisfied. And the price you pay in shame, guilt, and anger will make that gratification seem brutal.*

Putting It All Together

I grew up as an earnest believer but a misguided one. I thought pleasure was a temptation and a problem rather than a blessing and part of the solution.† If we want to cultivate and maintain long-term sexual satisfaction in marriage, we have to become friends with pleasure—our spouse's *and* our own. It is so much easier to maintain something that is mutually enjoyable than to force ourselves, out of guilt or obligation, to do something that feels like work.

If something feels good to you and to your spouse and it pleases and honors God, you've hit the mother lode! In a healthy marriage, the more enjoyable you can make sexual activity for yourself, while

---

* For those struggling with porn addiction, see Joe Dallas, *The Game Plan: The Men's 30-Day Strategy for Attaining Sexual Integrity* (Nashville: Nelson, 2005); Jay Stringer, *Unwanted: How Sexual Brokenness Reveals Our Way to Healing* (Colorado Springs: NavPress, 2018); "Conquer Series," 2 volumes, video series hosted by Dr. Ted Roberts, www.conquerseries.com.

† I wrote a book about this titled *Pure Pleasure: Why Do Christians Feel So Bad about Feeling Good?* (Grand Rapids: Zondervan, 2009).

simultaneously finding ways to bring pleasure to your spouse, the more you'll want to enjoy this wonderful path of intimacy. Mutual enjoyment leads to mutual satisfaction. Mutual satisfaction leads couples to cast those delicious smiles to each other in public later in the day. No one but the two of you knows what that smile really means: "If they had any idea what we just did . . ."

Both Debra and I (and we believe this is God's desire as well) would like to see many more married couples walking around with those kinds of smiles. Take charge of what gets *you* going, and you'll help get *your marriage* going as well.

chapter
seven

CHOOSE YOUR OWN ADVENTURE

On Sexual Positions and Perspectives

Gary and Debra

Liam was reading a book in bed when his freshly showered wife, completely naked, walked seductively up to the bed and sat down between his legs, her back leaning against his chest. "You can keep reading if you want," she said, "but I think I'll just sit here awhile."

Liam doesn't even remember putting the book down, but he does remember the feeling of his chest against her bare back, her neck and hair level with his lips, her body open to him in front, giving his hands free rein, and his wife responding so quickly . . . They started and finished in that position, with Liam leaning against the headboard the entire time.

Liam and his wife are in their late forties and have been making love for fifteen years, but "accidentally" starting out in a different position made Liam as excited as he's been in a long time. "It just sort of happened," he said, "but wow!"

One of the surprising things we've learned is that few couples talk about the sexual positions they want to try and why they end up in the positions they *do* use. This aspect of sex seems to be 90 percent spontaneous. It "just happens." A few couples may occasionally go to a website or a book to find a new position and may talk about it to figure out how to make it work, but the vast majority of the time, the why of the position, the meaning of the position, the ambience of the position, and the message of the position aren't even discussed.

We think that should change. Every sexual position can speak a different message and serve a different purpose in your relationship. Sometimes it may be all about raw passion and desire. Other times you may want soothing, quiet intimacy. Perhaps you want a good workout. Or maybe you're both looking for a quickie before the kids wake up.

Think about the positions from the perspective of how they serve your relationship and its needs at any given moment.

Anais and her husband have been married for twenty years. She prefers the missionary position above all others. "I like the closeness. The convenience of kissing. The weight of his body on mine. The protection. The covering. The strength of his arms coming through as he holds himself up over me." Even though it's not the best position for her to climax or to get stimulation in the "right" places, she says, "It's still my favorite."

As for other positions, Anais says, "Woman on top is okay because I have more control and I like watching it drive him crazy." But she's not a fan of the husband behind the wife (doggy style). "I find the position to be degrading. It isn't comfortable. And there's really only one person having fun, and I feel like I'm waiting for it to just be over." However, several wives told us they *love* the very position Anais finds degrading, which just demonstrates that every individual, and therefore every couple, is unique.

One of the benefits of changing sexual positions is that different positions stimulate different parts of each spouse's body. Moreover, different positions convey different emotional intensities. Some positions, such as the missionary position, lend themselves to face-to-face, quiet intimacy or bravely looking each other in the eye. Some, such as the "woman on top" position, speak of the wife enjoying her husband's body, being in control to put everything just where she likes it, to rub and move how she likes to rub and move.

Most of the couples we talk to have a position or two they enjoy the most and use most of the time. There's nothing wrong with that, and there's a lot right with it. Other couples crave more variety and will cycle through a dozen different alternatives before they go back to the tried and true. The marriage bed is a private, sacred place. You don't have to live up to any other couple's experiences. The ideas in this chapter are to help you reflect on what you choose to do; we don't intend to suggest in any way that something is lacking in your sexual repertoire if you and your spouse have mastered one or two positions and are content to enjoy each other in those ways nearly every time. You may not want to change what you're doing now, but keep in mind that this information may be valuable down the road as your bodies and desires mature.

The Positions (Gary)

You can find all kinds of resources with tasteful line drawings describing the various positions of intercourse.[1] Here are the most common:

1. The wife on top, either kneeling or prone
2. Side by side
3. Husband on top (he's lying down—the missionary position —or she is lying flat and he is kneeling)
4. Crosswise (the wife is on her back; the husband lies on his side perpendicular to his wife and enters her as she lifts up her legs)
5. Rear entry (either lying down—"spooning"—or with the wife on her knees, which is often referred to as doggy style)
6. Standing (what I jokingly call the "pre–emergency room position")

7. Sitting (the husband may sit behind the wife, or they may sit facing each other)
8. On the edge (the wife is lying down on the bed; the husband is standing)

Every position offers different sensations, emotions, and experiences. Some put the wife in control; others offer better visual cues; some will tax your muscles more than others. Some positions you'd be well advised to try *before* you hit the age of fifty. But every now and then, consider giving something new a chance.

Elements of the Positions

Following are some things to know in a practical sense that you otherwise might not think about.

Entry

One of the things I (Gary) was most surprised to learn when couples shared their experience is how, for many wives, *entry* was often the most pleasurable part of intercourse. Tabitha said, "Eye contact is key in this moment for me . . . We aren't generally a stare-into-each-other's-eyes couple, but this moment we try to. It's actually my favorite moment of the whole process."

Ariana said, "It's hard for me to describe the emotional and spiritual feelings that combine when my husband first enters me. When he takes his time and slowly slides in, I feel an emotional and physical bond. And then when he's all the way in, I sigh out loud as I anticipate what's yet to come. It is, for me, without a doubt, the most delicious part of making love."

Camille told me how she described the first thrust to her husband: "As crazy as the world is around us, the stresses that keep our minds occupied and all that tries to tear us apart, when I feel the warmth of you enter me with a tender look and a noticeably excited member, *everything fades away*. It's you and me against all odds, coming together and wildly in love. In that moment nothing else around us matters, all the worries about bills, or our children, ex-spouses, ornery aging parents, and the world gone mad are shelved. The first thrust completely connects you to me emotionally."

For most of us guys, this means *slow down*. Make this initial moment count. It's not primarily about the thrusting or how long we can last—it's about the wife welcoming her husband into her body, in a way a man can never understand because we'll never experience it. But make it special for her. Make sure she's lubricated. Figure out if she wants it to happen *right now*, or slowly, or by degrees. Different nights will likely mean different desires.

The position of your wife's legs will have a big influence on the experience. If her legs are closed and straight in just about any position, penetration won't be as deep; however, the clitoris will likely be stimulated more and the penis will probably feel a "tighter" sensation. When the wife opens her legs or brings them up toward her chest, the husband can penetrate more deeply and there will be more skin contact. Your genitals will connect more and there can be "grinding" on her pubic bone, which creates a different sensation for each partner.

Size Matters

Size matters, but we're not making a judgment here; it just is what it is. Depending on the length or angle of the husband's erect penis and the size of the wife's vagina, some positions other couples might enjoy could be painful or impossible. Size can have certain advantages and disadvantages, so we're not saying one size is better (in either case) than another. We simply recommend that you experiment to find out what positions work best for you. If you try one that, for whatever reason, just doesn't work (or takes more effort than it's worth), move on. Your two bodies can enjoy other positions in ways other couples will never know. Keep in mind that sometimes it's about figuring it out more than a physical limitation. When Phoebe and her husband, as newlyweds, first tried side by side, "we couldn't do it and my husband got discouraged and insecure and said, 'I'm not long enough,' but that wasn't true. We just needed more experience and time practicing. Now we are able to do it!" For the record, she added a smiley face.

Thrusting

Where the length of the penis doesn't help (and often can hurt) is during thrusting. While some wives say they enjoy a little "deep thrusting," when it comes to nerve endings (as Debra pointed out in chapter 3), a woman's vagina is most sensitive just one or two inches in. So, guys, while your wife may on occasion like the sensation of you filling her and going deep, other times shallow thrusts will awaken her nerve endings much more. Think of it this way: it's not the deeper thrusting that's making electricity happen; it's the *moving in and out*, especially the first inch or two, that is firing up your wife's brain. Shallow thrusts might be better for her. Mixing it up is even better.

Dr. Douglas Rosenau counsels, "Intermittently varying rates and depth of thrusting is a crucial skill of the mature lover. Intercourse thrusting might be charted like this: slow-deep, rapid-shallow, stop, rapid-deep, stop, rapid-deep, slow-shallow, slow-deeper, stop, rapid-shallow, and so on."[2] This isn't a formula; it's just a description of one approach to mix things up. Let your wife's movements and language guide you.

Here's a suggestion for men: Make love with your wife on top *and let her control the thrusting.* Notice the speed, the depth, and the angle. Does she grind or go up and down? How do her movements change as she gets closer to orgasm? *Don't think this is how she always likes it,* but be aware of the way she moves.

Another thing to keep in mind about thrusting is that you don't always have to! Try just moving around in circles, rocking, or even lying still. The wife can use her PC muscles to "squeeze" her husband. Enjoy simply being "one" in body for a while.

Positions Are a Part of Sexual Pleasure, but Not the Entire Meal

Some women rarely climax in any sexual position. Some positions will be more pleasurable to her than others, but it's perfectly acceptable for the wife to "finish" either before or after intercourse takes place. We hope by now readers will understand how important the wife's orgasm is, and that if she can't have one while her husband is inside her, the couple will find other ways to bring her to orgasm either before or after.

Taking a Different Path

Couples we talked to have given us a glimpse of how different positions create different relational dynamics. Choosing a position is tantamount to choosing a mood.

One of Bella's favorite positions is when Keir is on top and has his hands on the headboard. "His chest and arms look really strong and masculine in that position. It gives me the sensation of being safe in his strong and loving arms. In that position I have a deepened sense of trust, security, and closeness with him." Fortunately, that's Keir's favorite position as well: "I like when I'm on top of her and can look into her eyes. Her eyes are mesmerizing. They draw me in." Other times, Bella likes "when he folds me up like a pretzel under him. The angle feels really good."

Mark and his wife like to switch things around. "Most times I like to get at least a little time behind her because I like the view so much, but I ultimately prefer to finish with the classic missionary or wife on top, as there's a closeness I find in those positions that meets a deeper need. I like to see her smile, and it reassures me as a man somehow."

Shaunda likes to be on top because it becomes spiritually meaningful to her. "I find this position deeply communicates my vulnerability. It also confronts my self-righteousness and a perception engraved in me from childhood that sex is naughty or dirty. This position kills that." It also makes her feel like a woman who enjoys sex. "I can't hide how I am enjoying sexual intimacy. For me, being on top also confronts a deeply engraved perception that sex is for men's enjoyment only. I always reach climax in that position."

Not surprisingly, such a spiritual experience leads her to worship: "I thank God for engineering such pleasure and knowing what will lead to such wonderful marital contentment with each other. There's something about that position that makes me feel tender, gentle, loving, and vulnerable toward my husband. It makes me feel close to him, and I don't want to let go of him, even when we get back out in public. I just know I love this man!"

Maria and Matteo like to mix things up a lot, but Maria's current favorite position is "when I'm on the edge of the bed, lifted to a proper height so he has access to a particular angle that seems to send me to the moon very quickly. He loves to watch me when I climax, and we usually finish up in this position, smiling and laughing together."

That position produces the quickest, most intense pleasure for Maria and Matteo. When the emotional climate in their home is strained, such as when they've been arguing and need to experience closeness, Maria says, "I end up on top while he is sitting up, so we are eye to eye and can kiss. This position seems to put us back together. Another position that seems to express the depth of our love for one another is when he is on top. We rarely finish this way, as it doesn't reach that special spot for me, but it'll often be part of the journey." On those special nights when Maria is feeling "confident or exotic, I like to bend over in front of him."

Matteo and Maria seem to have discovered the key that it's okay to need or want something different from each sexual experience and to pick positions that foster that desire. Do you want it to be furious and passionate? Slow and sensuous? Playful and fun? Intense and long, so that you're both exhausted afterward? Each different experience with your spouse creates a different ambience and serves your marriage in a different way.

Savannah has a good take on this: "Good sex, in my book, isn't about always feeling the need to be adventurous, but about always connecting and walking away feeling satisfied. For us, that means me being on the top 95 percent of the time. It's face-to-face intimate, which is so connecting for us." Far from the same position being boring, Savannah says, "Honestly, twenty-seven years into this ride, sex has never been better!"

Choose Your Own Adventure (Debra)

When it comes to sexual positions, we want to reiterate that the main idea is to use sexual positions to serve your relationship. It's like a "choose your own adventure" book, in that reaching the end of the journey is always the goal, but getting there is going to look different for every couple. You get to decide what feels best, what you want to try (or not try), and how much you'd like to experiment. All too often, culture points to sexual positions as the recipe to a great sex life. But we know that the recipe to a great sex life has little to do with positions and everything to do with connection.

It's all about *understanding* your spouse, learning to listen to each other and to express what you each want and need in the relationship. You could say a good sex life is more about an emotional position, understanding where the other is coming from, than it is about a physical position.

The only obstacle, then, is each couple's comfort level in discussing their sex life. One thing I've observed in my work with couples is that the topic of sex and sexual satisfaction is something many are uncomfortable talking through. Sex is something most married people engage in, yet so few take the time to talk about it in detail. But in order to get better at it, we would benefit greatly to have a specific purpose and plan. We need to get on the same page and understand one another's perspective.

It took at least half a decade for my husband, John, and I to get comfortable talking openly, honestly, and in detail about our sex life. It was common for us to talk about frequency, for example—as in when we wanted to have sex, or how often. But when it came to the actual details of what felt good, what we each wanted to try, where we wanted the other partner to touch and how, what we liked and disliked, it took a few years for us to get comfortable with the conversation.

We both come from pasts where the topic of sex was considered "sacred"—so sacred, I might add, that no one ever talked about it. Which was problematic. Having healthy conversations about sex definitely wasn't something anyone ever brought up, much less taught us how to do before marriage. We've had to learn how to have these conversations along the way. It's times like these when I look back and feel deeply grateful for my training as a licensed counselor and the way my experience has influenced our marriage with regard to open and honest conversations about sex, and I want to share some of what I've learned.

1. Plan Ahead for the Conversation

When it comes to initiating a conversation about sex, the most important thing to remember is not to surprise your spouse. Raising the topic with your spouse shortly after a negative sexual experience ends up causing more harm than good.

James found himself frustrated after a sexual encounter with his wife in which he felt she wasn't very enthusiastic. He felt rejected and wondered if she was being intimate with him out of duty rather than desire. While they were washing up in the bathroom, he decided to bring it up. The problem was, it was already late at night and his wife wasn't prepared for the discussion. Things went downhill from there. She was irritated that he didn't see her selflessness in the situation, and he was frustrated that she didn't seem to care about their sex life. They ended up going to bed feeling distant and isolated from one another instead of feeling close after their sexual encounter.

If you have something on your mind that you need to share with your spouse, be sure to plan ahead and make time for it instead of choosing to bring it up out of the blue. For example, you can say something like this: "Hey, I'd love to make some time to check in about our sex life and discuss how we can make it even better. Is there a time that works for you in the next day or two?"

Even if you don't have anything specific on your mind, it's still wise to check in with one another on a regular basis. When was the last time you and your spouse had a good conversation about your sex life? Mark your calendar, planning a conversation every few months to connect on this important aspect of your marriage. For some of you, having these conversations may feel unnatural and difficult at first. I've worked with a few couples who had been married for more than a decade and still felt uncomfortable saying the words *penis* and *clitoris* out loud. You have to take into consideration the different comfort levels that exist around this topic and know that it's okay! With time and familiarity, talking about your sex life will become easier.

2. Start with a Lot of Affirmation

Opening with affirmation is nonnegotiable. In marriage counseling, we always encourage couples to give at least three affirmations for every one critique. Imagine how much more this strategy matters when it comes to an area as sensitive as your sex life. Begin by telling your spouse the things you love and appreciate about them, and specifically about your sex life. Here are examples of affirmations to get you started:

- I love the feeling of being wrapped up in your strong arms.
- I'm so attracted to your body. (Consider sharing the particular features you love.)
- I appreciate how you're willing to invest in our sex life even after a long, hard day.
- I love that you're willing to try new things in the bedroom.

Be specific about the things you appreciate and enjoy about your sex life. If your sex life is an area of struggle for you in this season of life, affirm the things you love about your spouse and your relationship. It doesn't have to be a sexual affirmation to make an impact. But you do have to begin with affirmation if you want the conversation to be effective.

3. Focus on One Area of Growth

I strongly advise that you tackle one area at a time. For example, if you want to have a conversation about sexual positions, keep the focus there. Don't bring up a list of other things you'd like to work on, because it may be overwhelming and discouraging for your spouse. Since this chapter is about sexual positions, let's look at some questions you can consider asking your spouse as you talk through this topic:

- What has been your favorite sexual position so far, and why do you enjoy it?
- What does this position [insert the name or description of the position] feel like for you?
- Are there any new positions you'd like to try?
- Is there anything I can do during this position to make it even more enjoyable for you?
- Is there anything I do during this position that causes you pain or discomfort in any way?
- Do you prefer trying different positions during one lovemaking session, or do you like to stick to one position?

If another topic comes up that you'd like to talk about as a couple, make a note of it and schedule it for your next "sex talk" time. There is no such thing as too many healthy conversations about your sex life.

4. Take the Time to Ask Questions and Be Sure to Listen to the Answers

Remember how I explained how important it is to understand each other's perspective? This is where that approach especially comes into play in the conversation. Oftentimes we go into conversations more focused on what we want to express than on what we want to learn from our spouse or on how they're experiencing the conversation. Tune in to the needs of your spouse, and make sure you're taking the time to ask questions and listen to the answers just as much as you're taking the time to share what's on your heart. For your reference, here's a list of additional questions you may want to ask:

- How do you feel about the frequency of sex in our marriage? How many times a week would you like to have sex?
- What time of day do you tend to enjoy sex the most?
- What's your favorite place on your body to be touched or kissed during sex?
- Is there anything you dislike during sex?
- What's your preferred way to initiate sex?
- What's your preferred way to communicate you're not in the mood for sex?
- Is there anything new you'd like to try during sex? A new place or position?
- What gets you most turned on and ready for sex?
- What tends to put a damper on your mood for sex?
- What do you enjoy during foreplay?
- Is there anything you wish I would do more for you during sex?
- Is there anything you would like me to stop doing during sex?
- How satisfied are you with how long it takes us to be intimate? Do you wish our times of lovemaking were longer or shorter?

5. End with a Practical Next Step

It's one thing to simply talk through issues like these, but another thing to come up with the next step. Let's go back to James and his wife. Once James decided to carve out special time for their sex conversation, he was able to begin by affirming his wife and listening to her before explaining his desire that she would show more enthusiasm during sex. He asked specific questions and found out that she felt most depleted at the end of the day. Having sex at the end of a long day, much less being enthusiastic about it, felt like a huge sacrifice of love on her part. They talked through some suggestions and were able to come to the realization that morning sex would be much more doable for her. Their next step was to schedule one morning lovemaking session per week—her preferred time for sex. When James understood his wife better, he was able to realize her lack of enthusiasm wasn't about her rejecting him but rather about her feeling wiped out at the end of a long day. Not only did their communication mature during this process, but they also were able to enjoy much more enthusiastic morning sex along the way.

As you think through your sex life and the topic at hand, be sure to come up with one "next step" for you and your spouse on this journey. It could be as basic as "getting more comfortable with conversations about sex by scheduling them once a month." Maybe it's deciding on a new position to try, the best way to say no when you're not feeling it without hurting the other person, or the frequency of lovemaking each week.

Also, remember that suggestions are much more effective than demands when it comes to next steps. Instead of demanding, "I want you to do this more . . . ," suggest it! "Would you be willing to try ____________ next time?" "I wonder if doing ____________ would help us enjoy it more?" "How do you feel about trying ____________?" "Maybe if you did ____________ it would help me reach climax a little faster." Suggestions come across as more inviting and less threatening in conversations about sex.

No matter what your comfort level is in terms of sexual positions, conversations, terminology, or experiences—remember that this is a process of becoming a better communicator as much as it is a process of becoming a better lover. You can use the ideas in this chapter to help you try different sexual positions if you choose, but always remember that the key to an exciting sex life is found in understanding your spouse's *emotional* position—knowing and understanding their perspective. The adventure of sex in marriage is uniquely yours, and you get to choose which way you want to go. Just remember to enjoy the ride!

chapter
eight

THE FIVE SENSES OF SEX

Gary

For the first few years of their marriage, Kyle and Abby enjoyed prolonged lovemaking sessions. Kyle can last a long time, and they took advantage of it. Now that they have four kids, however, they've learned to treasure quickies.

"Honey," one of them might say, "we've got *ten minutes*. Turn the television up loud and meet me in the bedroom."

Before they had kids, Abby wasn't into these kinds of encounters *at all*, but now she actually prefers them. "I've got four kids grabbing me all day long. When I can have an orgasm without getting pawed or pounded, I'm a happy girl."

But now Abby and Kyle are reevaluating this sexual rut that has become the norm more than they are comfortable with. "It wasn't just during the day that we got into the habit of quickies," Abby explains. "At nighttime, we're both tired and want to get to sleep, but we both know we need the physical release, so . . ."

They've come to learn that quickies are to a marriage what fast food is to a diet. They can be convenient, but they don't offer full relational health. Kyle and Abby have been trying to slow down occasionally and create more of a gourmet experience.

"We've realized it's not just about efficiency," they told me. "It's about connection. We just don't get the same connection when sex is fast and furious."

Thinking sex is only about getting to the orgasm is to sacrifice a potential thirty to forty minutes of the most delicious feeling and sensing for a five- to ten-second reflex. That's a poor trade.

Early on in their marriage, Haley experienced this with Lionel. Lionel was so focused on getting her to her orgasm—"Are you about there?" "Is this working?" "How does this feel?"—that it turned her off.

Haley's response is comical but is true to life: "If he would stop talking about my orgasm, I might just get there!"

The same is true for the husband's orgasm as well. Darrell explains, "Joanne and I made major strides when we both agreed to stop focusing on her having an orgasm. But the biggest step was when we also stopped focusing on mine. In the end, both of us usually do have orgasms, but we definitely enjoy the twenty- to thirty-minute banquet even more."

We don't intend to discount the importance of the wife's orgasm, which we believe is crucial for mutually enjoyed sexuality. Rather, we want to elevate the importance of the road *to* orgasm. Couples can increase their pleasure and sexual satisfaction enormously by focusing on the *process* that leads to orgasm, in part by utilizing different aspects of the brain and body. The idea is to *spend time* in desire rather than just *passing through* it—to taste, see, smell, hear, and feel the entire experience. Orgasm will probably happen, but the climax is merely one aspect of the lovemaking, not the entire focus. When we understand, respect, and incorporate all aspects of the mind and body that God has given us, we can enjoy the most intimate, satisfying sexual experiences in marriage.

My Brain, Your Brain, Our Brain

Your spouse's preferences—the sights, sounds, and smells that turn them on, the sensations each touch or movement brings, the way pleasure is received—likely vary widely from yours. Part of this has to do with our brains. A man's brain is very different from a woman's brain. Dr. Daniel Amen, a board-certified psychiatrist who spends much of his life looking at brain scans, points out that he can't tell if he's looking at a Caucasian, Hispanic, or African American brain, but he can tell if he's looking at a male brain or a female brain. And to complicate matters, when it comes to sexual excitement and pleasure, one woman's brain can be remarkably different from another woman's brain. God is a brilliant creator who paints with many different colors and combinations.

We'll suggest generalities in this chapter that may or may not apply to your spouse, so this is an especially important chapter to talk over with each other. As we've said elsewhere, treating your spouse the way most men or women like to be treated is a bad idea if that's not the way *your* spouse likes to be treated.

For example, most men are known to be aroused by sight more than most women are, while "women relate sexual desire to the quality of the relationship."[1] Sight is related to the limbic portion of the brain; judgments on the relationship are related to the neocortex. This explains why, in general, "a woman is more aroused by a man's reputation and social standing. A man is more apt to say he is aroused by a woman whose body fits his image of what is sexy."[2]

This generally has proved to be true for Lisa and me. As a young husband, I tried to excite Lisa with the things that were exciting for me, not realizing how different her experiences, desires, and attractions are from mine. Revving up our wives' engines, isn't always about doing more push-ups and avoiding the cheeseburgers and fries (though there may be something to both of those tactics); it may be about working hard to contribute to the family income. If you want your wife to desire you sexually, *engage her neocortex.* Self-proclaimed experts tell wives all the time to dress sexy. Put on makeup. Let your husband see you with the lights on. Fair enough—all of those things engage the limbic area of the male brain, and they usually work. But it's just as legitimate to challenge husbands to engage the neocortex of the female brain, because that works too.

Here's an analogy: At any given banquet, I'm looking at the food choices and wondering what will *taste best.* If it's high-quality barbecue brisket, a baked potato with creamy butter and bacon bits, and a salad with crunchy romaine lettuce, I'm salivating. In that instance, I'm catering entirely to my limbic system and feeling very satisfied.

At that same banquet, my wife is thinking entirely different thoughts: *Are those sweet potatoes organic, or were they grown with pesticides? Is the fish wild or farmed? How many calories are in that dressing? Is the salad made with iceberg lettuce or spring greens?* Lisa is walking up to the banquet table with her brain's neocortex in overdrive.

What if the same thing is true in the bedroom? Lisa has an outfit that makes my heart rate double. If she dabs on some essential oils, the world falls away for me. A nuclear bomb could go off next door and I wouldn't hear it. Even if I did hear it, I'd probably say, "Well, if the world is going to end, what better way to spend our final seconds?"

But because these things move *me* so much, I might think I need to find something sexy to wear and even spray myself with cologne to get Lisa going. First, I don't think many women want to see their guy in exotic underwear, and second, Lisa freaks out about the chemicals in cologne. She'd smell that cologne, and it would pass right by her limbic system straight into her neocortex and be an immediate turn*off.*

But what if I had been kind to her all day? What if I were to land a new book contract just as we were realizing we needed to do some home improvements? That would get her going a hundred miles faster than Calvin Klein underwear or Clive Christian men's perfume.

Victoria and her husband are both musicians. When she hears her husband practicing the piano, she often makes plans to seduce him later that night. One of the wives who participated in our private Facebook group is married to a pastor who preaches in a suit. She told me that when she listens to him preach a good sermon wearing a well-fitting suit, while others are taking notes on the sermon, she's thinking about what it will be like when she gets him out of that suit and into bed.

Husbands, sexual desire for many women begins in the neocortex part of the brain rather than in the limbic portion. We need to get away from the notion that the best way to make our wives want us more is to become a sexual athlete with supreme mastery of all parts of our bodies. While that may not hurt, a study on women's orgasms showed that the likelihood of a woman experiencing orgasm goes far beyond what's happening *physically* to what's been happening *relationally*, because she's more attuned to her neocortex when it comes to sexual desire.[3] So while there may be benefits to improving sexual performance, a full-on gourmet sex experience requires improving *relational connection.*

One of the most practical ways you can begin to understand how your spouse wakes up sensually is to put all five senses into play.

NOTE FROM DEBRA

What is *most* important—as Gary and I both mention throughout the book—is to be in tune with what really speaks to your spouse. We're all wired to feel most connected when the physical, the relational, and the emotional are in sync. My husband tends to be just as aroused—or more so—by how I've treated him that day (the emotional and relational piece) as by what I'm wearing. He might struggle to want to connect sexually if we haven't had a great day emotionally. In contrast, I can move past emotions a little more quickly. Even if we've had an argument or disagreement earlier, I tend to get aroused just by the scent of a certain cologne he has on, by seeing that he's wearing my favorite outfit, or even by watching him work out. Connecting physically helps me feel connected emotionally, even if we haven't had the best day. This may not be the usual "gender tendency," but it's who we are and what works for us.

It's important to understand these general concepts, and just as important to understand your spouse. Research and statistics are meaningless if they don't reflect the needs and desires of the one you love.

The Full Five

When it comes to planning a banquet, wedding, or other big celebration, the best event planners know they should engage all five senses in the process: from the scent of the flowers, to the taste of the food, to the sight of the décor, to the sound of the music, to the ambience of the room. Every sense we engage enriches the experience. The same holds true for sex. God gave us all five senses to enjoy intimacy with our spouse. Think of each sense as a tool to use to titillate, delight, and ultimately satisfy your spouse. In fact, expect intimacy to improve over time as you learn about your spouse's senses and enjoy the entire banquet instead of just focusing on the orgasm.

Touch

O that his left hand were under my head,
and that his right hand embraced me!
(Song of Solomon 8:3 NRSV)

Men, here's a big tip: "A woman's skin is at least ten times more sensitive than a man's. Women like and need to be touched more than men."[4] The feel of skin touching skin releases oxytocin. The fact that most women's skin is more sensitive than a man's explains the stereotype behind women wanting more foreplay and men rushing to intercourse. We men don't get *why* a light touch feels so electrifying, because to many of us, it *doesn't*. It also explains why women often complain about their husbands being too rough with their touches, while many men want their wives to be more direct with their touches.

The hands, feet, lips, and genitals take up the largest amount of brain space for stimulation, so touch involving these areas will be especially impactful. The area of the brain that processes genital sensations is right next to the area that lights up with foot stimulation. Their proximity partly explains why many women love foot rubs so much.

The hands themselves have about 2,500 receptors per square centimeter.[5] The amazing way that God has designed our brains means that in sexual touch, both the one being touched and the one doing the touching are having their brains activated, *even if the one doing the touching is using a tool* (like a feather, a brush, or a scarf). Neuroscientist Luke Miller explains that "the tool is being treated like a sensory extension of your body."[6] This is a wonderful twofer. *A giving touch becomes a receiving touch.*

Isn't God a master creator and designer?

So use a feather duster (one that's clean and set apart for "special" purposes). Wives, use your long hair (if you have it). Consider trying oils, lotions, or powders that alter how everything feels. Learn when to transition from a firm grab to a light tickle. Increase the variety of touches to heighten the intensity and the different brain responses.

One of Savannah and Craig's discoveries—decades into their marriage—was using frankincense with coconut oil as a lubricant. "Oowee, is it nice! Just warm enough and slick enough to make things feel extra good." When Joanie heard this, she asked Savannah, "Have you tried cypress and orange? Oh, mama!" These couples were combining touch and smell, and the responses "Oowee!" and "Oh, mama!" speak for themselves.

Barry couldn't enjoy either of these because he takes it personally that his wife needs lubrication to fully enjoy sex. For some reason, Barry thinks a lack of natural lubrication must indicate a problem either with his wife or with his technique, neither of which he is willing to accept. In Barry's mind, if *he* can't make her wet, relying on a lubricant is an insult, almost like having an affair. But without lubrication, the "touching" aspect of sex becomes painful for his wife.

This example may seem absurd, and I wish it was, but it's true. Barry's wife endured painful sex *for years* rather than admit to her husband that lubrication really helps. She didn't want him to be angry with her for not being wet enough or watch him pout that something was lacking in his sexual repertoire. To enjoy the banquet, you need to get over yourself so you can focus on your spouse. Your spouse's body is what it is; become familiar with the unique body you're making love to. The way each touch feels to you can be entirely different from the way it feels to your spouse. There's no right or wrong way for your spouse to process touch and pleasure; every brain is unique. The only thing that's guaranteed is that your spouse processes touch and pleasure differently than you do.

Gourmet banquet sex means you want your spouse to enjoy your intimate times together. Imagine dining at a restaurant where the chef prepared only the foods he liked to serve, not the kinds of food you like to eat, and it's the only restaurant you're allowed to visit for the rest of your life.

Sounds awful, doesn't it?

Pride is always destructive in relationships, but it is atomic bomb–level destructive in the bedroom.

Hearing

Let me hear your voice;
for your voice is sweet. (Song of Songs 2:14)

Danny was taking a shower on a Saturday afternoon, getting ready for the evening church service he plays at with the worship band, when a seductive Justin Timberlake song started playing through the bathroom speakers above him.

"Jocelyn's coming in!" he said with delight, and sure enough, his wife soon joined him.

Jocelyn knew choosing that song would be a signal. "For me, it's almost like doing something sneaky. He always gets ready to go into the church on Saturday at three, so I knew I could lock the door and we could have a little fun. Listening to dance or pop music gets me in the mood, and making it play loud feels like it takes over your senses. It also makes me feel confident that the kids won't overhear what's going on. When I'm less self-conscious, I'm more into the moment."

The beat, the sound, and the lyrics all proved to be a powerful aphrodisiac for this couple.

For most husbands, a wife can't be vocal enough—well, unless perhaps you're spending the night at your in-laws'. Sound is a particularly thrilling aspect of sex to put into play. This fact may be behind the exquisite experience of "hotel sex." When a couple is freed from concern about being overheard by family members, a wife's moans, shouts, or laughter can unleash new ways to thrill her husband.

But sometimes less is more. If you want to change the mood, wives, *whisper* something into his ear. It's a neurological reflex for the brain to pay close attention when the volume is dropped. But then change it up. Communicate what you want with surprising forcefulness or plead with earnest begging—whatever fits your mood, personality, or the moment. Consider how much the sexual climate will change if the wife acts in one of the following ways: demanding, begging, praising, moaning, cooing, shouting, laughing, or staying completely silent. Each form of verbalization creates an entirely different experience. Your voice can be rough, soft, urgent, soothing. Your words can be literal or provocative. But use them as much as you use your hands.

This advice applies to men as much as it does to women. Wives, how do you want your husbands to talk to you? Just as important, how do you *not* want him to talk to you? Tell him! We've discovered that husbands are just as likely to turn their wives *off* with their words as *on*, so be honest with each other.

Also consider Jocelyn and Danny's example and incorporate music into your lovemaking repertoire. It's one thing to make love to modern jazz; it's another experience to make love to classical music or romantic ballads. Darrell and Joanne are huge fans of Norah Jones and Barry White. Neuropsychologist Dr. Rhonda Freeman notes that listening to music during sex reaches three different areas of the brain: "the reward or pleasure system, the social affiliation or bonding system, and the limbic system (which processes emotions)."[7] Triggering the reward system releases dopamine and endogenous opioids. And the more your brain "fires," the more alive you feel. Dr. Freeman explains, "Those systems not only allow the pleasurable experience of sex to be amplified with music, but they also allow music to deepen your connection with your partner while subduing negative emotions."[8]

Music serves Savannah so well that she has created a special playlist of songs that will put her in the mood. Sometimes she listens to the playlist *before* her husband gets home so she can get her mind in gear before the festivities begin.

Outdoor or open-window sex can create new sounds—ocean waves crashing, rain falling (or thunder clapping!), birds chirping, the wind blowing. You may not be able to afford a hotel room at some exotic place, but you can always open a window . . .

Taste

Your lips drop sweetness as the honeycomb, my bride;
milk and honey are under your tongue.
(Song of Songs 4:11)

Of all the senses that couples disagreed about the most, how to incorporate taste into lovemaking was at the top of the list. Taste appears to be a supremely individualistic sense, especially during sex. Darrell explains, "While I am all for drizzling honey, dripping chocolate sauce, decorating with whipping cream and sprinkles, belly shots, edible underwear, flavored lubricants, and the like, Joanne has never gotten into it. She has tried most of these, but she says it's just not her thing. I respect her in this and leave all of that stuff in the kitchen."

The same difference of opinion seems to hold true for how each other's *bodies* taste. Some people are really into it; others see it as something to overcome rather than to delight in. One couple told us, "I truly enjoy the way my husband tastes, but my husband isn't such a fan. I don't know that there's much a couple can do about this other than focus on the other senses. It is what it is. Some people love cilantro, and some people hate it. You're not going to be able to change that, even if you want to."

One couple with disparate tastes during sex have found much to agree on *prior* to sex. The wife loves dark chocolate, and there's something about eating it before dinner that wakes her up to further pleasure. It sets her senses in motion, so to speak. The husband is a wine connoisseur and the wife is a foodie, so for them, while a high-class meal at an upscale restaurant is a huge turn-on, they don't like to bring taste *into* the bedroom.

If you're eating prior to making love and wondering what to choose, try putting some apples, almonds, and avocado on your salad. Neuroscientist Daniel Amen writes, "Apples not only clean the teeth and inspire the flow of saliva, but they also sweeten the breath, which is always a wonderful stimulus for the foreplay of kissing."[9] Amen explains that the smell of almonds has been reported to arouse passion in females, and avocados contain elements that enhance both male and female libido.[10]

For couples who enjoy it, food as part of lovemaking has a rich history. Dr. Michael Fenster points out that "food and sex have been bestest roomies since there has been food and sex; which is to say pretty much forever. Of all the senses, only taste and smell are predominately hard-wired directly into our brain. When we hear something, see something, or feel something, it is generally filtered first. But taste and smell home in on command central like a guided drone strike."[11]

Bella and her husband are fond of bringing surprising tastes into the encounter. One time when her husband was blindfolded, Bella put Nutella on her lips and kissed him. There was at first shock and surprise, then a lick of the lips, laughter, and a more passionate kiss in response.

Anthony, a chef, relishes taste and has learned to close his eyes while making love to his wife so that he can heighten the "sense of smell and taste for my wife—the smell of the nape of her neck, the residual taste of a great glass of wine in her kiss. For the chef in me, that awakens love."

Sight

[He:] How beautiful you are, my darling!
Oh, how beautiful!
Your eyes are doves.

[She:] How handsome you are, my beloved!
(Song of Songs 1:15–16)

In an earlier chapter we talked extensively about the importance of sight to men, but sight can also mean a lot to wives. So, men, if there are clothes that make you more or less attractive to your wife, what better reason do you need to wear them or get rid of them accordingly? I used to resist this until I realized that if something I wear makes my wife warm up to me, and something else makes her less attracted to me, why would I fight to keep that old shirt? (Unless it's a Boston Marathon finisher shirt; those should *never* be thrown away.)

When you are attracted to your spouse and you are staring into their eyes, you awaken activity in the ventral striatum, located in the limbic portion of your brain. This action creates a fun neurological spark that triggers your brain's natural reward system. Sex will feel more intense and pleasurable if you keep your eyes open and really look at each other *in the eyes*, especially as one or both of you orgasm.

Sight can be used to create sexual excitement even when you're not together. Abby's husband, Kyle, loves to receive provocative body shots texted to him. "I'm careful about where I open up any text from Abby," he says, "and when she sends me a picture in the middle of the day, I can't wait to get home to her. I'm thinking about her all day."*

Abby was at first reluctant to do this. What changed her mind? "It makes him so happy," she said. "He works really hard for us, and if I can sweeten his day a little bit, I didn't want to unnecessarily deny him something as long as God is okay with it."

She took the question to her women's Bible study where the opinion was mixed. The most common objection was, "What if it leads to him doing porn?"

Consider the Latin philosophical dictum *abusus non tollit usum*, which roughly translated means "abuse doesn't negate the proper use." Just because something can be abused doesn't mean it can't be used. In Abby and Kyle's case, the texting is creating intense desire for his wife, not for other women, and it hasn't led him to seek out porn. It also becomes all-day foreplay, so that when Kyle comes home at night, he's ready to go.

Shortly after they got married, Izzy did a boudoir photo shoot for her husband, Scott (the photographer was a woman). Scott calls the photos "awesome" and says they draw him toward Izzy again and again. With those pictures seared in his mind, his sexual interest is centered on Izzy, and neurologically he's less likely to be drawn to other women.

In a bit of a twist, sometimes intentionally *withholding* a sense can heighten the experience. Savannah says, "Sometimes I like the removal of sight so that I don't know what he's doing or where he's going next. He will blindfold me, and it can heighten the anticipation and excitement when he touches me or kisses my body simply because I don't know where he's going next."

---

* Note that some counselors strongly object to this advice, insisting that it's too dangerous for a wife to put photos of herself like this *anywhere*, lest they fall into the wrong hands. There are ways (and apps) to guard against this, but husbands, if your wife isn't comfortable with this, please don't pressure her.

Smell

Pleasing is the fragrance of your perfumes.
(Song of Songs 1:3)

If the Song of Songs has one message, it's that a lover smells wonderful. The wife says of the husband, "His cheeks are like beds of spice yielding perfume" (5:13). The husband says of the wife, "The fragrance of your perfume" is more pleasing "than any spice" (4:10).

Indeed, the female lover rejoices in both of their smells:

> While the king was at his table,
> my perfume spread its fragrance.
> My beloved is to me a sachet of myrrh
> resting between my breasts.
> My beloved is to me a cluster of henna blossoms
> from the vineyards of En Gedi. (Song of Songs 1:12–14)

Smell is the strongest of all the five senses and stimulates every aspect of our brain. It even elicits memories. Many of the couples we talked to mentioned this connection between smell and treasured sexual memories. Carrie wrote, "I bought a new lotion for a vacation in Cancun ten years ago. It was an amazing vacation—the best sex we've ever had. Now, whenever I use that lotion, we are both transported right back there." Bella keeps a bottle of the perfume she used on her wedding night and puts it on every anniversary, bringing both her and her husband back to that special event.

Citing the findings of neurologist Alan Hirsch, Dr. Daniel Amen writes, "There's a direct connection between the olfactory bulb at the top of the nose and the septal nucleus of the brain, the erection center."[12] For what it's worth, wives, Dr. Hirsch found that penile blood flow was enhanced in men by the smells of lavender and pumpkin pie—and doughnuts, licorice, and cinnamon were also among the winning scents.[13]

Dr. Hirsch studied vaginal blood flow in relation to smell and found that men's colognes actually *decrease* a woman's sexual interest, while baby powder is one of the most powerful scents to increase sexual interest.[14] Other positive smells associated with female desire are cucumber, licorice, lavender, and even pumpkin pie. Guys, think scented candles as your wife walks into the room! You should know, though, that the smell of barbecue apparently has a reverse effect on women's desire, so if you've been grilling, you'll probably want to take a shower and put on a new set of clothes.[15]

As with most things sexual, no two people have the exact same olfactory preferences. Though Dr. Hirsch found that cologne decreases *most* women's sexual interest, one wife told me that when her husband wears a certain musk-oriented cologne, "I melt in my socks and want to take off all of his clothes." So for that husband, it's probably best if he doesn't wear the cologne while getting ready for church and instead saves it for date night.

Jocelyn doesn't like either body odor or cologne; she just wants clean and unscented. "I don't mind coconut oil, but I'm not a fan at all of those scented lubes." Guys, you should know that a female brain is far more sensitive to smell than your male brain, which means just because you smell okay to yourself doesn't mean you smell pleasant to your wife. If there's any doubt, just take a shower and brush your teeth.

Meagan likes to light candles when she and her husband are in the mood. One winter, they laid a plush blanket in front of their fireplace. "The heat from the fire and the smell of logs burning really enhanced the experience."

Mark's wife has a special trick that drives him wild. There's a perfume that makes him crazy with desire, so she puts just a dab between her breasts. Mark calls it one of the most powerful turn-ons in their sexual relationship.

Candace and her husband fell into a fun kind of activity when they started using Listerine breath strips before having sex. "It's gotten to the point where if we smell the breath strip, we immediately think of sex. If you want to signal to your partner slyly that you're in the mood, you pop one of those bad boys in and the other immediately catches on. It has led to many memorable nights but has really ruined breath strips in any other setting, especially publicly."

By the way, before we conclude this section about the five senses, we should point out that there's one sexual act that engages all five senses at once: kissing each other on the lips. Think about it. Kissing on the lips with our eyes open involves touch, taste, smell, hearing, and sight. It's about the most intimate thing we can do. It's why some sex workers will do everything *but* kiss a customer on the lips. When a married couple stops kissing on the lips, it's usually a bad sign. When they perfect it to an art, their brains are firing on all cylinders with holy desire, pure passion, ecstatic longing, and thrilling pleasure. God gave us a hint of this rapture in the Song of Songs:

> [He:] May your kisses be as exciting as the best wine—
>
> [She:] Yes, wine that goes down smoothly for my lover,
> flowing gently over lips and teeth.
> (Song of Songs 7:9–10 NLT)

The Lifelong Journey

The sex life that served you well in your twenties or thirties may not work so well in your forties or fifties and beyond. Your erotic appetite will change as an individual and as a couple. The metaphor of a banquet is apt because a banquet speaks of many courses and many options. If you merely want to maintain your sexual pleasure, you're going to have to become more creative. The status quo may get boring. You may have to change, experiment, and explore just to stay even.

Author Ruth Buezis believes this concept applies especially to the wife: "I used to think my husband needed creativity in the marriage bed. I thought I needed to dress up, surprise him in new locations, or come up with a new move. It weighed me down and made me feel inadequate. Honestly, I don't think my husband really cared that much. I now understand that creativity in the marriage bed is something that I need. Women are the ones with fifty pairs of shoes, not our husbands."[16]

Dr. David Schnarch, who treated thousands of couples as a clinical psychologist, told married partners to "change your sexual style as you get older. If your sexual relationship stays the same, you are more likely to have sexual dysfunctions (and be bored to death). When your response thresholds exceed the total stimulation you get from 'doing what you usually do,' you'll start having sexual dysfunctions."[17] This may sound like a lot of work, but Dr. Schnarch made it seem like an invitation when he added, "You have dormant sexual potential that's ready and waiting to be developed."

In *Resurrecting Sex*, Schnarch teaches that we have two "response thresholds" or sexual trigger points—the amount of stimulation our body needs to stimulate sexual desire, and then again the amount of stimulation we need to reach orgasm. *This threshold changes over time.* Our brains may habituate to the "same old, same old," so the tried and true practices that worked in your twenties may not work in your forties and certainly not in your sixties.[18]

The important thing is to expect this shift and even anticipate it. Just because you may have more difficulty desiring or enjoying sex at any given moment doesn't mean your marriage has lost its spark. Hopefully, having read this, when it happens, you'll think, *Oh yeah, Gary and Debra told us this would happen. We need to switch things up.* The banqueting practices mentioned in this chapter can serve as your menu.

As couples, we may not talk often about what feels good. We just touch in the dark and keep silent, and if we hear a moan, we think it must have worked.

If you want to be a little more proactive, answer these questions together:

1. **Two of the five senses I think I'd most enjoy giving more emphasis to in our sexual repertoire are:**
   - ☐ touch
   - ☐ hearing
   - ☐ taste
   - ☐ sight
   - ☐ smell

2. **This is what I'd like to try related to those two senses:**
   - ______________________________
   - ______________________________

3. **After reading this chapter, here is one thing I believe would enhance our pleasure and connection in the bedroom.**
   - ______________________________

Your Unique Experience

After reading an early draft of this chapter, Danny sent me some helpful reflections:

> It was interesting for me to read this chapter and see things that other women really respond to but Jocelyn would be turned off by. That was the real lesson to me. We should use our senses and be open to new ideas, for sure, but remember that something that turns one woman on could really irritate another.
>
> Great marital sex is the by-product of understanding. If I learn all about Jocelyn, know her, pursue her, and become an expert about her, then we win. This is why monogamous, committed, faithful, long-term godly relationships get to have the best sex. It takes years to really know someone. Jocelyn is *special.* She's uniquely made by the Lord to be who she is, and I get to celebrate that. I enjoy her uniqueness,

> and I'm thankful that no other man could ever learn what I've learned without putting in the time. And the longer we're together, the more I get to learn about her, and the more we win in the bedroom.

Take all this information, talk it over with each other, and realize that you get the special privilege of creating a sexual relationship with your spouse that is unlike any other. When someone suggested to Alex that she and her husband would really enjoy shower sex, for instance, she cut to the chase: "I'm four foot ten, and my husband is six foot four." Though they've tried it "many times," shower sex for them isn't what it is for others, for understandable reasons!

This is what I love about marriage as God designed it: you have a lifetime to explore sexual intimacy together, so even if your marriage gets off to a weak start in this area, know that as you serve each other, the sexual experience will grow. At a banquet, nobody's plate looks exactly the same. Learn what your spouse likes, and enjoy the buffet that God has created you to enjoy!

chapter
nine

EN GEDI SEX

Gary

Lisa and I had been married for about ten years, and we had three young children. We lived in a small townhome where the bedrooms were very close together.

Very, very close.

We decided to get away for a one-evening romantic romp. I remember driving to the hotel late that afternoon, a babysitter at home with our kids. I don't remember which hotel Lisa and I were driving to, but knowing our budget back then, I can assure you it wasn't anything fancy.

This date was all about sex, and I was about as excited as a guy could be.

My vocational life was frustrating, to say the least. My financial outlook was bleak. The car we were driving died if it didn't get warmed up sufficiently or if we turned right too sharply. My physical fitness was compromised by a long commute and an obsession to become a writer, which meant I was tacking a couple hours of unpaid work onto a full-time job while suffering through Northern Virginia traffic before and after work. Add to all this my passion to spend as much time as possible with my kids, and exercise was something I *used* to do.

But none of that mattered in that moment. It was intense. I was going to have sex with my wife. In a hotel. We wouldn't have to be quiet. Lisa wouldn't have to bite a pillow. No young voice would yell out *at exactly the wrong moment* for a drink of water or because a shadowy monster lurked in their room.

Here's the thing: I don't remember what happened in that hotel room. I couldn't tell you how long it took, which position or positions we ended up in, or anything else. But boy can I remember the anticipation. I can remember driving there, seeing people all around us, and thinking, *I wouldn't want to be anyone other than me right now, driving to a hotel to have sex with my wife.*

Marriage isn't easy. But when we stay married, we can enjoy occasional moments of what I like to call "En Gedi sex."

When Solomon proclaims, "My beloved is to me a cluster of henna blossoms from the vineyards of En Gedi" (Song of Songs 1:14), he's referring to an oasis on the western shore of the Dead Sea. The Dead Sea is a famous wasteland, but En Gedi's springs and vineyards stand in stark contrast, helping to make living in a desert manageable.

En Gedi provides a powerful imagery for marital sexuality. Life can be dreary, weary, and teary. Nobody escapes the "desert" of occasional dissatisfaction, mind-numbing routine, and exhausting responsibility. This is a fallen world, and sometimes the fall feels brutal and hard.

But isn't God good, thoughtful, and kind? In the midst of these deserts, he has given us the opportunity to visit the oasis of En Gedi and forget all that is bad while remembering all that is good. When you walk out of the oasis of En Gedi, the desert will still be there, but you'll be stronger and ready to face it anew.

An Oasis for Facing the Future

Bella's husband hated his job and decided that he wanted to work for the railroad, like his stepfather had done for more than twenty-five years. The one railroad he had his eye on was holding open interviews at various locations across the country. Bella and Keir packed their bags and began traveling. Keir went to every interview—from Florida all the way up to Ohio. He had a great interview in Kentucky and thought he was going to get the job, but they ended up not calling him back for the second phase of the interview. Keir and Bella moved on and traveled a few hours to the next one.

Bella explains what happened next: "While he was at the interview, I stayed back in the hotel and prayed for him to get the job. When he came back from the interview, he walked through the door of our hotel room, tearing up and discouraged. I asked him what happened, and he began to share how the interviewers didn't give him the time of day and immediately and coldly brushed him off. As he shared, his lip was quivering, and I pulled him toward me to hug him. I could tell he felt rejected, unwanted, and inadequate. So I started to kiss him, rub my fingers through his hair, and tell him that it was their loss, that they missed out on a good man, that he is more than enough. He started to cry, and I started kissing his neck, undoing his belt, and taking off his clothes. I led him to the bed, and we began to make love. I whispered to him that he is enough, that he is intelligent, that he is a hard worker, that I'm thankful to have him as my husband, and so on. Afterward we lay in bed and held each other. He felt loved and encouraged."

In a desert of crushing disappointment, Bella invited her husband to the oasis of sexual intimacy. She initiated—that's the main thing—and then brought the "springs of refreshment" with her words: "You're enough," "You're intelligent," and "You're a hard worker."

Now for the best part: "And . . . surprise! That was when we conceived our daughter!"

Bella couldn't secure Keir's job for him, but with a tender moment of sensual connection, she could make the pain of not getting the job just a little easier to bear.

There's yet another surprise twist to this couple's story. In 2017 when Hurricane Irma (Bella refers to it as "Irmageddon") was heading for Florida, Bella and Keir packed their bags and evacuated. Bella had just graduated from college with a bachelor's in ministry leadership and started going through a long string of interviews to find a position as youth minister. By their very nature, job interviews can be soul-crushing and discouraging, but listen to this ending: "Long story short, Keir encouraged me the same way I encouraged him back in 2015. This time we conceived our son!"

An Oasis from the Past

Liz grew up with an unhealthy mindset about sex and then suffered through a horrifically abusive prior marriage (if you're going to be triggered by this story, feel free to skip over this and the next paragraph). Her ex-husband saw her as his "possession" and took sadistic pleasure in hurting her. "I have a high pain tolerance," she says. "The fact it hurt meant it *really* hurt." The abuse went on inside and outside the bedroom. When Liz was brushing her teeth, her ex would come in and slap her on the bottom so hard it felt like an assault, but her complaints would only increase his pleasure. Finally, whenever she saw him coming, "I would psych myself up for it and just take it. If I expressed pain, he'd only do it again."

I won't get into other specifics because what he did in the bedroom was even worse, with a total disregard for Liz's body and psychological health. "When he would line up shots of alcohol on the dresser with the bin of toys out, I knew it was going to be extra rough, so I would do the shots to numb the pain. It was anything but lovemaking." After the marriage was over, Liz needed multiple surgeries to repair the damage her ex-husband had done to her body.

With negative imprinting from her childhood and a horror show masquerading as sex in a prior marriage, you might imagine Liz would be done with sex. Fortunately, when she married Dan, she married a man who was as kind and gentle by nature as her ex was sadistic and cruel. The bedroom, which once was a dystopian desert, has become a wonderful oasis.

When they wake up, Liz and Dan cuddle for about fifteen minutes after the alarm goes off. "It sets the trajectory for the day and protects us from losing touch with one another. We do the same thing before going to bed at night. This deliberate time of nonsexual intimate touch sends the message that he values my presence in his life far beyond getting his sexual needs met."

Saying no wasn't an option in Liz's prior marriage, but now "even though turning Dan down isn't even on my radar, he presents making love as an option every time. He doesn't assume my willingness or desire and never demands, coerces, or guilts me into it. Being aware of our size difference, he will ask if I'm okay as far as his weight not hurting me and if I'm comfortable. He's far more concerned about me being okay than having his needs met. He's gentle and kind with his words, which makes it always feel like lovemaking rather than me just fulfilling his lust."

The end result for Liz is that "sex with my husband has been a healing oasis for me. I feel valued and protected. I don't feel like property to be harshly handled. Every time we're intimate, his consistently kind behavior is yet another piece of my healing from sexual brokenness. It redefines for me all I've ever known sex to be in the past. It's an act of acceptance, sending the message that I'm enough and that I'm valuable."

While many people have been hurt by sex, healthy sex—En Gedi sex—can gradually bring healing. We may have traveled through a desert of abuse, neglect, ridicule, or apathy to make it to the marital bed, but once we arrive, all of that can melt away as we enjoy, affirm, and love each other.

NOTE FROM DEBRA

While healthy sex can bring much healing and be an oasis from our past experiences, for many people, the journey toward healing is a long and layered process. Simply being married to a good person or being in a good place doesn't undo the pain and trauma of the past. For many people with a history like Liz's, filled with the horror of abuse, addictions, toxic experiences, or betrayal, they can't just will themselves into freedom. Sometimes, against our will, sex becomes a place of unwanted memories, a reopening of painful wounds, and a trigger to the trauma of our past.

If you're struggling through the pain of the past, there is hope for healing. There is a way to En Gedi sex, no matter how broken you feel or how much you've been hurt. But you have to remember that time doesn't heal all wounds; only Jesus can do that. And through the process of therapy, you can begin to unpack the hurts from your past, layer by layer, and find freedom and healing. En Gedi sex is for all. But we must always remember that the road to get there may be easier for some than for others.

An Oasis in the Present

Janell and Dale lived in Oklahoma, and Dale's mom, whose health was steadily declining, lived in North Carolina. Janell and Dale traveled out to see her every couple of months. On one trip they decided to go without their children. It was the first trip they had taken alone in sixteen years.

When they got to North Carolina, the nursing home personnel gave them a grim diagnosis and said Dale's mom wouldn't be able to move back into her apartment. In fact, they said she would never leave the dementia care building. That left Janell and Dale to move all of his mom's stuff out of her apartment and decide what was most important to keep so they could set up her new room at the nursing home.

"My mother-in-law was incredibly caring and had taken care of people her whole life," Janell says. "But she was also a hoarder who kept thousands of pieces of paper and every card ever sent to her. It was a monumental task to read all these and decide what to keep."

As sometimes happens in these situations, they also learned some "very troubling things" about Dale's parents' relationship. Janell could tell that Dale was having a difficult time processing all that he was going through, so the first evening after they were done, she surprised him with a generous offer of sex, including oral sex, "which was something I hardly ever did."

When Janell saw the relief this intimacy brought to Dale and the strength it gave him to press on, these sexual interludes became a pattern over the next nine days. "Every time things were getting intense with the cleaning or dealing with his mom's declining health, we would have sex. We had sex at least once a day, sometimes multiple times a day, and I'm pretty sure he got more blow jobs on that trip than in the rest of our marriage combined. We both agreed it was a fantastic way to handle stress and to lighten the mood. I was so glad to be able to be a support for him during that time."

That's what a wife did for her husband; here's what a husband did for his wife. Camille says, "I wear many hats, and exhaust myself because I am intense in my career, in my parenting, and when I can, in my time volunteering at the church. Like many women, I struggle with insecurity. I worry about our family, our finances, and if I'm honest I worry about what others think of me. The only place I am fully confident is where my husband and I come together as one in the bedroom. There are no phones, no internet, no social media—the world fades away and waits outside that closed door while he and I explore our passion in every created form imaginable."

Camille's husband, Brad, is intentional about making the bedroom and sexual intimacy an oasis for her. "He is terrific about knowing when

I've pushed myself too hard. Many times, I will come home and dinner is waiting. Afterward, a bath is drawn, with bubbles, lit candles, and a glass of wine. He has even given me a massage (we have a table in our room). It's because I know he isn't doing all of this for sex that I can't help but want to show him how much I appreciate the time to relax, the thoughtfulness, and I usually initiate it myself."

Husbands could learn a lot from Brad. Giving our wives a true oasis experience is the opposite of selfish posturing. Aim for this mindset: "I want to use this moment to help you feel rejuvenated." If that means she wants sex, so much the better.

Elizabeth was a woman who lived a hyperresponsible, take-charge-of-your-own-life existence, which her therapist, Dr. Esther Perel, discovered was hindering her sexual enjoyment.[1]

Elizabeth's husband, Vito, an Italian, prided himself on taking charge in the bedroom. Initially, that was a challenge for Elizabeth, who saw herself as always in control in all of her relationships, especially the romantic ones. When Vito introduced a different dynamic, a man taking charge, Elizabeth was shocked by how much she liked it and how much it turned her on.

"Because sex is a place where you can safely lose control?" Dr. Perel asked.

"Yes," Elizabeth answered.

"It is the one area where you don't have to make any decisions, where you don't have to feel responsible for anyone else."

"For me it's like a vacation . . . I don't have to be in charge. It's like being on a wonderful, distant island, far away from my ordinary life. I can just step out of my world and be somebody else, sexy and a little wild."[2]

If your spouse lives a hyperresponsible life with many people depending on them, your taking charge in the bedroom is like giving them, in Elizabeth's words, "a vacation." And vacation sex is often the most enjoyable sex.

Take Each Other Away

When I was doing a book tour in Germany, Lisa researched some natural springs with curative thermal waters for a birthday trip for me. When she mentioned the possibility of going, I was skeptical, as I'm not into "public pools." But that was only because I had never been in waters like these. After we'd spent a day there, Lisa told me, "You look ten years younger."

After five days back in Houston, Lisa laughed and said, "Well, the springs' effect has worn off!"

En Gedi sex is an oasis of pleasure in a wasteland of responsibility, pressure, stress, and sometimes disappointment. The "cure" won't be permanent, but this refuge adds a wonderful dimension to life. And unlike my foray to the thermal springs in Germany, we can keep going back time and again to renew that oasis feeling.

En Gedi sex is birthed in empathy and expressed in generosity and compassion. It provides a safe space to focus solely on your spouse, whether to help them heal from the past, deal with an ongoing frustration in the present, or face an uncertain future. It's an oasis of pleasure, caring, and service in a world of anger, apathy, and disappointment.

Visit the oasis of En Gedi as often as you can to find new strength, refreshment, and encouragement for your marriage.

chapter ten

SACRED SIMMERING

Gary

One of the great challenges of sexual fulfillment in the twenty-first century is that there's so little time and energy left over to enjoy sex. I get sympathetic laughs in my talks whenever I mention "hotel sex." Two of the main reasons hotel sex (or vacation sex) creates such a different experience are *time* and *energy.*

Most of us who are older than thirty will find that our sexual desires aren't like a light switch. We can't just flip them on, even if we really want to. I know many wives and husbands feel terrible (because they tell me so) when their spouse is really in the mood and they just aren't. They wish they could be. They may even try to get there. But sometimes it feels like they just can't.

Sex therapists recommend a practice called "simmering." Debra is the therapeutic professional here, not me, so I'll offer my amateur's definition: *simmering is letting sexual tension build without bringing it to a boil.* It's not foreplay; it's fore-foreplay. The purpose behind simmering is simple: it's much easier and quicker to go from simmering to boiling than it is from cold to boiling. Too many of us live in a sexually cold manner most, if not all, of the time. Pursuing simmering sets us up for the occasional boil.

While simmering may seem like a new concept in modern therapy, "sacred simmering" is thousands of years old. Let's take a look at how a husband and wife describe their sacred simmering in the Song of Songs. We'll listen in on the wife's longing first:

> Daughters of Jerusalem, I charge you—
>   if you find my beloved,
> what will you tell him?
>   Tell him I am faint with love. (Song of Songs 5:8)

This wife is so distracted by her desire to be sexually intimate with her husband that she feels "faint," even to the point of telling others, "Hey, if you see my husband, please tell him I can't wait to have sex with him!"

She wants him so much it is difficult for her to think of anything other than making love to her husband. She is the supreme example of "simmering."

But notice that this simmering doesn't just happen. She is intentional in the way she thinks about him, which builds anticipatory desire:

> My beloved is radiant and ruddy,
>   outstanding among ten thousand.
> His head is purest gold;
>   his hair is wavy
>   and black as a raven.
> His eyes are like doves
>   by the water streams,
> washed in milk,
>   mounted like jewels.
> His cheeks are like beds of spice
>   yielding perfume.
> His lips are like lilies
>   dripping with myrrh.
> His arms are rods of gold

> set with topaz.
> His body is like polished ivory
> decorated with lapis lazuli.
> His legs are pillars of marble
> set on bases of pure gold.
> His appearance is like Lebanon,
> choice as its cedars.
> His mouth is sweetness itself;
> he is altogether lovely. (Song of Songs 5:10–16)

Why did I take the time to quote such a long passage? To make this point: *the Bible contains a lengthy poem describing how a woman is meditating on the sexually desirable aspects of her husband.* By the time she's done thinking about him, she's ready to pounce! If it was wrong to think about our spouse sexually, the Bible wouldn't describe it this way. And because the Bible does describe it this way, such meditations are more than acceptable; they're *recommended.* We honor and obey God when we think about the most sexually enticing parts of our spouse to the point where we become distracted with desire.

The husband does the same thing in the way he thinks about his wife. Let's look at how the Bible describes a husband's sacred simmering:

> How beautiful your sandaled feet,
> O prince's daughter!
> Your graceful legs are like jewels,
> the work of an artist's hands.
> Your navel is a rounded goblet
> that never lacks blended wine.
> Your waist is a mound of wheat
> encircled by lilies.
> Your breasts are like two fawns,
> like twin fawns of a gazelle.
> Your neck is like an ivory tower.

> Your eyes are the pools of Heshbon
> by the gate of Bath Rabbim.
> Your nose is like the tower of Lebanon
> looking toward Damascus.
> Your head crowns you like Mount Carmel.
> Your hair is like royal tapestry;
> the king is held captive by its tresses.
> How beautiful you are and how pleasing,
> my love, with your delights!
> Your stature is like that of the palm,
> and your breasts like clusters of fruit.
> I said, "I will climb the palm tree;
> I will take hold of its fruit."
> May your breasts be like clusters of grapes on the vine,
> the fragrance of your breath like apples,
> and your mouth like the best wine. (Song of Songs 7:1–9)

Men, if you're returning from work or a business trip and you close your eyes to think about how great your wife looks when she's naked and what you want to do with her and for her when you get home, you're simply applying this passage. You're learning what it means to "simmer." Thinking about the sexually desirable qualities of your mate is a biblical thing to do! Simmering is healthy and holy, and it prepares your mind and body to enjoy your spouse.

Looking at pornography to see nameless naked women or reading erotic novels that celebrate a fictional man you're not married to undercuts marital intimacy and risks setting up comparison. But, guys, fantasizing about what your wife's naked back looks like in the candlelight? Bringing back that glimpse of her breasts as she was getting dressed in the morning? Remembering her smell as she crawled into bed and cuddled up in your arms? That's as biblical as it gets! It's a direct application of Scripture and is as far from lust as winter is from summer.

Wives, to set simmering in motion, intentionally ruminate on how it feels when your husband first enters you, when you feel his strength surround you, or when he holds you on the cusp of orgasm before lovingly bringing you over the edge. Imagine the best, most delicious parts of sex, not the "duty" parts of sex. These are holy meditations when they center on the marriage bed. If you need a fantasy break to get through a tough day, start to imagine the sexual thrills that await you at home.

NOTE FROM DEBRA

Another thing to remember about simmering is that it doesn't just mean imagining physical and sexual attributes. Other aspects of simmering are the emotional and mental components. For many women (and men), simmering begins with the way we think about our spouse throughout the day. As much as I love my husband's strong and sexy arms, for example, nothing is sexier for me than ruminating on his character and love for me—feeling my heart overflow with gratitude for my husband, remembering how he kisses me in the morning before we part ways or locks eyes with me after one of us walks in the door after a long day, seeing him play with the kids and be such a great dad, noticing the ways he helps me with things around the house, recalling how he listens to me when I'm stressed and need to talk. Those moments that demonstrate the character of my husband—and not just from the past twenty-four hours (because we've all had our bad days) but throughout the entirety of our marriage—create a constant simmer inside me like nothing else can. I've heard this same testimony from so many other women.

But the opposite happens too, and that's where we truly have to be careful. When my mind is filled with criticism and critique or my heart is filled with bitterness or resentment, when I'm only able to see flaws and failures and spotlight what's lacking in him instead of what I have in him—in those moments, my sexual flicker gets extinguished faster than the blink of an eye.

I've realized that so much of the attitude of simmering is something for which we hold personal responsibility when it comes to how we think of our spouse in our mind and feel about them in our heart.

Savannah has a favorite musical playlist that puts her in the mood. When she listens to music that she has orgasmed to, those wonderful sensual moments in the past help her anticipate tantalizing moments in the near future.

Several wives we talked to mentioned how they put lingerie on to get their *own* minds going as much as they want to fill their husband's eyes. "Sometimes it seems silly," one wife said. "The more he likes the lingerie, the sooner he wants to take it off of me."

We talked about Abby sending Kyle risqué photos at work. If that gets him thinking about her body, we're all for it. The way the couple in the Song of Songs banters with each other, it's not difficult to imagine what they would have done if they had cell phones back then.

Your simmering could be a prolonged hug or kiss in the morning. Jocelyn greets Danny with a full-on-naked body hug every morning. "I just press my breasts against him." Ninety percent of the time it doesn't lead to sex. But it leaves the thought of her beauty in Danny's mind 100 percent of the time, and Jocelyn loves knowing his thoughts will be tethered to her throughout the day.

Andrea likes little connections of a varied kind throughout the day: "It may be a pat on the behind or a quick kiss in passing, taking a moment to hug and slow down in the kitchen, a quick five-minute connection through conversation."

Brad and Camille are a bit more explicit. To get ready for those rocking Friday and Saturday nights, they'll walk around in the nude on "off day" mornings. Camille intentionally wears a "mood-striking gown" on an off night, setting up this Song of Songs atmosphere with Brad: "You have stolen my heart, my sister, my bride; you have stolen my heart with one glance of your eyes, with one jewel of your necklace" (Song of Songs 4:9).

Camille and Brad have also mastered the use of provocative, anticipatory words: "Your lips drop sweetness as the honeycomb, my bride; milk and honey are under your tongue" (Song of Songs 4:11). They've developed their own private love language, lingering on common words that have sexual innuendoes for just the two of them.

Anais once paid a visit to her husband's workplace and found a discreet place to stick a Post-it note while he was on the phone that read, "We need to have sex." In Anais's words, "He nearly lost it." This reminds me of the wife in the Song of Songs, who said:

> The mandrakes send out their fragrance,
>   and at our door is every delicacy,
> both new and old,
>   that I have stored up for you, my beloved.
>   (Song of Songs 7:13)

Using sticky notes instead of mandrakes, Anais was telling her twenty-first-century husband, "Just wait until you experience what I have stored up for you!"

This couple's testimony of learning the importance of simmering is inspiring. Anais told me that while she and her husband read what I had written about simmering, they both realized their heat was usually set too low. They both value sexual intimacy, but they came to realize that when they live at "cold" for too long, suddenly heating up can be difficult. They have renewed their commitment to live at "simmer" and are thrilled at how it's raising the level of their sexual intimacy, excitement, and enjoyment in their marriage.

The point of simmering is to sustain a low level of sexual interest throughout the day so that we're not trying to go from ice-cold to boiling in what little time we have left at the end of the day. Foreplay may be too big of a leap for couples who feel distant or distracted. Simmering sets us up for foreplay. If we keep sexual interest simmering, we'll be much more likely to find that perhaps we *do* have at least a little energy left when the moment presents itself.

We've learned that some younger couples may feel wary of the concept of simmering because the wives express concern that it *must* lead to boiling all the time. Our perspective is that it's not too big of a deal for a young husband to get a little bit of an erection and have to wait. He won't explode, and if he's spiritually healthy, he can spend his day thinking about how to please his wife instead of turning to pornography. Similarly, it's healthy for wives to feel a little stir and know that fulfillment won't come until the end of the day. Sexual tension won't kill us; on the contrary, it will focus our thoughts on our spouse and make us yearn for one another. That's a good thing, right?

Radiant Routine

Erica has four young children, and she calls her care for them a twenty-four-hour-a-day job. Her husband, Timothy, helps, but he works outside the home, which means decisions throughout the day tend to fall on her shoulders alone.

In the face of this reality, their sex life took a nosedive. Both Erica and Tim mourned their diminished lovemaking without casting judgment on either partner. They both felt tired and overwhelmed at the prospect of finding a surprise thirty-minute window and having the energy to act on that window—all while trying not to be distracted by the fact that the thirty-minute window would soon end, even if things didn't progress.

Their counselor suggested planning their times of sexual activity, an idea both Erica and Tim thought sounded horrible. "The last thing I need is another task on my to-do list," Erica complained. "That will only make things worse."

But then the counselor explained the concept of "simmering sex." She urged them to wed that concept with planned sex: "Make the entire day a routine of getting ready for sex." And the "call to duty" that Erica feared became a hot appointment she didn't want to miss.

Erica started taking a few minutes longer for her Friday morning showers (their planned day of lovemaking), making them more sensual. She thought about what she would wear during the day—underneath her clothes and on the outside as well. She and Timothy started sharing some text messages and even, on occasion, a photo or two.

Timothy learned to get home a little early on that day to help with the household duties. He took charge so Erica could enjoy a few hours without having to make a decision. Things took a huge step forward when he started bringing dinner home without asking Erica what she wanted. He figured out that "making another decision" was part of mothering for Erica, and on Friday nights, she wanted to leave mothering far behind.

The need for Erica to experience a momentary escape from mothering is why, if they got a babysitter and went out to eat, Timothy made sure every child was tucked in while Erica went straight to the master bedroom. He knew that for Erica to simmer on those days, he had to keep a wide berth between her and her mothering tasks.

Over time—it took them a few months to work everything out—Fridays became ritualistic. Erica's long morning shower, her dressing in an intentional manner, the desire-inducing text messages, and Timothy's commitment to removing obstacles that stole Erica's desire (making decisions and mothering) all created a simmering atmosphere. Now Erica says planned sex is one of the best things that ever happened to their marriage.

A caveat here: Guys, don't assume that your wife's hindrances are identical to Erica's. Maybe your wife doesn't mind making decisions and would be offended if you didn't ask her opinion about what to bring home for dinner. Maybe kissing her kids good night puts her in the mood to connect with the father of those children. The key is to figure out what turns your spouse on and what turns them off and then start to "simmer" accordingly.

Let your *entire day* be the provocative conclusion to the Song of Songs:

> Come away, my beloved,
> 	and be like a gazelle
> or like a young stag
> 	on the spice-laden mountains. (Song of Songs 8:14)

chapter
eleven

PROBLEM SPOTS

Debra

Sexual compatibility. It's a buzz phrase we hear a lot these days, especially outside of Christian community. It's an excuse people often use to justify sex before marriage. "You've got to explore, understand, experiment, and get to know yourself" is the conventional wisdom. But our culture makes far too much of the concept of sexual compatibility. In the beginning of any relationship, I believe most of us will find that we're more sexually *incompatible* with our spouse than we are compatible. Take any two people and put them together to have sex for a few years, and there will be some sort of sexual misunderstanding, sexual problem, or sexual incompatibility.

Every two people who come together in marriage will have their own unique set of sexual struggles. No one comes into a relationship sexually compatible, because every person is so different you can't possibly know how best to please your spouse. A fulfilling sexual relationship is something you create *together*. I've counseled many couples who felt sexually incompatible but who went on to learn and grow together toward great sexual satisfaction. It's part of the process for all of us. The idea that we need to explore, understand, experiment, and get to know ourselves is absolutely true—when applied in the context of marriage. One thing I wish I could tell every single couple before they enter marriage is that understanding your sexual incompatibility is simply the first step in creating a marriage marked by sexual enjoyment, intimacy, and satisfaction.

Problem Spots

For years, sexual problems in marriage were something no one dared to discuss. Couples who struggled assumed they were the only ones struggling. So they kept quiet and continued to struggle alone. Culture began to shift a little at the end of the 1990s with the introduction of medications like Viagra. Those who are younger than thirty-five have grown up with television commercials revealing and normalizing the problem of erectile dysfunction. For the first time, people realized they weren't alone in their sexual problems. And since then, the conversation has slowly moved in the right direction.

Everyone faces sexual struggles at some point in their marriage. Some of the problems will fade away as we become more accustomed to each other, but new problems will emerge as we age and our bodies change. When we asked married couples to tell us the biggest challenges, or problem spots, they had faced in their sex life, not surprisingly, many different problem spots came to the surface. I'll use the next few pages of this chapter for two main purposes: (1) to remind you and affirm to you that if you are struggling with your sex life, you are not alone; and (2) to give you some next steps as you identify and begin to deal with these common problem spots. Let's talk through some of the most common sexual problems people are facing.

Differences in Desire (or No Desire Altogether)

In a survey of more than one thousand married people, 61 percent reported that differences in sexual desire, or a lack of desire altogether, was the number one problem spot they were facing in their sex life.[1] It's common to have seasons when sex drive is mismatched in a marriage.

And interestingly enough, in different seasons and stages of marriage, we often see a flip in which the lower-drive spouse becomes the higher-drive spouse. The bottom line is that if not handled well, these differences in desire can cause serious tension.

Which brings us to an important question: How often does the average married couple have sex? About 30 percent of respondents to our survey said they were having sex two to three times a week. Fewer than 5 percent of people reported having sex four times a week.[*] We also noticed responses in our research group revealing that most cases of more regular sex were early married couples or empty nesters, because having young children in the house clearly can change the frequency of sex in marriage. But the most interesting fact was that the rest of the group, the *majority*, more than 50 percent, reported having sex once a week or far, far fewer times than that. A few (6.5 percent) even reported they hadn't had sex in years.[†]

The bottom line: the answer to how often married couples are having sex is all across the board. But the clear reality is that most people aren't having sex as often as they would like. When we consider the intimacy, connection, and bonding that sex is meant to cultivate between a husband and wife, we understand why Scripture tells us not to allow too much time to pass by without it, because "Satan has an ingenious way of tempting us when we least expect it" (1 Corinthians 7:5 MSG). Whether the temptation comes in the form of emotional disconnection, relationship tension, sexual temptation, or something else, our relationships are not the best they can be when we're not connecting sexually. We need to take Scripture's admonition seriously, viewing it not as an obligation to have sex, but as an opportunity to come together in this sacred way.

As you read this chapter, take time to consider the frequency of sex in your marriage at present. Not what it was ten years ago, but what it is today. While I don't think there's a one-size-fits-all number for how

* See appendix 1 for research information.

† See appendix 1 for research information.

many times a healthy married couple should be having sex per week, I want to challenge you to look for the *why* behind the number. I asked a few couples to do just that, and here is a sampling of what they said about the frequency of sex and the why:

- *We have sex three to four times a week. The why is because we reconnect in the best way during sex. It helps us focus, relax, and unwind.*
- *We have sex daily, or as often as possible. The why is because I seem to have a really high sex drive. I know it causes tension because my wife isn't always on the same page.*
- *For us it's two to three times a week. There isn't a specific why. It's just the rhythm we've found over the years. If we go longer than that without sex, it makes us feel disconnected.*
- *Sex happens about one to two times per month for us. It's not that we don't want to be close, but I think the why comes down to the fact that our lives are too busy and our schedules are just crazy.*
- *We have sex a handful of times a year. The why is because we're facing health issues that prevent us from being intimate as often as we'd like.*
- *Sex for us has been problematic lately, happening maybe once a month. The why is because as much as I want to, I just don't feel a physical desire to be close. I don't need sex these days, but my husband still does.*

As a licensed counselor, I believe the why to the question of sexual frequency and desire is even more important than the number of times a couple has sex. When there's a healthy motivation behind sexual frequency—a why that revolves around connection, closeness, love, and learning consideration for one another—the actual frequency doesn't hold as much value. But when the why is rooted in poor prioritization, frustration, bitterness, or unaddressed physical or relational problems, you could be having sex with your partner three times a week and it would still cause tension. So getting to the root of your why is crucial for dealing with this particular problem spot. Let me give you a few tips to help you do just that.

1. Communicate with Your Spouse

When we're struggling with differences in desire, we need to be proactive about checking in with our spouse on a regular basis and discussing our sex life. I talk in detail about this process in chapter 14. Often a solution can be found by simply *communicating*. This was the case for Julio and Anais, who early on in their marriage dealt with tension around their differing desires. Julio often felt rejected by Anais's lack of desire and carried his unspoken resentment into their interactions. Anais felt unsupported by Julio and couldn't understand how he could "ask for more" from her sexually at the end of an overwhelming day. Over the years they learned to open up to one another about their sexual needs and desires. Julio shared his insecurities and how he felt when Anais said no to sex. Anais shared that she was feeling empty and opened up about her desire for support and help. Communicating what was going on underneath the surface allowed them to understand what they needed from one another. They learned to have empathy for each other and give to each other in more specific ways. That simple understanding and the accompanying shift of behavior allowed them to be more in sync with their sexual frequency.

2. Understand Your Spouse

Sometimes a difference in desire points to the fact that one spouse is struggling to enjoy sex. This is an important point to discuss, because an increase in frequency isn't likely to happen if one person is struggling to enjoy sex altogether. We hope you've already picked up some strategies and techniques throughout this book to help you make sex the best it can be for both you and your spouse.

Sometimes physical and emotional factors affect a person's desire for sex. Certain medications, such as SSRIs (anti-depressant medications), are known to inhibit and decrease sexual desire. Being overweight or having an increased body mass index is another physical factor that can influence personal desire. Physical illness and health issues can have a significant negative impact on your desire for sex. Hormonal ups and downs (from menstrual cycles to menopause) can affect your sex drive and your ability to reach orgasm altogether. Additionally, struggling with mental health issues such as depression and anxiety can put a powerful damper on desire. If you notice your spouse is struggling with their desire for sex, seek to understand your spouse before you take it personally or even blame them.

If *you're* the one struggling with desire issues, feeling extremely low to no sexual desire on a regular basis, consider getting a full physical exam and sharing your struggle with your primary care doctor. Many medicinal and therapeutic options are available for dealing with the physical and emotional struggles that inhibit your sex life. Don't rob yourself of the enjoyment of sex! Take it seriously, and take the next step.

For the woman with the low to no sex drive. The majority of women who struggle with this issue can trace their low libido to some common issues: (1) a low emotional and relational connection to their spouse; (2) a physical/medical condition or illness, or an underlying hormonal imbalance or changes; (3) a lack of physical energy due to fatigue or exhaustion, which could be situational or medical; (4) a reaction to or side effect of a medication; or (5) relationship struggles or a husband who doesn't make her pleasure a priority. If you find yourself having minimal desire for sex, consider talking through these potential factors with the help of a counselor and a medical practitioner. Depending on the root issue, the next steps may include marriage therapy to enrich your relationship with your spouse; a physical exam to check for hormonal or physical issues, which can often be resolved with medication; or a psychiatric evaluation to rule out such things as depression and anxiety.

Also be aware, as we've said throughout this book, that sometimes all it takes is a mind and heart shift, as well as a change in schedule and priorities, for your enjoyment of sex to begin to increase. But if you've struggled with a low sex drive for more than three months, it's time to take the next step to uncover any underlying issues that may be inhibiting you from desiring and enjoying sex.

For the man with the low to no sex drive. In working with men with low to no libido, I've discovered it often can be traced to a few common things: (1) a diagnosis of depression or anxiety (or another mental health concern) that is dampening desire; (2) a reaction to or side effect of a medication; (3) physical or mental exhaustion or stress; or (4) problematic pornography use that misdirects sex drive toward something other than your spouse.

First and foremost, don't feel shame if you're the spouse with the lower libido. Men especially need to take this advice to heart, since low male libido isn't the common spoken narrative. Let me be clear: it's a common problem but is not commonly discussed. Depending on the root issue you identify with, take next steps to pursue counseling to address underlying mental health issues or pornography use, or schedule a medical evaluation to rule out underlying physical causes and get recommended medication alterations if necessary. The key is *don't wait.* Whether you are a man or woman with low libido, don't rob yourself of enjoying the gift of sex when a few appointments could get you back on track.

3. Give to Your Spouse

We mentioned earlier that the best sex happens when both parties are giving sacrificially, seeing sex as a way to love and serve one another in the context of a healthy marriage. If you struggle with frequency issues in your marriage, carefully think about how you're giving to one another. Has the focus been on getting your own needs met, or on giving to your spouse? Do you feel like your spouse is giving to you? Or maybe the problem stems from the fact that you're giving to everything and everyone but don't have enough at the end of the day to give to your spouse.

Often, a focus on your own needs is the "why" behind frequency, but when you can shift your perspective to see sex as an avenue for loving and serving one another, issues of frequency tend to become less significant. Take inventory of your emotional connection and the health of your relationship. Take inventory of your own emotional health and how full or empty you feel, because this awareness can play a big role in solving the problem of frequency in a marriage.

As I mentioned earlier, many of the couples we surveyed reported that dealing with outside stress and feeling physically and mentally exhausted are huge factors in their sexual infrequency issues. In essence, their biggest sex problem is they're too stressed and exhausted for sex! From caring for newborn babies to dealing with the realities of full schedules, along with managing home and business concerns, financial affairs, health problems, and life stress, we can easily see how feeling depleted, exhausted, and overwhelmed can impact a couple's sex life. This is such a common occurrence that the term "sexual anorexia" was coined by author Patrick Carnes to describe the lack of sexual frequency many couples face in their relationship.[2] The bottom line is, we could use more sex in healthy marriages!

What boundaries are you setting around your life and your relationship? What needs to be cut out to make more time for rest and fulfillment? Is it possible to call in reinforcements for help, such as family members, friends, doctors, or therapists? To be able to give to your spouse, you first must take inventory of your own fullness.

Some Tips to Fight Stress and Have More Sex

- Reserve one specific evening a week for a date night that includes a time of emotional connection as well as sex!
- Commit to having sex a set number of times per week, just like you would commit to doing a workout a set number of times per week. See sex as an opportunity to strengthen your marriage, just as exercise strengthens your body.
- Take inventory of your family schedule so you're not overloaded. Weigh each incoming commitment accordingly before you say yes, remembering that every yes takes up time and energy that could be focused on your spouse.

- Remember that sex isn't just a nighttime activity. Carve out special times for sex in the morning or for a quickie in the afternoon.
- See your sexual intimacy as an investment in your marriage. Don't always wait to feel "in the mood," but rather choose to engage out of love and affection for your spouse.
- Consider the outside stressors in your life, and work on setting boundaries to eliminate those stressors or consider seeing a professional counselor to help you manage the ones you can't eliminate.

Vaginismus

Let's move on to a more specific sexual problem that affects many couples. Vaginismus refers to female sexual pain during intercourse. For women with vaginismus, the muscles of the vagina contract during sex, causing pain and discomfort and making male penetration difficult and sometimes nearly impossible. I once worked with a couple who hadn't been able to have traditional intercourse after four years of marriage, due to the unaddressed problem of vaginismus.

Vaginismus is considered to be a psychological disorder; there is no *physical* problem with the genital area. If you and your spouse struggle with this problem, let me assure you that there is light at the end of the tunnel! For most couples, vaginismus is a temporary problem that can be resolved with a two-prong approach of counseling and physical therapy. The most important part of the process of healing is to get to the root of the muscle tension response through counseling. The vaginismus response can be caused by a number of things, such as anxiety, past abuse, or strong feelings of guilt and shame.

Once you get to the root of the psychological response and begin to work through it with your counselor or psychologist, you can begin learning to overcome the physical response through physical therapy. Your OB-GYN can refer you to a reputable pelvic floor therapist in your area to get you started on some physical exercises, often including dilators. For some women, the thought of using a dilator may seem uncomfortable or even inappropriate. But this type of therapy is of utmost importance for working toward healing. Just as our physical bodies require exercise equipment to train, so do our sexual organs and muscles. There's nothing wrong or shameful about moving toward sexual satisfaction in your marriage! It's what God wants for you.

Let me assure you that you're not a failure if you experience this type of sexual reaction. Many women do. But too many people allow shame to prevent them from seeking help, which ends up negatively impacting their marriage. Don't waste another day struggling through the pain and frustration of vaginismus. Make an appointment with a licensed counselor and with your OB-GYN, and get started on the process of healing today.

Erectile Dysfunction or Premature Ejaculation

I'm addressing these two male sexual problems in the same section, although they are different problems. Erectile dysfunction is the inability to achieve or keep an erection when desired (this tends to be a problem in the later years). Premature ejaculation is when a man ejaculates too quickly (this tends to be a problem in the earlier years). Both of these problems can be addressed at the same starting point. First and foremost, we can't deal with a sexual problem until we acknowledge it. Because of unnecessary feelings of shame, many men may try to deal with sexual problems on their own, perhaps viewing explicit materials such as porn, masturbating, or avoiding sex altogether.

If you're dealing with either of these problems in your marriage, the best thing to do is to talk about it, acknowledge the issue, and then support one another in taking next steps toward healing. My first recommendation is always to begin by discussing the problem with your primary care physician, since a medical or physiological reason often exists. I've counseled couples before where the man was taking an SSRI for depression and had no idea it was having an impact on his sex life, causing issues with erectile dysfunction that could have been dealt with easily through a dosage or medication change. Erectile dysfunction has been linked to diabetes, heart disease, circulation issues, and high blood pressure, to name just a few. Premature ejaculation has often been linked to hormonal imbalances, inflammation of the prostate or urethra, stress, depression, and relationship problems.

My second recommendation is to recognize the emotional component of the physical problem. Once medical issues have been dealt with or ruled out, the main cause of continued struggle is rooted in the emotional response of anxiety. Even when a physical problem is primarily at play, an emotional reaction can exacerbate the physical problem. In other words, the anxiety about the problem worsens the problem.

Craig struggled with premature ejaculation, which created a great amount of stress. As much as he wanted his erection to last, within just a few seconds after penetration he would climax. He sensed this led to frustration for his wife, who was nowhere near climax, which in turn caused shame and embarrassment for him. For Craig, sex began to trigger anxiety, because he was worried he would climax before he wanted to. Ironically, his anxiety would increase his adrenaline and cause him to ejaculate even more prematurely than he normally would. One issue fueled the other. He was caught in a cycle of struggle, until eventually he just wanted to avoid sex altogether. Instead of sharing this struggle with his wife, he isolated himself and sought out sexual relief through masturbation. Their sex life dwindled, and when his wife caught him masturbating, she felt confused and hurt.

The good news is that for every problem, there is a solution. Sometimes more than one! After ruling out medical issues, premature ejaculation can be dealt with by means of emotional awareness paired with behavioral exercises to help your body respond slower to stimulation and deal with the underlying anxiety response. Medicinal options are also available to aid the process. Again, working with both a licensed counselor and a medical doctor is the best next step in dealing with sexual problems. For an in-depth look and additional practical suggestions, Gary and I recommend a book called *Resurrecting Sex* by Dr. David Schnarch.[3] While it's not a specifically faith-based book, it offers a thorough examination of the most common sexual problems and solutions.

Inability to Reach Climax

The inability to reach orgasm during sex is another problem people struggle with. It tends to be a bigger problem for women than men. Our surveys revealed that close to 70 percent of men report experiencing orgasm ten out of ten times during sex, while only about 18 percent of women report having an orgasm ten out of ten times during sex. The majority of women reported general inconsistency with achieving orgasm during sex, ranging anywhere from one out of ten times to nine out of ten times.*

When it comes to achieving orgasm, for the majority of people the problem can be solved with increased emotional support in the relationship paired with increased stimulation. By increased stimulation, I don't necessarily mean touching more, but instead touching properly. If your wife is struggling to reach orgasm, just rubbing a little harder isn't going to get her there. To achieve greater chances of orgasm, the focus should be on the quality of touch versus quantity of touch. I've discussed this in more practical terms in chapters 3 and 5.

Achieving consistent orgasm must be your *mutual* goal as a couple, because it involves a lot of communication. You first have to understand what feels good to you in order to be able to communicate it to your spouse. I often encourage newlywed spouses to lie in bed together and allow the person who struggles to achieve orgasm to guide the hand and body of their partner, showing and telling them exactly what feels good and what doesn't. Be specific about the types of strokes, the speed of touch, and the level of pressure that feel good to you. Too often, people allow sex to be a guessing game instead of taking initiative to

---

* See appendix 1 for research information.

guide their spouse. If you're struggling to reach orgasm, don't hesitate to teach your spouse how to touch you.

It's also important to get rid of the expectation that we must reach orgasm together. In fact, our surveys show that the vast majority of people do not reach orgasm at the same time, with 0 percent of people reporting that they orgasm together all the time. The goal is not to orgasm at the same time but to learn to help each other get there.

Additionally, as we mentioned earlier, certain medications can be linked to an inability to reach orgasm. As a result, we'll need to understand the side effects of any medicine we're currently taking.

For most people, achieving orgasm consistently is something that has to be practiced and perfected. It's one of the reasons couples tend to orgasm more frequently as they get more experienced in their marriage. For many women, reaching orgasm early on in marriage requires manual stimulation (the husband has to use his fingers to help her achieve orgasm), but they often become able to orgasm during intercourse as they learn about their bodies and feel comfortable with their spouses.

In case you've never been able to achieve orgasm through manual stimulation or otherwise, I suggest you make an appointment with a medical doctor and a licensed therapist to help you address your specific situation and develop the steps to get there. If you take those steps, you may be in what sex therapist Dr. Schnarch calls the "pre-orgasmic" category.[4] With a little understanding and effort, a good orgasm is just around the corner!

NOTE FROM GARY

To deal with sexual issues and dysfunction in marriage, we must address the difference between false guilt and real guilt. The treatment of premature ejaculation, vaginismus, erectile dysfunction, or the inability to achieve orgasm is no more a "moral" issue than a doctor's treatment of indigestion or sinus congestion. Yet those issues that have to do with sex sometimes get shrouded in morality concerns. Even though physical therapists use tools of all types (elastic bands, weights, and so forth) to help a patient recover from surgery, Debra and I have both encountered couples who believe that physical "exercises" or "instruments" used to treat sexual dysfunction are somehow tainted. Wanting to experience sexual satisfaction in marriage is no less moral than wanting to regain the use of your knees or sleep without snoring.

Here are some guidelines to help us move past false guilt:

- Sex is a good thing created by God. Both spouses will be blessed by healthy sexual expression. Therefore, exercises that point to this healthy expression are good and holy, even if we are given individualized exercises to lead to the fulfillment of that goal.
- The genitals aren't immoral. Exercising them or doing the physical things that may be necessary to help them function sexually is no different in the sight of God than rehabbing a knee, shoulder, or wrist.
- Feeling pleasure isn't immoral. If some of these exercises result in pleasurable feelings, we have not done something wrong. God created nerve endings in body parts that sometimes need to be mastered. It may not be possible to exercise them without feeling pleasure, but since feeling pleasure isn't immoral, it is not a matter of conscience.
- We don't need to pay for past sexual immorality by suffering from premature ejaculation or the lack of orgasm. Jesus paid for our sins so we don't have to. Thinking that enduring a substandard sexual relationship with our spouse makes up

for past sexual sin is to discount the power of the cross and the finality of Jesus' sacrifice.

- Because sex outside of marriage and inappropriate sexual expressions carried over into marriage are so common, many make a one-to-one correlation between sexual pleasure and guilt. Reread chapter 1 to reset your mind and embrace the glorious truth that God's will is for you and your spouse to learn how to have a supremely pleasurable sexual relationship.

Porn Use, Sex Addiction, or Infidelity

The sad reality—but one that must be addressed—is that our problems with sex often come from outside influences rather than organic physical problems. Nearly 25 percent of couples surveyed reported their biggest sexual struggles stem from the negative influence of pornography in their marriage. More than 43 percent of couples reported their sexual struggles arise from other emotional and relational problems in marriage.* These types of things have the power to ravage our sex life in the worst way because they break trust—which is the foundation of great sex. If trust is like a chain, whether we take out just one link or a hundred links, the chain is still broken. And when the chain of trust is broken, it must be rebuilt in order for us to move forward in healing.

For many years, Jasmine struggled to desire sex after she discovered her husband's six-year battle with pornography. He had been hiding his problematic behavior from her, and when she unexpectedly found out, she wondered if she'd ever be able to trust him again. After getting caught, her husband sought healing, joined a 12-step group for accountability, and worked hard to be free of porn for more than twelve months. Yet Jasmine still struggled to feel the closeness and intimacy

* See appendix 1 for research information.

she once felt. She couldn't let her guard down. How could she, after what he had done?

Jordan found out his wife had been emotionally cheating on him with a man she met online. When he confronted her about it, she quickly confessed, deleted the chat apps from her phone, and immediately ended the contact she was having. But Jordan was left with a gaping wound he didn't know how to deal with. He felt hurt, distant, and disconnected from his wife and found himself wanting nothing to do with her in the bedroom. Where was he supposed to go from there?

Miranda had a hard time coping after she found out about her husband's affair early on in their marriage. Even though they both agreed to reconcile and move forward in their marriage, she was still haunted years later by memories of the past. Trust had been broken, and it was affecting their marriage, as well as their sex life. Could it ever be fixed?

These kinds of difficult situations aren't something couples should just try to "push through." When it comes to porn, infidelity, sex addictions, or other major relationship problems, there's no predictable pattern for how these hardships will influence a marriage or sex life—only the guarantee that they will. Even when both parties have committed to healing, honesty, and fidelity, broken pieces still need to be gathered and put back together again. Boundaries still need to be established, and a plan to rebuild trust needs to be put in place. Just moving forward doesn't make past experiences go away. We address this topic in chapter 13—how to go backward to go forward—but these struggles sometimes occur in the present as well.

Whether past or present, if you're dealing with these kinds of relationship struggles in your marriage, there is no better time to seek counseling than today. You need a guide to help you walk through these murky waters and get you to the other side. You need someone who can objectively see the role that each of you plays in rebuilding the chain of trust. Just pushing through, forcing yourself to be intimate when you feel unable to trust, doesn't make the problem go away. In fact, it can cause you to become even more bitter and resentful along the way. Consider this type of problem an emergency situation, and don't wait another day to get plugged in to therapy.* Even if your spouse refuses to come along, begin the process for yourself. In order for your marriage and, in turn, your sex life to be rebuilt, trust must be rebuilt. This will take time, consistency, boundaries, transparency, and clear expectations. Healing is possible and trust can be rebuilt, but it will take effort and a clear plan to get there.

Whatever your unique experience is when it comes to sex in marriage, know this: for every sexual problem there is a solution. The solution can come in the form of medication, behavioral changes, relationship growth, education and experience, rebuilding of trust, perspective shifts, counseling and therapy, or a little of all of the above. The important thing to remember is that every couple will face a sexual problem at some point in their relationship. The question is this: What will we do when we get there?

---

* See appendix 2 for information on how to find a therapist.

chapter
twelve

SHADES OF GRAY

Gary and Debra

A. J. is one of the most earnest, committed young men I (Gary) have ever had the blessing to work with. He is resolute about following God, and his passion for obedience is inspiring. Premarital sex was never an issue for him, but because obedience matters, he sincerely wanted to know, "After we're married, what's allowed?"

As people of freedom who are called to live lives of freedom, Christians don't need to concoct a lot of "don't do this, this, or that" lists. Paul specifically attacked that line of thinking in Colossians 2:21–23. Any sexual activity *outside* of marriage is clearly forbidden, but within marriage, there are many "shades of gray."

Debra and I receive questions from people on a regular basis asking us our opinion on whether a specific activity is "right" or "wrong" when it comes to sex in marriage. Sometimes there are clear-cut answers; other times the answers lie somewhere in the middle—somewhere in the gray. And 1 Corinthians 10:23 reminds us that even if something is "okay" to do, it's not always beneficial.

This chapter is our best attempt to give clear pastoral *and* clinical responses to the most common questions we receive, but keep in mind, the two of us don't always entirely agree with each other in these areas. We offer our opinions to help you come to your own conclusions and set your own boundaries as a couple. When we asked couples to tell us the areas that caused confusion or controversy in their sex life, these are the top conversations that emerged.

Masturbation (Gary)

No Scripture clearly prohibits masturbation, though Jesus does, quite starkly, prohibit all forms of lust (Matthew 5:28). In this section, I discuss masturbation on its own, not masturbation joined with pornography or as part of voyeurism or anything that is obviously sinful.

In general, the act of masturbation is not, in and of itself, sinful. A couple doing this together as they enjoy each other is not sinning. A wife who in the midst of lovemaking touches herself to increase her own pleasure is likely increasing her husband's pleasure as well. I would even suggest that a woman who is learning how to orgasm is ultimately serving her marriage. The fact that something is pleasurable does not make it sinful. Likewise, the fact that something is *sexually* pleasurable does not make it sinful.

But what about masturbation done alone, when someone is married, simply for "sexual release"?

The answer to whether it is appropriate depends. For men or women in recovery for sexual addictions, masturbation is sometimes (not always) seen as resetting the date of their sobriety. The thinking with these groups is that if someone has developed a sexual relationship of any kind (including porn and the like) outside of their marriage, solo masturbation must stop completely so the recovering addict can reset their mind to view sex as relational.

But what about men and women who aren't in recovery? Dr. Mitch Whitman, a clinical psychologist who has dealt with sexual issues for more than three decades, teaches that a man or woman traveling on their own is, in the face of sexual temptation (an affair, pornography, or strip clubs), much better off masturbating to thoughts of their spouse than acting out in a way in which they find sexual pleasure with someone else (or even with thoughts of someone else). I'm inclined to defer to Dr. Whitman's practical expertise but would add that if the trip is relatively short, wouldn't riding the waves of sexual hunger until you get home make the reunion all the sweeter? I'm not one to make a bunch of rules here; the guiding principle in my view is responding to sexual hunger in a way that focuses on your spouse, at the very least in memory if not in anticipation.

Does that sound indefinite? I'm sure it does. But then, so is the Bible's silence.

In the case of a long military deployment, however, when you are talking to twenty- and thirtysomething soldiers who might be away from their spouses for months at a time, my advice has been to make every sexual experience focus on their spouse. Connecting via a secure phone connection is easier to do now than ever before in human history but still isn't always possible, depending on the conditions of the deployment. If a guy is beside himself, teetering on the brink of falling into temptation, I'm not going to shame him for pulling out a picture of his wife. The same thing is true if a guy's wife is deep into pregnancy (or recovering from childbirth) and can't even stomach the thought of intimate contact, and he just wants to be "free" to focus on loving his wife in nonsexual ways.

What about when the spouse isn't traveling but is at home? Here I think in many cases a spouse who habitually masturbates while at home with their spouse is flirting with disaster. I'm not speaking of a wife who is learning how to orgasm. I'm not chastising a husband who may be training to control his orgasm. Those are simply physical exercises designed to help a spouse perform in marriage, and that's a good thing (but wouldn't they be even better when done together?).

In this scenario, masturbation may well be acting as a substitute for mutual pleasuring. If the marital bed either lacks sexual touch or is marred by relational frustration, better by far to use the tension as motivation to address what's happening between the couple rather than simply to release the tension as an individual. I suspect that the majority of secret masturbation within marriage ultimately leads to resentment and anger toward the other spouse. Whether or not an act is sinful isn't the only question; an act that makes us resent our spouse and builds a wall of bitterness between us and our spouse is undeniably an unhealthy thing to do.

Recognize that sex hunger is a universal struggle that we can respond to in unhealthy ways, relatively healthy ways, and the healthiest way. The healthiest way is one in which sex is part of being one with your spouse.

Dr. Steve Wilke, who has been a marriage and family therapist for more than thirty-five years, recommends a healthy, nonlegalistic way for couples to deal with masturbation. Because our sex life is created and designed for both of us, we should have no secrets in this area of our marriage. If a husband or wife is separated from their spouse and concerned about sexual pressure, the couple should talk about masturbation beforehand and agree together about what sexual behavior is appropriate. Dr Wilke also recommends—and I strongly agree—that there should be zero masturbation while spouses are separated if either spouse is sexually unfulfilled in the relationship.

Dr. Whitman adds a helpful warning: if husbands are masturbating while thinking about their wives, their thoughts should be realistic, centering on something their wife really can (or will) do. Don't create an "idealistic" version of your wife—regarding the way she looks or behaves—so that you end up feeling dissatisfied with your real wife and more drawn to the fantasy wife. Every act of sex should make us cherish our spouse more, feel closer to them, be more appreciative of them, and have a greater desire for them.[1]

NOTE FROM DEBRA

I generally agree with the points Gary made, and his comments about the exceptions of long separation due to military training and mutual masturbation. (Though a three-day business trip doesn't count as a long separation, in my humble opinion! Call your spouse and enjoy some phone sex instead.) But when it comes to choosing the solo act of masturbation rather than engaging with our spouse, I find it to be a slippery slope. First, mentally focusing on our spouse when they aren't present can be difficult—the temptation of giving in to lust and allowing our mind to wander to dangerous territory is ever present when we're alone. To expect someone to regularly masturbate and keep their mind on their spouse 100 percent of the time is just not realistic.

Second, I think there is a danger in allowing masturbation to become a regular part of our lives for "release," even for a specific season, because it trains our body to respond to our personal touch rather than to the touch of our spouse. Because I am in charge of what feels good, and I know every nook and cranny of my body in a way my spouse can't, masturbation can become the competition. Men and women who regularly masturbate can ultimately begin to lose enjoyment when their spouse touches them because their body has been trained to feel, *I can do it better on my own.* Dr. Mark Laaser, a recovering sex addict who is a leading voice in the world of recovery from infidelity and sex addiction, calls masturbation "the secret that can ruin your sex life."[2] I believe it is the enemy of a healthy sex life.

Is it the end of a marriage if a spouse masturbates on their own? Absolutely not. It's not infidelity (especially if your focus is on our spouse), but it's not the best option. Moreover, if it becomes a regular habit, it can have a negative effect on our sex life. I also believe that in the case of solo masturbation, we should be more than willing to open up to our spouse and tell them about the experience. They should know about it. We should be open about everything in marriage, and this topic of conversation is no exception. To get to the heart of my question at the beginning of this paragraph, I think we need to ask another question: Does this act bring us closer together or move us farther apart? The answer will give us clarity for how to move forward.

Sex Toys (Gary)

I don't remember which holiday it was for, but I do remember being excited about getting my wife a Theragun. It looks (and sounds) like a drill, and many professional athletic teams use it for percussive therapy massage. Lisa lives with a lot of pain; any gift I can give her that relieves even a smidgen of her pain is something I'm eager to find and enthusiastic about surprising her with.

But what if a massager isn't about relieving pain but instead is about giving her pleasure? Does that make it wrong? Not one person in a million would have a problem with my buying my wife a Theragun. We wouldn't even think to hide it, and in fact we've recommended it to many others.

It's likely that our discomfort with what are commonly called "sex toys" comes from a suspicion of sexual pleasure in general. It may also be based on the understandable fact that most of the stores that sell such items are garish, juvenile, and flat-out embarrassing. Putting these issues aside, an aversion to sexual pleasure is not a good enough reason to restrict something that could be a special treat for your spouse. Think about it this way: you can buy something to massage your wife's neck but not to massage . . . elsewhere? Is that consistent?

But there are some things to keep in mind. While occasional novelty can serve an already strong sexual relationship between two lovers, it is not so good at restoring sexual interest. As an aid, sexual toys are like seasoning on a steak. As a substitute, they are like popping a teaspoon of cinnamon in your mouth and calling it dinner. When a couple requires a box of toys to enjoy their time together, there may well be some deeper issues worth attending to. The other harm, as Debra mentioned in her comments on masturbation, is that your body becomes accustomed to the feeling of getting aroused by a sex toy instead of getting aroused by your spouse—for example, the wife who needs a vibrator to reach orgasm rather than patiently teaching her husband how to get her there. When we require a sex toy to reach climax, the problem is that we're missing out on "the real thing." Don't allow the aid to become the main event.

The moral objections we hear most often about sex toys are usually centered around the concern that they will lead to selfish masturbation and thus alienation. We remind you of the Latin adage *abusus non tollit usum*—"abuse does not cancel use." There's a vast difference between something that enhances a couple's shared sexual experience and something that becomes a solo stress release. Let's keep this as a discussion about something that will be shared.

Another objection we hear is this: "What if my spouse prefers the toy to me?" If that's the case, other issues are involved that are probably larger than the toy, and I recommend you stop using sex toys, at least until those issues in your marriage are addressed.

As in everything, I urge couples to respect each other's boundaries. From the start of our marriage, I told Lisa I would never want her to do anything in the bedroom (or elsewhere, for that matter) that violated her conscience. I want a wife who is more eager to please God than she is to please me. Where you can experience *mutual* freedom and enjoyment as a couple, please do so. But don't try to build your pleasure on a spouse's aching conscience. Spiritually and psychologically, that is not a wise thing to do.

Oral Sex (Gary)

The Bible doesn't prohibit oral sex, and in fact some biblical scholars believe the Song of Songs speaks of both a husband (2:3)* and a wife (4:16) receiving oral pleasuring. I'm not a Hebrew scholar, so I can't argue this definitively, but let's look at it this way: I don't know anyone who would suggest it is immoral for a husband to kiss his wife's nipples, even though, in some instances and with some women, that alone can lead to orgasm. How then could we possibly suggest that a husband can't kiss a wife's genitals or vice versa? The distinction seems to be arbitrary and based on an assumption that there is something "dirty" or "distasteful" about this part of our spouse's body.

I don't believe oral sex is governed by biblical prohibitions, but as always, marital sex should be mutually enjoyable. If either spouse can't get over the feeling that such an act is wrong or distasteful, the matter of whether or not it is allowed isn't the issue; kindness is. If a spouse becomes convinced that their hesitation or revulsion is based on poor teaching, then perhaps evaluating their thinking on the matter can set them free. But if a spouse simply feels repulsed by oral sex, there's no need to get Scripture involved—care for each other will lead the couple to abstain.

NOTE FROM DEBRA

I've worked with many couples who shared that oral sex was something they had to grow into in their marriage. The thought of something that was "gross" or "uncomfortable" in the beginning slowly became one of the acts that brought them the most pleasure and enjoyment in their sex life. I remember one woman

* The word *apples* is used throughout the Song of Songs to refer to a male's genitals.

in particular who cringed at the thought of giving her husband oral sex in the early stages of their marriage.

The reality is, it's not uncommon for people to cringe at oral sex initially, because so often their understanding of oral sex has been tainted by an inaccurate view of it or an unhealthy experience with it. Maybe they connect oral sex with the pornography industry and so they see it as something dirty or wrong. Maybe they've experienced oral sex as a result of past abuse or past sexual interactions, and the thought of it elicits feelings of guilt and shame. Maybe the way people have talked about oral sex or the things they've learned about it have caused them to see it as degrading, inappropriate, or gross. If any of those mindsets describes your perspective, you'll want to think through the emotional attachments you have to the concept of oral sex—and whether they come from a healthy perspective. I certainly don't believe every couple needs to engage in oral sex, but I do think it's important to consider your perspective and where it came from before deciding to avoid it altogether.

Back to the story above. Years later, I met with the same woman, and she told me that after she had worked through some of her negative notions of oral sex and tried it, the giving and receiving of oral sex became one of her favorite sexual activities! As she and her husband got used to one another and increased in comfort with each other and in their sex life, oral sex became another way to share pleasure and show each other love. In a way, it's almost like an acquired taste for some people. It may take a few tries to really learn how to enjoy it.

Many women have reported to me that the more "turned on" they feel, the easier it is to give and receive oral sex. It's as though they need to be in the right frame of mind to let go and enjoy oral pleasuring. And remember this tidbit as a rule of thumb:

the fresher and cleaner you are, the easier it will be to enjoy it. There's no need to force this experience on your marriage, but at the same time, there's no need to write it off entirely if you've never tried it. It may even become one of your favorite things!

Anal Sex (Gary)

Once again, there is no biblical prohibition of this kind of sex between a husband and wife, but doctors frequently raise alarms about possible or even likely physical damage to the wife's body during this act. Sex should be pleasurable and according to God's design. A woman's anus isn't designed for something to go *into*—quite the contrary. Whereas the woman's vaginal area is therapeutically clean, the anus has all kinds of bacteria that aren't meant to be exposed. So my hesitation would be based on natural law more than God's law. God designed a woman's vagina to be sexually active; the same is not true of her anus.

I've talked with two seasoned counselors who specialize in sexual issues in marriage, and both have told me that the men they have treated who most frequently insist on anal sex have watched pornographic acts that they want to reenact or have been abused and have adopted reenacting the abuse "in reverse" as a way to deal with the trauma. Both reasons should give us spiritual chills and be cause for great concern. Any wife who has any hesitation should not feel even the slightest pressure to consider this act. Since her body isn't designed for anal sex, it cannot be considered a reasonable marital expectation.

But what about situations where a wife says she truly enjoys it and the couple has figured out a way that the act isn't harming her in the short term or long term? I can't cite chapter and verse to say you are offending God. To be honest, I don't even understand the allure. The way God designed sex seems supremely pleasurable to me in a way no other option could ever compete with. But my preferences are irrelevant to yours. Let love guide you here. At the very least, however, please don't let a spouse's hesitancy about this one act be seen as selfish or unloving. In my view, based on health concerns alone, anal sex is a largely unreasonable request.

Sex during Menstruation (Debra)

I've heard couples give two primary reasons to explain why they refrain from sex when the wife is having her period: (1) they point out that it's messy, and the mess makes them uncomfortable; and (2) they cite the Old Testament biblical teaching in Leviticus 15:24 about uncleanness. Most theologians agree that, because of Jesus, we no longer follow the Levitical mandates that were set for the Israelites. We use them as lessons and principles that remind us of our "unclean state" because of sin, and ultimately point us to our need for a Savior. So if you think it's no longer a sin to wear linen and wool together (Leviticus 19:19), you have to see this reference to a woman's menstrual period in the same light.

With that out of the way, we tackle the question of comfort. Many couples report that they avoid intercourse during the first few days of a woman's menstrual cycle because it tends to be the heaviest and messiest stage of menstruation. They opt to wait it out or choose alternate ways to pleasure one another, such as manual stimulation. Other couples choose to have sex throughout the menstrual cycle, because they notice that a woman's sex drive tends to be higher during menstruation. The hormonal changes bring about an increased libido, which can often be a long-awaited feeling for a woman who normally struggles with low libido. The enjoyment of mutual pleasure outweighs the mess—which a couple can easily deal with by laying down a towel and taking a shower afterward (or even having sex in the shower)—so they go for it. Other couples choose to wait until the cycle is completely over.

Whether or not you choose to engage in sex during your menstrual cycle is up to you and your spouse. It's probably more of a personality issue than anything else. In fact, one woman who was feeling quite aroused during her cycle told her husband to "have some courage and get to business!" But it's something you need to discuss together and feel comfortable with.

Naughty Words (Gary)

One of the most intriguing questions I've ever received as a pastor was from a fellow pastor. Two church members came to him with a sincere question. The wife occasionally got so excited during sex that she let the words "Oh my God!" slip, and she wondered if she was sinning. She never used the Lord's name in vain in any other setting, but when she was close to climax or her husband unveiled a new move, the words just came out.

The pastor assured her that in this context, the words could be taken as worship. It pains me (literally) whenever I hear God's name taken in vain—including if it were to come out of my wife's mouth—so I might be a little more sensitive to this issue than most people. Accordingly, I ran the thought by some other pastors I greatly respect. One of them provided a very thoughtful response:*

> I think it's all about the heart and meaning when it comes to the words being expressed.
>
> If the words are lifted with a heart thankful for God's good gift of covenantal love . . .
>
> If they are expressed in response to the beauty of the gift of sex . . .
>
> If they are screamed or whispered in the ecstasy of sexual intimacy or climax between a man and woman in the context of marriage and in the privacy of the marriage bed . . .

* The pastor wanted to remain nameless, so I'm honoring that request.

> Words like "Thank you, Lord!" "Praise you, Jesus!" "Yes, Lord!" "Good God!" "Oh my God!" "Oh my Lord!" "Thank you, Jesus!" "Thank you, God!"—all these seem like they could be an expression of worship and celebration that brings honor to the God who invented sex and who delights when it is expressed in the context he designed.

And what about couples who get excited using words they would never utter outside the bedroom, words they wouldn't want to hear their kids use? If naughty words get you *mutually* excited in private and it's not a turnoff to your spouse and doesn't feel demeaning to them, I'm inclined to say let's not try to rein in the forceful passion of sexual enjoyment in marriage. When you have sex with your spouse, you're doing what you would never do in front of someone else—and that's perfectly okay. So I think it's a fair comparison to suggest that you might also *say* something you'd never say in front of anyone else. Let the marriage bed be private, and don't let an overly active conscience rob you of the joy, freedom, delight, and ecstasy that God designed marital sex to elicit.

Fantasy and Fantasizing (Debra)

It takes hard work to block out all the sexual mental noise around us. We're bombarded with sexual images and stories every day as we turn on the TV or pick up our phones to scroll through social media. And for a couple who is struggling to reach orgasm or going through a dry spell in their sex life, the temptation to let their mind wander to something they've seen or want to experience through the realm of fantasy is a real issue. It could be flashbacks of a person they found sexually attractive, a sexual image they saw in the past, or something else that they use to turn them on in the present.

But I believe that any form of fantasizing about anything or anyone other than our spouse is, strictly speaking, considered lust (which

Jesus takes a step further in Matthew 5:28 and calls adultery) and is harmful to our marriage. We have to train our brain to stop doing it. In counseling we call this "thought stopping," which we discussed in chapter 6. It's the concept of learning to dismiss a harmful thought and focus on something more beneficial. During sex, we may not be able to keep a sexual image or thought that has nothing to do with our spouse from popping up in our brain—but what we do with that thought is entirely our own responsibility. For those who struggle with fantasizing on a regular basis, some mental training may need to occur, as well as some boundary setting to limit the things our eyes take in. Training our thought life is just as important as training our physical body. It rarely can get to a healthy place on its own. If fantasizing is a struggle for you, consider connecting with a Christian licensed counselor to learn how to set boundaries and make progress in this area of your life.

Finally, what about fantasizing within the context of your marriage, with your spouse as the object of your thoughts? By all means, feel free to do it! Some couples enjoy sharing with one another their fantasies (which I recommend) or the things they have dreamed of doing to their spouse or having their spouse do to them. Your spouse belongs to you, and you to them. There is so much freedom in that truth! The only danger, as Gary mentioned earlier, is the temptation to paint your spouse into a picture that isn't true to who they really are. Doing that can only set you up for disappointment, hurt, and frustration.

In all of the gray areas mentioned above, the guiding rule should always be this: Does this particular sexual activity bring us closer to one another or cause us to feel farther apart? When we start relying on anything or anyone (including ourselves) other than our spouse to fulfill our sexual needs, we've crossed the line into dangerous territory. While many things may be "okay" to do, the bottom line is whether these things are benefiting our spiritual life, our sexual life, and the state of our marriage, and whether they are enhancing our love, grace, and respect for one another. If we can answer a resounding yes, then by all means . . . enjoy!

chapter
thirteen

GOING BACKWARD TO GO FORWARD

Debra

Meredith and her husband had been married for ten years. They had a decent sex life, but as she put it, "I know it can be better." Before she met and married Ben, Meredith had a few sexual encounters during her college years. She was a Christian at the time, but she found herself caving under the pressure and stress of being so far away from home, surrounded by people who didn't believe what she believed. In fact, her first sexual experience happened at the hands of a guy she hardly knew. And the mixture of adrenaline, apprehension, and the power of her raging sex drive caused the details of that encounter to be seared in her mind. When she thought back to that time, she was filled with an intense mixture of both guilt and desire. Guilt, in that her first sexual experience was with a man she barely knew, but also desire, in that it was an explosive moment of sexual energy unlike anything she'd ever experienced sexually.

She hated that she had experienced such an intense moment with a man who wasn't her husband. But more so, she hated that she found herself recalling that moment more often than she should. Sometimes when she and Ben were struggling to get her to climax, she would find her mind slowly drawing on that memory. But after she climaxed, her mind wallowed in guilt and shame. Guilt that it took a fantasy of another man to get her to climax, and shame that she was withholding this information from her husband. How could her past still have such power in her life? How could such a fleeting experience take up so much space in her mind? How could she even begin to explain all this to her husband? Meredith felt paralyzed. Paralyzed by the experiences of her past.

The past can wrap its deadly tentacles around our lives, holding us back, keeping us from moving forward. I know this to be true, because I've experienced the pain and power of the past in my own life. Not only that, I've seen it played out in the lives of thousands of people—men and women who have been ravaged by the pain of the past. Not only can the past impact our present lives, but it can have devastating effects on our sex lives.

I've seen hearts that have been bruised by past sexual experiences, wounded by the pain of sexual abuse, or scarred by past sexual choices their partner has made. No matter the history, if we don't deal with our issues in a healthy way, the past can cause significant pain in the present.

Meredith is not the only person who has struggled with her past. I think of another client named Andrew, who found himself frustrated in his sex life because his nine years of porn addiction had completely ravaged his expectations of what sex in a healthy marriage should look and feel like. Or Michelle, who found herself feeling paralyzed at the thought of even undressing in front of her husband because it brought back memories of the sexual abuse she had endured as a child. Or Daniel and his wife, Jessica, who avoided sex because it usually ended in tears and frustration for Jessica, who found herself feeling inadequate and insecure in light of Daniel's extensive past sexual history.

In the Old Testament, God told a man named Lot to take his family and move out of the city of Sodom—a city filled with dysfunction. God wanted Lot and his family to experience something better, something healthier. On their way out of the city, God gave them a warning: "Don't look back" (Genesis 19:17). There was a lot of pain back there. A lot of poor choices and difficult experiences. A lot of things that happened outside of God's best for their lives. God knew that focusing on the past—staying there—could keep them from moving forward. And so he warned them.

But according to Scripture, as they left the city, "Lot's wife looked back, and she became a pillar of salt" (Genesis 19:26). I read this passage literally, and I believe that's exactly what happened. But I also read this passage figuratively as I apply it to my life and the lives of so many others: the past truly can be paralyzing. When our gaze is fixed on the past, we find that we're unable to go forward.

But what I know to be true as a healed daughter of God and as a licensed counselor is that in order to be *freed* from the past, we have to learn to *deal* with the past. Coming to Jesus doesn't make the past simply "disappear." My friend Christine Caine said that "the blood of Christ doesn't give us amnesia."[1] We don't forget just because we come to know the Lord. We're forgiven of our past the moment we ask for forgiveness, but that doesn't mean we forget. If we want to stop gazing at the past, looking back again and again and again, feeling stuck and paralyzed, we have to go back so we can go forward.

Going Back to Go Forward

One of the values I hold near and dear to my heart is efficiency. I'm acutely aware of the value of my time, and I don't like to waste a minute. If there's a small corner I need to cut in order to make the most of my time, I'll take it. My husband, John, is the opposite. He values the details and doing things as thoroughly and as perfectly as possible. So when we decided to tackle the project of refinishing our dining room chairs, you can imagine the struggle we faced. Before we could paint the chairs with the new color, we had to remove the old paint color. I don't know about you, but I didn't think that was totally necessary. A quick sanding was fine with me. Let's move on to the fun part—new paint! But the problem with my technique is that with the wear and tear of time, my chairs didn't hold up. Over time, the old paint slowly began to peel off, taking the new paint with it. I should have taken the time to take off the old before putting on the new. And because I didn't do that the first time around, it cost me extra time in the end.

Life is sort of like that. In order to move forward, you first have to go back and deal with the layers of the past. It's the opposite of what most of us want to do. We want to take the shortcut, to plow straight through, to put on the new and just move forward. But eventually the old layers begin to impact the new ones. The past starts chipping away at the present.

One of the things I love about being a Christian who happens to be a licensed counselor is that I find so many beautiful and healing truths in the pages of God's Word. Scripture contains so much "therapy" if we just open our eyes and look for it. Ephesians 4 is one of these special passages in which we're taught, step-by-step, what it looks like to deal with the past. Let's take a look at how we can apply its truths to the process of dealing with our past.

Step 1: Take Off the Old

To deal with the past, the first step is to actually acknowledge the past. For many of us, our history is something we'd rather not bring up again. Some people falsely believe that recalling it will make it worse, when the truth is that ignoring or repressing the past is what gives it the most power. When it comes to dealing with our sexual history, we must understand that by just ignoring it, we're allowing it to take up space in our life. Ephesians 4:22 reminds us that the first thing we need to do in the process of transformation is "put off your old self, which is being corrupted by its deceitful desires." In order to take something off, we have to acknowledge it. We have to recognize it. It won't just "come off" on its own.

I worked with a young woman named Laura who was seriously struggling with her sex life with her new husband, in part because she had never opened up about her past history with masturbation. For many years, she had struggled with compulsive masturbation and lustful thoughts as a single woman, and the buildup of shame and guilt each time she masturbated slowly attached those terrible feelings to anything sexual. More than a decade later when she got married, those same feelings of guilt and shame intruded into her sexual experience with her husband. She couldn't handle the thought of him touching her genitals with his fingers because it brought back the immense guilt and shame she felt when she had touched herself years ago. The only thing was, she didn't recognize the connection. Her past struggle with masturbation happened so many years ago that she failed to recognize its significance in the present.

One of the first steps in dealing with these feelings from Laura's past was having her talk with me about the details of her sexual history. This wasn't an easy process for her, and in fact, she didn't even want to say the word *masturbation* out loud. For a little while, she'd simply refer to it as the "M-word." And that's okay! The important part was that she had the courage to go there. She had the courage to face her past rather than ignore it. Without talking through her sexual history, we never could have made that important connection to the shame she was feeling in the present.

Have you taken the time to really talk through your past? To take off the old, one piece at a time? Talking through (or writing out) our past history in *detail* is crucial to the process of healing from the past. If you've never done that before, please consider engaging in this process as a vital piece of the puzzle of dealing with your past.

I'll often ask my clients to create a timeline of events, recording both the beautiful and the painful moments that have shaped them over the course of their life. Some of those experiences are sexual, while others aren't. But no matter the experiences, this can be a very important process as you seek to be freed from the past. Make a list of the things that stick out to you from your past, things you want to ask forgiveness for, things you still carry feelings of guilt and shame about. Acknowledging those hard things is so important. After you've done that, take the next important step of intentionally sharing your list *out loud*. Talk through the details of your sexual history with a counselor or even a mentor or trusted friend—someone you can speak freely to and confess to, someone who will pray for you as you share what you've experienced. It can help to be specific during your prayer time about the things you want to confess from the past, the things you're asking God to heal, and the ways you want to change and grow as you look to the future.

If you've been a victim of past sexual or physical abuse, I want you to understand the unique importance of this process for you. These types of life-altering experiences cause significant trauma, and the wounds of trauma need to be healed one layer at a time with the help of an experienced professional. There are counselors who specialize in this very thing, and they can offer you hope and freedom. You can thrive, even in the face of past abuse. I know this to be true because I've seen hundreds of people released into that freedom. Abuse may have stolen the innocence of your past, but it can't steal the joy of your present unless you allow it to.

Step 2: Renew Your Mind

How we think is the number one thing that affects how we live. Our thoughts are powerful, and they are responsible for writing the script of the story of our life. In fact, modern neuroscience shows us that our brains are malleable, and we can reshape our brain function based on the thoughts we allow ourselves to think.[2] When we begin to think better, we begin to live better. So much of dealing with the past comes down to how we think about both the past and the present. This applies to our sex life just as much as it does to any other part of our lives. What story do we tell ourselves about the past? Is it a story that lifts us up and calls us toward the abundant life God has for us—or is it a story that takes us down in guilt, shame, fear, insecurity, and doubt?

God knows the power of our thoughts, and in Ephesians we're introduced to step two of dealing with the past: "Be made new in the attitude of your minds" (4:23). To live right, we have to start thinking right. Past experiences will always have power over us until we start to think differently, replacing toxic thoughts with truth. Throughout Scripture we're asked to take responsibility for our thought life. In fact, these tend to be some of my favorite passages in God's Word:

- "We take captive every thought to make it obedient to Christ" (2 Corinthians 10:5).
- "Finally, brothers and sisters, whatever is true, whatever is noble, whatever is right, whatever is pure, whatever is lovely, whatever is admirable—if anything is excellent or praiseworthy—think about such things" (Philippians 4:8).
- "Do not conform to the pattern of this world, but be transformed by the renewing of your mind. Then you will be able to test and approve what God's will is—his good, pleasing and perfect will" (Romans 12:2).

Think through any issues you face as a result of your past and ask yourself: Is my thought life encouraging me to move forward—or is it holding me back? Are my thoughts filled with scripts of shame, guilt, doubt, resentment, insecurity, and fear—or are they filled with hope, redemption, grace, forgiveness, and mercy? The story you tell yourself is crucial to moving you toward healing and wholeness.

Roberta had struggled with an eating disorder for most of her life. In fact, the shame and insecurity she felt about her body started at a very young age and grew larger and larger as she faced bullying, teasing, and harassment from boys in high school. Sometimes life felt so out of control, and controlling her weight through purging was the only thing she felt she could do. She was determined not to gain weight and put a lot of emphasis on her physical appearance. This mentality continued into her college and young adult years, until her eating disorder got so bad she had to be hospitalized for a short time. This was a wake-up call. She realized how much value she was putting on controlling her appearance rather than embracing her true identity in Christ—an identity that superseded how she looked, how much she weighed, and even what people said about her. She started on the journey toward healing, and by the end of college, she felt like she had made real progress in this area of her life.

Fast-forward about ten years. Roberta had met and married Bradley, and together they had their first baby girl. At about six months postpartum, she realized that life was beginning to feel a little out of control again. With the toll that pregnancy had taken on her body, paired with the feelings of exhaustion that come with adjusting to life with a new baby, Roberta's physical insecurities came back with a vengeance. She found herself going into another room to change if Bradley happened to be close by, afraid to let him see her postpartum body. Having sex with the lights on was absolutely out of the question, and she found herself trying to hide under the covers as quickly as she could. Even when he touched her in certain places, she found herself pulling back with discomfort, because all she could think about was the extra pounds, the rolls she was convinced he was feeling, and the fact that her body seemed unrecognizable.

She kept all these feelings to herself, but slowly Bradley began to feel distant and detached from his wife. He didn't understand why she was pulling away. He questioned her love for him and wondered what he had done to cause this distance. Soon their sex life began to wane, and they eventually went from routinely making love two to three times a week to being intimate barely once a month. Roberta blamed it on the baby and the exhaustion, but deep down she knew she was seriously struggling with physical insecurities. She felt a deep sense of shame as she looked in the mirror—shame that was affecting her life and beginning to sever her relationship with her husband.

When I met Roberta, she had been struggling alone for quite some time. Her relationship with Bradley was getting more and more distant. Not only was their sex life a disaster, but what was of greater concern was that their marriage seemed to be hanging on by a thread.

Roberta was caught in a series of toxic thoughts that were seeping into her relationship with her husband. The story she had been telling herself was a script full of shame, hatred, and insecurities: *I'm not good enough to be able to have a baby and keep my body fit. I'm not attractive enough to satisfy my husband in the bedroom. My husband will be disgusted if he sees what I've become.* And just like that, she found herself transported back to the script she had told herself many years ago, a script that allowed her value to be defined by the bullies in high school, the teasing remarks, the size of her waist.

In order for Roberta to be healed from the past, she needed to take seriously the power of her thoughts. She needed to learn to take those thoughts captive and rewire her brain into believing healthy, truthful things. She needed to change—"to be made new in the attitude of [her mind]" (Ephesians 4:23). If she wanted to be freed from the past, she needed to combat the lies she was believing with the truth.

The truth was that the postpartum period is hard on every woman.

The truth was that she was a strong, capable mother who was filling her God-given role with grace and strength.

The truth was that her waist size and stretch marks were not a reflection of her worth.

The truth was that her body was strong, miraculous, and powerful. It had conceived, birthed, and sustained a child!

The truth was that she had a husband who was crazy about her and attracted to every part of her body.

The truth was that every extra pound, every stretch mark, and every wrinkle represented a battle wound reflecting her strength and dignity as a woman.

The truth was she could either allow the toxic thoughts to rob her of joy or allow the truth to fill her with joy. The choice was up to her.

If you want to remove the old from your life, you need to make sure you take inventory of your thoughts and the story you tell yourself. Each and every thought, each and every word you tell yourself, will either carry you one step backward or take you one step forward. Roberta learned to recognize those toxic thoughts—thoughts that sometimes can be so subtle, so automatic, they can be easy to miss. She learned to recognize them and then replace them with the truth. And soon she was able to let her husband in on her struggle. She was able to assure him that she didn't want to feel disconnected from him, and together they worked to heal and restore their marriage.

Take a moment now to make a list of the negative thoughts that have intruded into your mind, especially as they relate to your sex life. They could be thoughts you've harbored for many years, or ones that only recently have begun to creep into your mind. They could be negative and harmful thoughts about your past sexual encounters (or past partners), about your body, or even about your spouse. Maybe you've found yourself thinking and believing things like this:

- *I'm irreversibly blemished because of the sexual encounters I've had in my past.*
- *My body is not good enough for my spouse.*
- *I shouldn't fully enjoy sex because it's not a godly act.*
- *Sex is awful because it reminds me of the pain and abuse of my past.*
- *My husband only wants me for sex; he doesn't really care about me.*
- *I can't measure up to all the other men she's been with.*
- *I'm too old to have sex anymore.*
- *The sex I'm experiencing isn't as exciting as what I've seen and watched on my phone.*

Whatever it is you're battling, remember that so much of the quality of your sexual experience in marriage begins (or ends) in your mind. The things you allow yourself to think about and dwell on will shape your sexual encounter with your spouse more than anything else you could do. In order for the past to loosen its grip on your life, you must recognize what it sounds like and then begin to replace the voices of the past with the voices of truth:

- No matter what you've engaged in in the past, you are forgiven and freed, and there is no condemnation for those who are in Christ Jesus (Colossians 2:14; Romans 8:1).
- You are fearfully and wonderfully made, and your body is a sheer gift to be enjoyed by both you and your spouse (Psalm 139:14; 1 Corinthians 7:4).
- Sex was God's idea, and sexual satisfaction between a husband and a wife is an act that brings glory to God (Proverbs 5:18–19).
- God wants to redeem the pain and trauma of your past, and what people intended for evil, God is able to transform into grace and goodness in your life right here and now (Genesis 50:20).

What are you allowing to fill your mind and heart? Scripture is full of truth that can overwrite the script of your past. Take a moment to identify every one of the negative thoughts that are holding you back. Over the next week, I challenge you to examine those thoughts, one by one, and ask the Lord to reveal to you the passages in Scripture that can help you overwrite those negative and harmful thoughts with God's truth. As you write out God's truth, remember that this isn't a one-and-done experience. You'll need to go back to that list of truths again and again, each time shaping your brain, transforming your heart, and aligning your mind to begin believing this new script of truth.

NOTE FROM GARY

While some of you haven't taken your sexual baggage seriously enough, others of you may be making more of it than you should. How much your past robs you of sexual freedom and enjoyment is actually up to you. Anxiety about sex and even about regretful sexual actions is, frankly, a normal part of sexual development. Few people enter marriage with a perfect scorecard. Everyone gets hurt and fails in this area in some way and to some extent. Our *anxiety* about what happened to us and residual guilt about what we did can do almost as much damage as the original offense.

Be kind to yourself. You didn't learn to drive without hitting a few curbs or tapping the brakes too aggressively. Some of you may have even totaled a car or two. Those past actions don't necessarily make you a poor driver today. In the same way, you likely made some mistakes as you sought to understand, explore, and control appropriate expressions of sexual desire and release. Christians have Christ's sacrifice to fall back on to be freed from our shame, hurt, and guilt. God is generous to forgive, and he is a great and gentle healer.

Step 3: Put On the New

A little part of our brain, called the amygdala, is responsible for the big job of emotional memory. This part of your brain stores any experience you've had that is attached to some sort of emotion. Let's say you walk into Grandma's house and smell chocolate chip cookies baking just for you. Your body is flooded with feelings of comfort, knowing you're loved and appreciated. That experience gets stored in your amygdala.

But just as our amygdalas store positive emotional memories, they also store negative ones. Let's say you get into a fender bender on your way to work. During the accident you experience fear and anxiety, and your body gets a little banged up. Your amygdala holds on to those emotional memories as a way of protecting you, and the next time you get into a car, you start to feel fear and anxiety as your brain alarm goes off: *Hey, don't get into that car! Remember what happened last time? It's dangerous!*

These emotional memories have the power to bring joy to our life, and they also have the power to protect us through a positive use of fear. But sometimes the amygdala can overreact. Sometimes the fear is unwarranted. Consider the fender bender example. Just because you got into a fender bender once doesn't mean it's going to happen every time you get into a car. But your brain doesn't know that. Its only job is to protect you. So it fills you with fear and anxiety that keep you from stepping foot in that car. A lot more can be said about this incredible emotional reaction God has given us, and you can dive deeper into that subject in my book *Are You Really OK?*[3] But the reason I bring it up now is that I want you to see that in order for us to recalibrate our amygdala's response, sometimes we need to overwrite the "bad" emotional memory with a new, "good" emotional memory. We have to replace the old with something new.

And this imagery brings us to the third step in the beautiful process of dealing with our past: *put on something new.* Ephesians 4:24 says it this way: "Put on the new self, created to be like God in true righteousness and holiness." We have to put on something new to replace the things of old. This is exactly what we do in the therapy process when we're working with hard experiences from the past. After we've acknowledged and worked through the details of the past, replacing the negative thought processes of the present with truth, we move on to create new experiences as we look to the future.

In the case of the fender bender story, we push through the fear and eventually get back into the car. We remind our amygdala that much more often than not (as in, almost always), driving to work is a safe and convenient experience. We create *new* emotional memories in an attempt to replace and recalibrate.

All of this brings me back to the story of Meredith I told at the beginning of this chapter, the story of the woman struggling with fantasizing about her past sexual experiences. Meredith felt stuck, paralyzed by her past. When she came to see me, she felt no hope because those experiences were seared into her brain. But what she didn't realize was that her thoughts didn't have power over her; she had power over them. For Meredith to begin to heal, we had to start by going back. We talked through the details of her sexual history, and as she confessed and acknowledged those encounters, she purposefully asked the Lord for forgiveness along the way.

Meredith had been a Christian for many years, but she had never taken the time to take responsibility for those encounters. Just to do so was a freeing act for her, but there was more. The next step was to set mental boundaries that would help her make sure she was aware of the times she had allowed her mind to go to unhealthy places. Specifically, she needed to engage in thought stopping—not allowing her mind to wander to those encounters during sex with her husband. She had to be an active participant in what she allowed to happen in her brain. Through practice, Meredith began to realize she could control what she thought and force her brain to think about something beneficial. She filled her mind with truths instead of with the scripts of her past.

Finally, Meredith and her husband, Ben, had to create new experiences. They had to put on something new as another step in overcoming the past. As we analyzed their sex life, Meredith explained that she longed for more creativity and adventure in their sex life, but out of guilt, she had never voiced this desire to her husband. Oh, she had often complained and showed signs of frustration after sex but had never articulated what she wanted him to change or do differently. Ben hadn't been able to meet her needs because she had struggled to express her needs. As she opened up and let him in, she was finally able to convey what she desired. And Ben, loving husband that he was, quickly and excitedly obliged. He wanted to try new things too but had never initiated because he hadn't wanted to push her outside of her comfort zone. He knew she had a sexual past, and so he wanted to be sensitive and let her lead the way in this area.

Now that they were both on the same page, it was time to create something new together. It didn't happen overnight, but eventually, after ten years of marriage, Meredith and Ben's openness and honesty with one another took their sex life to a whole new level. They tried things together they had never tried before, and by the end of the year, Meredith had many new experiences stored up in her emotional memory that began to write over the old encounters in a way she never imagined possible. What a joy and delight it was for her to realize that her husband was the one who satisfied her like no one else could! Her past no longer held her captive. But she'd had to deal with her past in order to be freed from her past.

Here are a few other practical examples of ways in which people have "put on the new" as they pursued the next step toward freedom:

- For Paul, a man who struggled with a past history of pornography use, putting on the new meant being deliberate about speaking aloud words of affirmation to his wife during and even before sex and acknowledging in detail the parts of her body he enjoyed. This helped him focus all his sexual attention on her and helped her feel valued in his eyes.
- For Laura, a woman who struggled with the guilt and shame of past masturbation, putting on the new meant allowing her husband to use his hands and mouth to touch her genitals, giving herself the chance to replace feelings of guilt and shame with his love and affection for her.
- For Michael, who had a long history of sexual experiences before marriage, putting on the new meant being deliberate to stop his thoughts from wandering to other women or experiences and being intentional about filling his mind with thoughts of his wife and their moments of sexual intimacy.

- For Greg, who had a past history of sexual abuse, putting on the new meant eventually permitting his loving wife to engage him in oral sex, allowing himself to enjoy it rather than avoiding the experience altogether, as he had done in the past.

NOTE FROM GARY

Men, if your past has been marked by selfish behavior, your concrete steps of "putting on the new" might include sexual sessions in which your wife receives all the attention. Put the kids to bed while she takes a bath. Give her a long, sensuous massage. Pleasure her with your hands or mouth. And then let her go to sleep. Make it *all* about her.

One man said, "I like to go down on my wife because this is something I'm doing *for her.* And afterward, sometimes *that's it.* We're done when she's done. Guys might wonder, *What are* you *getting out of it?* and my response is, *Intimacy, closeness, and connection.* When I get her to the point of full release, I feel good because of how I was able to make her feel."

Whether your issue has been sinful reluctance or sinful selfishness, take concrete steps to act in the opposite direction, thereby creating a new dynamic in your marriage.

Whether a struggle with pornography has held us back, insecurities have snuck in as a result of our spouse's sexual past, old emotional wounds have made us question our worth, or the shame we've carried has kept us feeling paralyzed, we all have some sort of a past.

No matter what is behind you, it doesn't have to overshadow what's in front of you. You have the power to face and acknowledge your past, to rewrite the story you're telling yourself in the present, and then to begin creating new experiences as you look to the future. If you're still feeling stuck, please remember that professional counselors can help you walk through the hard moments of your past so you'll be able to move forward in freedom. Don't let another day go by. Don't allow the past to steal one more moment of your present. Sometimes you have to go back in order to go forward.

chapter
fourteen

ABOVE THE SHEETS

Debra

"They have no clue what kind of fun we had last night," she said with a mischievous smile on her face.

I was a single college student at the time, sitting across the table from my fiftysomething-year-old mentor and friend, and we were talking about her marriage. She was telling me how fun it is to be a pastor's wife, sitting in the front row while her husband preached, but holding on to a secret that no one else in the congregation knew. The secret was this: they had an incredible sex life. The night before, making love with her husband had brought an overwhelming ecstasy that nothing could compare to. She wanted me to know that when two people love God and love and serve one another the way God calls them to, their sex life gets taken to a whole new level.

Since that conversation many years ago, I've come to realize that there's a big difference between making love and having sex.

If sex is the physical act by which two people connect their genitals, making love is the emotional act by which two people connect their hearts and souls. A deep and meaningful union occurs when two people become one as they intertwine their bodies and connect their hearts (Genesis 2:24).

In the process of making love, there is an emotional penetration of the heart just as much as there is a physical penetration of the body. Because the emotional and relational connection is so vital to the process of making love, what happens above the sheets in a couple's life is just as important as what happens under the sheets. In fact, the former fuels the latter. When a problem arises in one of those areas, there's often a problem in the other as well.

In our survey in which we asked couples to share the problem spots they've faced in their sex life, one of the top concerns that came up revolved not around actual *sexual* issues but around *emotional* issues that ultimately impacted their sex life.* Couples who struggled the most sexually found that the strain was a direct result of problems they were facing relationally. Sex isn't just about the physical act of sex. It's about so much more. And the state of our sex life is often a symptom of what's going on beneath the surface of our relationship.

Couples will often come into my practice with what they think is a sex problem. They're frustrated that sex isn't "working" the way they want it to. But as we unpack the layers, the sex problem actually ends up being a relationship problem deep down. All the sexual techniques and strategies in the world aren't going to cure a sexual problem that's not actually a sexual problem. That's why we need to understand the connection and begin to track the health of our relationship. Recognizing the correlation between emotional and sexual intimacy is an important step in dealing with any sexual problem, because more often than not, satisfying sex is an overflow of a satisfying relationship. But we don't always recognize this truth at first glance.

Edward and Janice

From the very start of their relationship, Edward and Janice fell into their default roles. As the oldest of six and the most responsible child,

---

* See appendix 1 for research information.

Janice always found herself in the caregiver role. Naturally, when she met Edward, she carried that role into their relationship as well, which was easy to do, because Edward was the youngest in his family of origin, and he loved to be taken care of. He was a laid-back, fun-loving kind of guy who brought out the fun side of Janice. Her responsible, serious nature was quickly drawn to his fun, carefree personality.

Fast-forward twelve years into their marriage when they came to see me, and they were struggling in their sex life. For the past two years of their marriage, Janice hadn't been able to reach climax, and nothing Edward did seemed to get her there. The problem had started much earlier than two years ago, but it was two years ago that her orgasms had come to a complete halt. Their sex life had become such a point of contention that Janice was dropping hints that maybe it was time for her to say goodbye to their marriage. He couldn't please her, and she wondered if he would ever be able to do so.

All the "bedroom" strategies in the world wouldn't be able to help them get over this hurdle if their sexual struggles were in reality a symptom of their emotional struggles. This is where we had to dig a little deeper to try to uncover what might be happening underneath before we could begin to rebuild.

I discovered that Janice found herself "caring" for Edward in more ways than she bargained for. Because of her take-charge nature paired with Edward's laid-back personality, she ultimately became responsible for managing their finances, running the household, organizing their family schedule, and being the primary caregiver for their two children—all while holding down a part-time job. It was easy and natural for her to take charge, but over the years, she found herself slowly feeling burned-out and resentful that Edward got to have all the fun while she assumed all the responsibility for the household. Edward had in effect become like another child in her eyes, just another body she was responsible to feed, take care of, and motivate.

It's important to understand that when a husband gets put into the category of "child," the power dynamic in the relationship changes, and ultimately so does the level of sexual attraction. When we constantly care for someone in the form of giving and giving and giving in the relationship—losing our expectation of receiving anything—we will find that our desire and affection toward that person begin to fade. We become the caregiver instead of the lover. We become the parent instead of the partner.

And that was exactly what had happened in Janice and Edward's marriage over the years. And now their relationship dynamic was preventing Janice from feeling excited and aroused by Edward in the way she used to feel at the beginning of their marriage. He couldn't help her get to climax, essentially because she wasn't *allowing* him to get her to climax. She had been carrying so much responsibility in their relationship for so long that she didn't even realize how much of the struggle stemmed from underlying bitterness, resentment, and control issues. Edward had to learn to step up to the plate of their marriage, and she had to learn how to begin expecting him to—and then allowing him to.

It didn't happen overnight, but eventually, with a lot of therapy and sustained effort from both of them, Edward and Janice were able to restore balance to their relationship, which ultimately led to balance in their sex life. In fact, their relationship came out of that experience healthier and stronger than it had ever been. And so did their sex life.

Better Relationships = Better Sex

If you're struggling sexually, the first thing to do is step back and ask yourself how you're doing emotionally and relationally in your marriage. What is the relational temperature of your marriage, and is anything causing tension, a power struggle, distance, stress, or conflict that you haven't addressed? Do you think of your spouse primarily as a lover or as a parent? A child? A bother? An enemy? A threat? Maintaining sexual desire for your spouse requires you to keep your roles as lovers intact.

While not all sexual problems stem from underlying emotional or relationship problems, the more connected and in touch you are with one another, the easier it will be to identify the problem and come up with a plan to work on it together.

Anthony and Veronica had a strong and healthy marriage, yet she found herself continuing to struggle with very low sexual desire. She *wanted* to want her husband, but she just couldn't get her body to cooperate. It was easier to get to the root of this couple's sexual struggles because they had already done the work on their relationship. With the relational component out of the way, Veronica was able to identify her need for medical intervention and made an appointment with her primary doctor to discuss medication and hormone options to get their sex life back on track.

But most couples aren't like Anthony and Veronica. Most couples have some work—or in many cases, plenty of work—to do on the emotional and relational health of their marriage. In a survey of more than one thousand married people for my book *Choosing Marriage*, the majority of couples reported engaging in zero to thirty minutes per week of quality conversation with their spouse.[1] I assure you that there is absolutely no way healthy relationships are happening in the context of zero to thirty minutes of communication per week. If we really want to work on the health of our sex life, we have to take the health of our relationship seriously.

Both Gary and I have written books about things we can do to strengthen our emotional and relational bonds.[2] For the remainder of this chapter, I want to give you a practical checklist to help you discover which emotional and relational areas may need attention in your marriage.

Your Sexual Struggle May Be a Relationship Struggle If . . .

- ☐ Sex is something you fight about often, but the fighting ends in tension and bitterness rather than resolution and intimacy.
- ☐ You feel like sex is the only time you physically or emotionally connect as a couple.

- ☐ When you feel hurt, you use sex to cover up the relationship problem rather than talk about it and deal with it.
- ☐ You find yourself blaming your spouse and harboring resentment for the sexual problems in your marriage.
- ☐ Your sexual struggles have gotten so bad you think about leaving the marriage or imagine what it would be like being with someone else.
- ☐ Your sexual struggles have led to fantasizing about others or engaging in pornography or masturbation.
- ☐ You commonly see sex as a duty and an obligation rather than something you want to enjoy with your spouse or a way to express your affection.
- ☐ You have no interest in sex and, frankly, very little interest in your spouse in general.
- ☐ You've experienced serious relationship wounds like adultery, addictions, or abuse in your past that seem to be triggered by sex.
- ☐ You feel anxious and uncomfortable around your spouse during sex and find yourself filled with insecurities.
- ☐ You never feel aroused by your spouse or interested in them sexually.
- ☐ You go into sexual intimacy with the automatic assumption that it's not going to be a good experience.
- ☐ The only time you touch or kiss is when you're having sex.
- ☐ You're generally disengaged from what your spouse is feeling unless he explodes with anger or she breaks down crying. They have to express some monumental emotion for you to notice.
- ☐ You're no longer curious about each other—what your spouse has done during the day, how they are feeling, how you can help them, what their opinion would be.
- ☐ You can't remember the last time you laughed together.
- ☐ You fear the thought of being alone together for any significant period of time other than when you're sleeping.

These are just some of the signs that your sexual problems may be rooted in emotional or relational problems. If you connect with one or more of the above statements, I challenge you to take seriously the emotional health of your relationship. Have an honest conversation with your spouse about the aspects of your relationship that bring satisfaction to each of you, as well as the things you believe need to change. Gaining healing in your relationship is an important step toward gaining healing in your sex life.

NOTE FROM GARY

Healthy sex serves a relationship; unhealthy sex *becomes* the relationship, which is asking too much of sex. Sex should be an expression of what is, not a way to temporarily and artificially create what we hope to be true. Our culture tries to make sex be the pathway to intimacy rather than reminding us that healthy sexuality is an expression of intimate connection.

By nature, sex can last only so long and be performed only so often, and sexual chemistry eventually slows down. *Sexual desire simply cannot sustain a lifelong marriage. But an intimate sacred marriage can sustain a tremendous lifelong sex life.*

When sex becomes the relationship, it's like trying to support a fifty-story hotel on a foundation made of toothpicks. We build a healthy sexual relationship by building a healthy marriage on all levels—emotional, spiritual, intellectual, and relational.

Wise couples avoid asking too much of sex *or* too little of sex. A spouse who says, "The rest of our relationship is so strong you shouldn't need sex," is just as misguided as the spouse who says, "Our sex life is so good you shouldn't need anything besides sex." We can fall off the rails on *either* side of the equation—asking sex to do too much or failing to take advantage of its power altogether.

Naked from the Inside Out

One of the most beautiful things two people can share is the vulnerability of being physically naked together. Naked, yet loved. Naked, yet desired. Naked, yet accepted. Every flaw is exposed; every blemish is on display; every insecurity is out in the open in front of a spouse who sees you just as you are and loves you anyway. But just as beautiful, if not more so, is *emotional* vulnerability—the "nakedness" of the heart. One of the things that brings sex to a whole new level is the ability to feel fully known and fully accepted emotionally by our spouse. It's the safe place of knowing that in this relationship, *I have nothing to hide.* It's a true nakedness that starts from the inside out.

A man who has nothing to hide becomes a safe place for a woman to hide her heart. But this is just as true the other way around. A woman who is living authentically and honestly becomes the safest place for her husband. A marriage in which we have nothing to hide is a marriage we have to work at, because that type of intimacy and authenticity doesn't come naturally to any of us.

We live in a world where we're taught to put our best foot forward. And through the culture of social media, we're conditioned to live in a way that presents the best version of ourselves to the world. But sometimes we can get so accustomed to this way of living that we allow this mentality to affect our closest relationships—we bring it into our marriages. We want to present our best self, and so we put our sins and struggles on the back burner. We may even convince ourselves that they don't really exist.

One of the best things you can do for your marriage, and in turn for your sex life, is to think about how naked you are being emotionally. How vulnerable are you with your spouse? How much do they know about the inner workings of your heart, your weaknesses, your struggles, your hardships? If they could see inside you, would they be surprised at what's really going on there? Are you living a life in which you have nothing to hide? Can you say you're truly naked from the inside out?

One way my husband, John, and I have tried to be intentional about this level of nakedness in our marriage is through what we call our "Sunday night check-ins." Every Sunday night, we sit down together at 9:00 p.m. after the kids have gone to bed for a time of sharing, confessing, and encouraging one another. We talk about our struggles, share the things we're stressed about, and confess the ways we've sinned against one another and then ask for forgiveness.

Let me be real: this was not an easy process in the beginning. And sometimes it still isn't. Sharing weaknesses and struggles, being vulnerable, and confessing what we've done wrong takes a lot of courage. But this emotional nakedness is what brings intimacy like nothing else can. By engaging in those moments, we're choosing to live a life where we have nothing to hide from one another. We're choosing to be naked from the inside out.

Since we started this ritual about a decade ago, it has truly transformed our marriage. We started this process because, simply put, our marriage desperately needed it. We were going through a difficult time in our relationship and weren't connecting the way we needed to. John was stressed-out and working crazy hours as a medical resident, and I was dealing with the postpartum hormones and complete exhaustion of having a new baby, all while taking care of our one-year-old. We were both struggling in different ways, but we weren't being totally transparent about what we were going through and what we needed from one another. The gap between us got a little larger with each passing day, because hiding always inhibits intimacy.

I think about the story of Adam and Eve in the garden after they had eaten from the tree that God commanded them not to eat from. They were struggling, and instead of choosing to lean into God, they chose to run from him. "The man and his wife heard the sound of the LORD God as he was walking in the garden in the cool of the day, and they hid from the LORD God among the trees of the garden" (Genesis 3:8). That's essentially what we're doing when we keep things from one another in marriage. We're choosing to hide instead of choosing to connect. Choosing distance instead of closeness.

But when we choose openness and honesty in our marriages, we invite intimacy. For me and John, this level of openness brought an emotional connection far beyond what we experience in any other relationship in this world. And not only that, it also brought our sexual intimacy to a deeper level. In fact, I remember one specific Sunday night check-in. I had just finished talking through some of the dark anxiety I was struggling with at that time in my life, and John was there to listen, encourage, and offer words of support. He had just finished sharing about some stress he was facing, as well as ways he was being intentional to keep the lure of lust out of his life. We prayed together, hand in hand and heart to heart. And let me tell you, nothing is sexier than the honesty, support, and vulnerability of a loving husband. Nothing is more attractive than a man who will be real with you, engage with you, and pray with you. What started off as a Sunday night check-in, an act of emotional vulnerability, turned into making love on the couch. Our emotional connection led to a deeply satisfying physical connection, because the former will always fuel the latter. We were able to engage with one another with complete freedom and security.

When we feel emotionally safe, we can feel sexually safe. When we feel emotionally secure, we can feel sexually secure. When we've been emotionally naked, physical nakedness is just an external representation of something so much more meaningful—it's the outworking of deep intimacy between two people.

Practically speaking, what does this check-in time look like? What are some things you should share with your spouse? What are some areas in which you need to choose to be emotionally naked before them? And is there such a thing as "oversharing"? Drawing from both my personal experience and my clinical experience as a licensed counselor, let me share some of the most important topics that can usher couples into emotional nakedness.

Current Sins and Struggles

The book of James tells us to confess our sins to one another and pray for one another so that we might be healed (5:16). Confession and prayer lead to healing! In marriage, we have a built-in accountability partner—someone to confess to, pray with, and seek healing with hand in hand. So often we fail to take advantage of this beautiful opportunity, and instead we isolate and withdraw from one another in our sins and struggles. Is there any sin or struggle in your life that you've kept in the dark from your spouse? What could it look like to begin the process of confession and healing?

If you're struggling with secret sins or even leading a double life that you've never before confessed to your spouse—maybe you're battling pornography, committing sexual sin, feeling trapped in deceit and dishonesty, or engaging in something else that could cause harm to your marriage—I recommend that you choose to share your story for the first time with the help and guidance of a professional counselor to walk you through the process of disclosure in a healthy and productive way.

Past History

I have worked with many clients who are struggling in the present because of problems from the past. Whether it's experiences of trauma or abuse, a sordid sexual history, or past mistakes and failures, the past is holding too many people back from living fully in the present. But if we don't deal with the past, we can't be freed from the past. Is there anything significant or painful in your past that you've failed to share with your spouse? How could that past experience be affecting your present life?

Relationship Struggles

When it comes to relationships, I try to teach my clients that we can't hold someone responsible for something we never told them they were responsible for. Maybe there's something in your relationship that's bothering you—an unmet expectation, a wounded heart, a difficult disappointment, an unfulfilled need. Sometimes it's a small unexpressed need, like that of the wife who didn't want to have sex at the end of the day because her husband failed to unload the dishwasher when she was tired—but she had never told him how much that irritated her. Or the husband who felt neglected at the dinner party while his wife roamed the room, socializing with everyone else—but he had never let her know how he truly felt.

Sometimes the unexpressed needs run even deeper. Like the woman who longs for more affectionate physical touch outside of the bedroom but hasn't had the courage to express that desire to her husband. Or the man who feels criticized and critiqued by his wife but keeps his hurts to himself.

No matter how small or significant the unexpressed need may be, you're responsible for being an active participant in sharing your needs and desires. Don't mistake passivity for selflessness by keeping things to yourself; instead, take a step toward your spouse by gently and graciously sharing what's on your heart and mind. The truth spoken in love has the potential to bring profound healing to a relationship.

Mental/Physical Struggles

I'm so passionate about mental and emotional health that I wrote an entire book about it,[3] no doubt in part because I've suffered through both clinical depression and anxiety, which led to a host of other physical symptoms. Whether we're struggling with physical health or with mental and emotional health, the truth is that these issues can seriously impact the quality of our marriage if we try to walk through the situation alone. An attitude of openness means being real with our spouse about how we're really doing, inviting them into the process and journey. Sometimes people don't want to burden their spouse with difficult information, but by keeping these things from our spouse, we're creating distance that leads to isolation instead of to the intimacy that closeness brings. Are you letting your spouse into every part of your life, no matter how vulnerable it might make you feel?

People often ask me what it looks like to live a life where you have nothing to hide. *Can't too much honesty damage a relationship? Aren't there some things your spouse is better off not knowing?* One practical way I encourage spouses to be open and honest is to imagine their life like a book. It's important to share a summary of every chapter of your life with your spouse, but it's not necessary to take them through it word for word. For example, while they don't have to hear the nitty-gritty details of your past sexual history, they *do* need to be aware of your past partners. While they don't need to know the exact details of your past traumatic experience, they do need to understand the things in your past that have shaped you into the person you are today. While they don't need to know the exact names of the people you lusted after today, they do need to understand you're struggling in this area and working to transform your heart and mind. Share the summary with your spouse, and share the details with the Lord. And then wait and see how this level of openness and authenticity brings an intimacy to your marriage that you've never experienced before.

Spiritual Intimacy

Husbands, let me tell you one of the most powerful aphrodisiacs you can give your wife: *praying for her out loud*. If she is feeling judged by your mom or hers, nervous about speaking to a friend, anxious about work, or stressed by anything else, take a moment to ask, "Can I pray for you?" Put your hand on her shoulder while you pray, hug her afterward, and then, later in the day, follow up and ask her how she's doing or how the anxiety-producing situation went.

Some of the deepest and most powerful moments of intimacy in a marriage happen above the sheets, in the spiritual connection between a husband and wife. When we share our heart and bare our soul before God, with our spouse by our side, a supernatural bond brings us together like nothing else can. When the Lord is the third party in our relationship, the marriage is stabilized and strengthened because "a cord of three strands is not quickly broken" (Ecclesiastes 4:12).

As I look back on my relationship with John, I realize some of our most intimate moments had more to do with prayer than sex—moments when we were broken by the hardships of life, sitting hand in hand on our bed, crying out to the Lord together for our children, our families, and one another. If that's not intimacy, I don't know what is. And I'm not the only one who resonates with this sentiment. Across the board, all the couples I interviewed recognized the power of spiritual intimacy in their marriage and, also most interesting to note, acknowledged how the spiritual connection positively affected their sexual connection:

> *When my husband and I are in sync spiritually, it impacts everything. It even brings a new level of freedom to our sex life.*

> *When we aren't connecting spiritually, sex can almost feel flat and impersonal.*

> *When we have a genuine spiritual connection, sex is always so much more intense.*

> *When we aren't connected, sex feels like work at the beginning. I almost always end up enjoying sex, but it takes quite a bit of warming up and a ton of mental work on my part, where I have to constantly refocus my mind and ask the Lord to help me engage and serve my husband. It can feel very impersonal to me and sometimes like a Band-Aid fix for the spiritual intimacy that is lacking in our relationship.*

I want to address a false notion that can have a great impact on our sex lives. We're often told that men are *just* wired to be visual, or that they're simply physical or sexual beings. And while men may be more inclined toward a physical experience of sex, to put them in such a small box is not only degrading but inaccurate. Men are fueled by emotional and spiritual intimacy because God wired them that way. The need for a deep and meaningful connection with another human being is not a male/female thing—it's a human being thing—human beings who are made in the image of God. Let's not underestimate this truth or make light of the need for emotional and spiritual connection. Mature men understand this need and work to achieve a deep connection in their marriage. In fact, one of the most insightful responses to our question about spiritual intimacy came from a man married for twenty years:

> When we're not connected emotionally or spiritually, it has a chilling effect on our sex life. When it feels like we're disconnected, I don't want to initiate sex. I don't want Janell to feel like she has a duty to have sex with me even when she's not in the mood, and if we're not truly connected, she's not likely to be in the mood.
>
> Early in our marriage, I didn't understand this. I thought, *We know how sex works and we both enjoy it, so why shouldn't it bring us together even if there are other aspects of our relationship that aren't perfect?* Basically, I thought that as long as we had sex, everything else would work itself out eventually.
>
> Of course, it's more complicated than that, and I've since figured out that obligatory, perfunctory sex is just not that great. It's still sex, sure, but it leads to a lot of hurt, and it's definitely not what God intends a fulfilling marriage to look like. I do believe that God can use sex to bring healing to other areas of a marriage, as we've both experienced, but the healing came from God and not from the act of sex itself.

The quality of our relationship above the sheets impacts the quality of our relationship under the sheets. How are you nurturing your personal relationship with the Lord, and in turn, how are you allowing that relationship to overflow into the life of your spouse? What does your spiritual connection with your spouse look like today, right here and right now?

Human beings are holistic. We're made to connect on every level—emotionally, mentally, spiritually, and physically. When all of these components are in sync and aligned, the outcome is a deeper satisfaction, joy, and intimacy than you ever thought possible. But when one of these components is off, it will inevitably impact the others.

All of this matters because once the initial sexual chemistry in a marriage has waned, a healthy sex life is a reflection of the overall health of a relationship. But a struggling sex life is often a reflection of a misalignment in one or more of these areas. It's a symptom of an emotional or relational disconnect in the relationship. No strategies, techniques, or sexual positions are going to give you what you need in your sex life if you don't care for the health of your relationship overall. But as you work on the other areas of your marriage, your sex life will ultimately reap a great reward. As you take time to learn about strategies for under the sheets, I challenge you and your spouse to take a moment to think about how you're doing above the sheets.

chapter fifteen

BETTER PEOPLE, BETTER SEX

Gary

Dustin told his wife, Lexi, no for perhaps the first time in a decade. Lexi had a pattern of dropping everything whenever her younger brother got into trouble—which was often. On this occasion, Dustin and Lexi had planned to take their two daughters to a movie, followed by ice cream. On their way out the door, Lexi's cell phone rang. As soon as Dustin realized it was Lexi's brother, he could write the script. Lexi would say, "You know I'm there for you," and begin to make up some excuse as to why she couldn't go to the movie, wanting Dustin to deliver the news to their daughters.

"Lexi," Dustin said firmly, "you've promised your daughters this would be a family night."

"My brother needs me," Lexi said.

"Your daughters need you," Dustin said. "And I'm not going to cover for you. If you ditch them to go bail him out one more time, I'm not going to lie to them. You're going to have to own this."

At first, Lexi was furious. "I can't believe you would put me in a situation like this." She clenched her fists, let out a cry of exasperation, and said, "Fine! I'll call him back."

For years, Dustin had caved to Lexi's anger and guilt-inducing accusations. As a people pleaser, he could hardly stand it when Lexi was displeased with him for any reason. Worse, this was a Saturday night, and Saturday night was their customary night for sexual intimacy. Even so, Dustin had been seeing a counselor and was intent on resetting the course of his marriage, facing his issues even if Lexi wouldn't face hers. After Lexi backed down, Dustin expected a chilly experience in the movie theater. He actually got the opposite. One-third of the way through the film, Lexi started some provocative touches. They weren't scandalous—the girls were with them, after all—but direct enough to let Dustin know "Saturday night" was still *on*.

Dustin was puzzled by what had happened, but it's what one counselor calls "begrudging respect." Even when we take a stand that may seem to frustrate our partner, if we are acting in good faith (not like a jerk or a powermonger), our spouse is likely to eventually see our good intentions and *our strength*. Strength is a turn-on for both men and women, even when it seems to work against us.

It makes sense if you think about it. A weak man or a wimpy wife is going to be pitied more than they are going to be wanted. Strength of character builds our sex appeal. If you want your spouse to want you in the bedroom, be someone they can respect outside the bedroom. A better *you* can actually lead to better *sex*. The longer I work in marriage ministry, the more convinced I am of how essential respect is—from the husband to the wife, and from the wife to the husband. If either the husband or the wife is disrespected, things start to fall apart, especially in the bedroom. Sex without respect gives me the chills.

This is just one example of why growing in the Christian faith serves our sexual intimacy. A Christian is never "not" a Christian. When the apostle Paul tells the Colossian believers what they should strive for and what they should avoid, he's telling us to apply what he says wherever we are, whether on the ball field, in the boardroom, or even in the bedroom. We can take Paul's words in Colossians 3 about what to take off and what to put on as indicators of how we can most enjoy and benefit from sexual intimacy. If we pursue biblical character, our sexual pleasure will likely be enhanced and protected.

Taking Off the Vices

Before Paul tells us to put on certain virtues, he urges us to get rid of harmful vices. Not coincidentally, these vices are the relationship traits most likely to hinder a satisfying sexual intimacy. Here's what we need to take off:

> But now you must also rid yourselves of all such things as these: anger, rage, malice, slander, and filthy language from your lips. Do not lie to each other, since you have taken off your old self with its practices and have put on the new self, which is being renewed in knowledge in the image of its Creator.
>
> *Colossians 3:8–10*

Anger and Rage

Sabrina caught glimpses of Reggie's anger before they got married—occasional road rage, embarrassing tirades directed toward sloppy customer service. But she never imagined his rage would be turned on *her* after they got married. When it was, the sexual relationship that had been "Hall of Fame" quality nosedived in just the second year of marriage.

The fact that Reggie and Sabrina had enjoyed "tremendous" sex before shows they knew *how* to have sex. Reggie was great in bed. But his anger made Sabrina never want to *be* in Reggie's bed. The key wasn't Reggie's improving his sexual technique; the key was his dealing with his anger.

Anger tends to crater sexual desire. The authors of a study on the relationship between anger and sexual behavior concluded, "Anger seems to have a negative effect on sexual excitement, 'shutting off' the desire to be involved in sexual intercourse."[1] Even when sex does occur in an angry relationship, the presence of anger changes the nature of the sexual experience from one of "connecting" to the more soulless and often independent pursuit of pleasure for its own sake. The study offered this additional revelation:

> Anger-prone individuals share a tendency to . . . consider partners as sexual objects, neglecting their personality, and to express aggressive tendencies during the sexual act. Overall, anger-prone individuals are primarily interested in seeking sexual pleasure rather than committing to a deep relationship: They are essentially interested in satisfying their own needs and desires, neglecting those of their partners; they also experience their sex life without emotional closeness, commitment and love.[2]

This is soulless sex in which the angry person just needs a body—*any* body—to work out their issues.

When a counselor pointed out to Sabrina that Reggie's anger needed to be addressed before their sexual intimacy could thrive, everything finally made sense. Now she knew why she didn't enjoy making love to the same man she used to crave sexually. Angry sex *was* different. It felt different. It left her in a different place. Anger had wrecked a once beautiful connection.

As a physical picture of its spiritual devastation, anger often leads to erectile dysfunction in men, partly by making the blood rush to their face (which is not where you want the blood to rush before intercourse), which of course makes certain kinds of sexual activities impossible. If you're prone to anger, I urge you to see a counselor before you try to "fix" things in the bedroom.

Malice

Getting rid of malice is part of what makes it so difficult for me to embrace the BDSM (bondage and discipline, dominance and submission, sadism and masochism) practices made popular by the *Fifty Shades of*

Grey novels. These "mini" acts of violence have been romanticized, but a desire to create pain is the very thing Paul tells us to take off. From a Christian perspective, we should never want to hurt *anyone*, least of all our spouse. I'm not challenging a consensual playful spank on the rear end, or fingernails unconsciously scratching a lover's back when things get particularly intense. I'm talking about deliberate and cruelly creative ways of causing pain.

To make sure I wasn't simply pushing my own prejudices, I checked with some psychologist (PhD) friends. They confirmed my suspicions and said in their experience the desire for pain can be a yearning to reenact abuse or submit to dysfunctional power struggles. Since we see marital sex as designed to heal, not to reinforce, early injuries, this is a real cause for concern. I want to be open about my prejudices here; it is all too easy a temptation to judge something we find personally distasteful, but let me try to make the case from common sense: the nature of marital sex (with the same person for life), makes pain a short-term strategy with dangerous long-term potential. Neurologically, to get the same effect from sexual pain, we have to consistently *increase* the pain, since our brain learns to tolerate it. Obviously, if we must increase the pain to increase the pleasure, we're going to run out of "safe" pain in a long-term relationship.

If you think your spouse has any malice toward you, how can you surrender? How can you trust? How can you make yourself naked and vulnerable? It would be foolish to voluntarily enter the vulnerable intimacy of sexual union with someone who may want to do you harm.

Malice is just as deadly to sexual intimacy *outside* the bedroom as it is inside. Healthy marital sex is about wanting to pleasure someone you would die for. Malice—having an agenda to inflict physical or psychological hurt, shame, or pain—is the very opposite.

Filthy Language

By filthy language we don't mean "sexy talk" used as terms of endearment (though if sexy talk turns your spouse off, we recommend you don't go there). We don't mean you can't use inside the bedroom words or phrases you would never use outside the bedroom. The Song of Songs contains plenty of "colorful" language we may not want to use in public.

The kind of filthy language Paul is talking about is language that demeans, hurts, and puts down. It's the opposite of the language used in the Song of Songs, where two lovers praise, extol, and celebrate each other. Filthy language is worse than coming to bed with three-inch-long toenails, garlic breath, and an unshowered body. It destroys the basis of sexual intimacy, which is about caring, affirming, honoring, and cherishing. *Every* one of our words throughout the day is either setting up our spouse to desire us and surrender to us or rather building walls of distrust, hurt, avoidance, and anger. We cannot sustain healthy, pleasurable touch in a climate of filthy, demeaning talk. Hear me on this: *one sentence can unleash weeks of hurt and alienation.*

Lying

You know what bothers many spouses who learn about their spouse's affair or pornography use? The lying that covered it up. This realization surprised me as a pastor. You'd think a betrayed spouse's anger would be focused on the sexual acts. It's not as if they *aren't* angry about those acts, but the constant lying that covered up the acts is equally hurtful, and sometimes even more so.

As I reflected on this, it began to make more sense. Sex is based on intimacy and trust—you're naked together! You're exposed physically and spiritually. Desires that you'd never speak about in public often get shared in passionate whispers. Good, healthy sex is the antithesis of lying.

If you've been misled for several years, you'll find it difficult to trust again. If you want long-term sexual satisfaction, you have to "take off" any kind of lying and deceit. Being naked physically is no substitute for not being naked emotionally and spiritually. A relationship built on deceit is like sliding into bed and offering sexual favors as long as you remain fully clothed.

Putting On the Virtues

A healthy sex life is not just about what we "take off." Sexual pleasure is enhanced by what we "put on." The word *virtue* may seem far removed from the thrill of sexual excitement, but becoming a better person can actually lead to better sex. In this context, the virtues are road maps to delight, laughter, and even ecstasy.

Men, we know where our brain goes if our wife walks into the bedroom wearing lingerie, or if freshly showered, she walks into the bedroom, gets our attention, and dramatically drops her towel, smiling that seductive smile.

Kaboom!

Want to have that same effect on your wife? Rebekah shared what works for her: "There's nothing that makes me desire intimacy on all levels more than my husband demonstrating intentional kindness to myself and our children."

Foreplay for many women can be intentional acts of virtue throughout the day that make them feel connected to us.

Savannah and Craig were at a sexual impasse. Sex matters a lot to Craig, but when this couple found themselves unemployed and living with the in-laws, Savannah's libido was nonexistent. Craig felt like he needed sex *more* than normal, not less, because nothing else in his life seemed to be working.

Craig paused long enough to realize that Savannah's hesitancy was about their relationship more than it was about sex, so he asked Savannah to open her heart back up to him. He assured her he wasn't asking her to be sexual with him, but he wanted her to drop her guard emotionally while he focused on his character.

A new sexual technique can't woo a woman who wants nothing to do with sex. But a change in character can do wonders to soften a woman's heart.

"I wasn't sure I could open my heart back up," Savannah confesses, but she did, and here's why: "As Craig continued to pursue Jesus and my heart, he began to exhibit more compassion, gentleness, kindness, patience, and humility. The greater those qualities became in his life, the more I found myself not only opening up to him but actually *wanting* to open up to him."

Craig didn't learn a new sexual technique; he learned a new way to relate, and that made all the difference in the bedroom. "The fact that Craig is embodying kindness, compassion, gentleness, patience, and humility makes him *exceedingly* desirable, and my heart knows it is safe and cared for with him. Because my heart is safe, I'm willing to entrust my body to him without hesitation. It's such a sweet place to be."

It's not just wives who are moved by the virtues. Brad went through a difficult year after his mom died. He knew he was neglecting responsibilities, but he felt lost in a "fog of sorrow, frustration, and a solid dose of anger at God. The grieving process was excruciating." Sex, which had been "indescribably fun and an integral part of our relationship," all but stopped. For *more than a year*, Brad was barely present in his relationship with his wife. Instead of resenting Brad's grief or asking him why he couldn't get over it, "Camille shouldered the load with grace and dignity; she was *gentle.* Her heart was broken with mine; she was *compassionate.* She never spoke a word about taking up the slack; she was *humble.* She spoke words of life and healing into me; she was *kind.* And she never tried to rush the healing process, though I know it was exhausting; she was *patient.*"

Now that the grief has lifted somewhat (it will never be fully gone), Brad finds Camille to be more sexually attractive than ever. "Now, when I look at her, I find her to be the most amazing and desirable woman I've ever seen. She is truly my standard of beauty, not merely because she is outwardly attractive but because she displays the heart of God."

Sexual Kindness

One wife asked another wife a delicate question. "Come on, be honest," she said. "Do you actually *like* giving your husband oral sex?"

"It makes him so happy," the other wife responded.

When this conversation was relayed to me, I was struck by where the second wife placed the focus. The first wife asked, "Do you actually *like* giving your husband oral sex?" but the second wife answered, "It makes *him* so happy." One wife was evaluating a future act by wanting to know if *she* could get joy out of the act; the other wife found her joy in her husband's happiness.

Two men had a different conversation. "Don't you feel threatened to think that your wife may enjoy a sex toy more than she enjoys you?" one husband asked.

"First of all, she doesn't use it alone," the other husband responded. "And besides, anything I can do to make her feel good—in a way that's not sinful—is exciting to me. I love it when I can see that she is fully satisfied, sometimes in a new way. She works so hard. She's an amazing mom, and she loves me. I want her to have something special to look forward to now and then."

The same dynamic that had been at work between the two wives was true for these men. One husband was thinking of himself—his pride, his skills as a lover, his security. The other husband was intent on thinking about his wife's pleasure.

We could describe the motivation revealed in both of these conversations as *kindness*. Kindness, by its very definition, focuses on someone else. We are motivated to do good to someone. We're not thinking about ourselves; we're thinking about them, how we can bless them, help them, or, in the case of the bedroom, pleasure them.

In his book *Leading with Love*, Alexander Strauch wrote, "Kindness is a readiness to do good, to help, to relieve burdens, to be useful, to serve, to be tender, and to be sympathetic to others. It has been said, 'Kindness is love in work clothes.'"[3]

Is your attitude in the bedroom motivated by a sincere desire for your spouse's pleasure? Are you marked by a readiness to do good to your spouse? If so, when it comes to sexual intimacy, your first thought will be, *I bet she [or he] would really like that*, and that may be all the motivation you need.

Kindness also means, however, that if we think our spouse really would *not* like a particular sex act or would feel demeaned or harmed by something, we wouldn't even think to ask it of them, and we certainly wouldn't make them feel like less of a spouse because they're just not into that. Kindness dictates what we do for our spouse and limits what we ask of our spouse. In both cases, we're motivated by what serves, pleases, and affirms them.

Sexual Compassion

Paul urges the Colossians to clothe themselves with another virtue—that of *compassion.* Compassion is the feeling of sympathy that inspires action. Jesus healed and fed the crowds as an expression of his compassion for them (see, for example, Matthew 9:36; Mark 6:34). He could see they were needy and hurting, and he wouldn't just leave them in their hunger. *He was moved by compassion to reach out to meet their needs.*

Because sex can feel so rewarding, its temptation is to make us focus on ourselves—what we want, even what we think we need. Compassion moves us to have mercy on, concern for, and empathy for our spouse. Belgian psychotherapist Esther Perel had a great response when she counseled a husband who was frustrated with his wife's sexual reticence: "I point out to him that she might be more receptive today if he paid attention to cultivating her desire rather than simply monitoring it."[4]

Sex as God designed it is to be an act of love. Its motivation, its expression, its mechanics—all should be governed by love. Saying sex should be governed by love is the same as saying it should be governed by God, because God is a God of love.

The heart of love is *sacrifice.* Jesus put it this way: "My command is this: Love each other as I have loved you. Greater love has no one than this: to lay down one's life for one's friends" (John 15:12–13).

So in sex as God designed it, I'm laying down my life for my spouse, using my body to affirm her, please her, serve her, cherish her, and adore her. Tim Alan Gardner asks, "If there's anything you could do to make your spouse's life easier or more fulfilling, and if there's anything you could do to make your mate feel more loved, more cherished, and more valued, why do you hesitate to do those things?"[5]

Of course, we can remove any immoral actions from obligating us in any way, as well as any actions that would compromise our health. But if nothing like that is holding us back from applying what we've discussed in this book, what is? If we know our spouse would like a better sex life and that we're the only one who can provide that, why don't we just do it?

Gardner suggests that the reason is often (but not always) selfishness: "Any attempt to justify not choosing loving actions toward our mates is an argument rooted in selfishness. Love, from God's perspective, is always about doing, not just about feeling. Love is about commitment and the choices we make. It's about deciding not to be selfish."[6]

You may have been inspired by this book and picked up a few tips. You may be more informed. You may even be a bit convicted. But if you don't *do* what we've talked about, this book won't help you.

Much has been said—indeed, we've said it ourselves in this book—about the unhelpfulness of having sex primarily out of "duty." Making sex an obligation owed by our spouse crushes sexual delight. At the same time, when we choose to get married, we *are* declaring that we will be reasonably available for sexual activity. It's most helpful to examine the relational issues that crater sexual desire, but we also need to search our heart for any spiritual issues that may be getting in the way as well. I don't want to make sex feel like a sacrifice for my spouse, nor do you. That sounds horrible. But God can use the sexual relationship to reveal our own selfishness, which is crucial because selfishness never restricts itself to one arena of life. If selfishness finds a foothold in our heart, it will work its way into our parenting, our friendships, our marriage, our finances, and, yes, the bedroom.

It is not healthy for sex to always (or even mostly) feel like a sacrifice. But it also is not healthy for a spouse to think sex should never feel like a sacrifice. I can't think of any other aspect of marriage that doesn't have some sacrificial element to it. Feeling mentally exhausted from a long day of writing is no excuse for tuning out my wife during the evening when she wants to talk and needs me to listen and even ask her questions.

I've seen manipulative people who insist their spouse jump through ten hoops for the previous seventy-two hours just so they can eventually say, "Aha! So I *don't* have to have sex with you tonight." That's a contractual understanding of marriage ("you do this, and I'll do that"), not the heartfelt concern of a compassionate spouse.

A compassionate husband thinks about what his wife is feeling and how he can make her feel better. He recognizes her natural fears about her body and reassures her of her beauty. He knows she has limited energy, so he does his best to help out. He empathizes with what his wife must feel to have children pawing at her body all day long, so he goes out of his way to offer *giving* touches, not *taking* touches. He is able to say, "Life isn't easy for you," so he seeks to make it a little better, to help ease her concerns rather than add to her burdens.

Some wives (by no means all) who read this may think, *That means he needs to be leaving me alone!* But does it? Perhaps at times, but if God designed you to be desired by your husband, adored by your husband, celebrated by your husband, and sexually pleased by your husband, wouldn't "sexual compassion" motivate him to adopt an approach that allows him to accomplish this in a way you find inviting and exciting?

I don't always want to exercise, but I need to do it at least five days a week. I don't always want to eat vegetables, but according to my wife I need to several times a day. "I don't see where you got your seven servings of vegetables today" is one of her favorite sayings. Nothing delights me more and her less when I playfully respond, "Don't worry, I had a salad *yesterday*. I'm good."

Does Lisa encourage my vegetable consumption to lord it over me? Does she do it just because she wants me to eat everything she has prepared? Or does she do it because she has compassion for me? Her motives may be mixed at times, but in the end, I know there's compassion behind her actions.

David Schnarch counsels that "compassion requires making room in your relationship for your partner."[7] Because of the mutuality of sexual intimacy in marriage, your refusal to pursue a flourishing sexual relationship comes at a high cost to your spouse. Schnarch writes, "Marriage never offers you the simple choice: 'Do you want to resolve your sexual problems or not?' The choice always includes: 'Do you want to let this fall on your partner or not?' . . . Repeatedly, you will have to choose between stifling your partner's growth and happiness, or growing up yourself. Good sex involves compassion, openness, sharing, and generosity that are not confined to your sexual technique."[8]

Sexual Peace

What's the greatest threat to the sexual satisfaction of most couples? Is it busyness? Is it the prevalence of pornography? Is it past hurt?

Dr. Schnarch believes one of the biggest assaults on sexual satisfaction is *anxiety*: "I've counseled men who have premature orgasm, delayed orgasm, or erection problems who have no idea how completely anxiety-ridden they are. Some women haven't a clue how anxious they are in bed because they've never experienced anything else. They can't relax because all they know is 'red alert.' Many people who read about performance anxiety still have no idea how tortured they are during sex."[9]

For sex to be truly enjoyed, we have to lean into it. It requires finding freedom, letting go, not trying to perform but focusing on our spouse or sometimes on our own pleasure. All of this means that growing in peace will greatly increase your satisfaction in the bedroom. Peace means learning to face your anxieties without letting them have the upper hand. We recognize the threats (embarrassment, poor performance, fear, distraction) but move forward anyway because we realize that the best things in life all involve varying degrees of anxiety. By allowing sex to help us learn to manage anxiety, we can become more mature believers.

Marriage should be a safe place where we know that one unfulfilling episode of sex won't threaten our relationship or destroy our spouse's respect for us. Our spouse's commitment isn't dependent on us lasting longer, having an orgasm, or being able to "perform."

What if many sexual issues arise from anxiety more than from physical inability? Schnarch believes that sexual satisfaction "often involves realizing you are more frightened, tense, anxious, and insecure than you thought—and more embarrassed, humiliated, intimacy-intolerant, angry, narcissistic, vindictive, self-centered, petty (add your favorite) than you imagined. Although these difficult realizations can trigger uncomfortable feelings of being unlovable, they will enhance your capacity to love. Just hold on to yourself, calm yourself down, and let yourself finally relax."[10]

Amelia is anxious because it takes her so long to climax, and she's afraid her husband might get bored. Here's what she needs to know: if her husband is healthy, he's enjoying the journey as much as she is. If he's not healthy, learning to serve Amelia sexually is making him healthier, so Amelia shouldn't get in God's way of "growing" her husband by pretending she's done when she's not! Besides, trying to force herself to respond more quickly is certain to delay her satisfaction even further.

Physiologically, the female body and brain can experience sustained and heightened sexual pleasure far more than a male can. Especially as we age, men require more recovery time, and before we age, we may have a difficult time enjoying pleasure without finishing before we want to. God designed wives' bodies in such a way that their pleasure can be greater for a longer period of time, and more frequently, than is true for their husbands. This knowledge excites me as a husband; it's not a burden!

The physiological mechanics of sex mean that wives can increase their pleasure by remembering what we said earlier: "My pleasure increases his pleasure." And husbands can prolong their pleasure by remembering this: "Her pleasure increases my pleasure." Wives, be at peace! Sex seems designed to give husbands more pleasure when they give than when they receive. What an atrocity when books on sex make it seem as if the husband "needs" sex and the wife "needs" to serve! Actually, the husband needs to serve. And when he does, *he* is served. Only God could come up with something so brilliant.

The Song of Songs mentions Solomon and the Shulammite as the two lovers.* *Shulammite* is a feminine form of *Solomon*. Both words are taken from the Hebrew root word *shalom*, which means "peace." Sexual satisfaction leads to a divine contentment whereby we can be satisfied, at rest, free of anxiety, filled with *peace*. Haven't you ever had a wonderful time of intimacy with your spouse and just let out a sigh: "Aaahhh"?

Addicts frequently mention the shame and anxiety that consume them when they act out. Married couples should experience the opposite as they lie quietly in each other's arms—the contented peace and restful satisfaction resulting from intimacy-building pleasure.

NOTE FROM DEBRA

As Gary mentioned, an atmosphere of sexual peace is vitally important, but it doesn't just happen on its own. You have to be intentional in creating this atmosphere by watching what you're communicating to your spouse both inside and outside the bedroom. When I feel loved, accepted, affirmed, and desired in my marriage, I find that all of these things translate to how I relate in the bedroom. As a spouse, take a moment to consider how you affirm your spouse outside the bedroom. Do you make them feel wanted and secure or unappreciated and rejected? Do you encourage more than you criticize? Do you tend to lift up your spouse or tear them down? What you communicate outside the bedroom will carry over into your sex life.

But what if you're the spouse who struggles with anxiety in the bedroom? No matter how affirming or encouraging your

* This isn't to suggest that the entire book relates to Solomon and this woman. Most modern commentators read Song of Songs as a series of love poems, not the chronological development of one particular story or couple.

spouse is, you can't seem to see past your own insecurities. You worry that your climax is taking too long; you're filled with self-loathing over your physical appearance; you're afraid your spouse won't be attracted to you.

Mandy's struggle with this type of sexual anxiety was so intense that it was hindering her desire for sex and her performance in the bedroom. No matter how much her husband affirmed her, she just couldn't get past her own insecurities and negative view of herself. She was reaching the point where she hardly wanted sex because of it. As I worked with Mandy, we came to realize that the root was deep-seated insecurities that stemmed from her high school days. She had been a star athlete and great value had been attached to having the perfect body and build. Now, years (and five children) later, she was still measuring herself by the same unrealistic standards, which was destroying her sex life, preventing her from feeling the freedom and affirmation she could be experiencing with her husband.

Your spouse may be wonderfully supportive, but ultimately *you* are responsible for dealing with your own sexual anxiety by getting to the root of the cause. If this struggle is one you're facing, I encourage you to reach out to a counselor and begin to deal with your underlying insecurities and fears.

Hope

We live as fallen people in a fallen world, which means the bedroom will sometimes feel like an area of brokenness. Growing in the virtue of hope will help us press on toward better times.

David Schnarch writes, "Hope will get you further than safety and security, because hope is part of human resilience. Hope is what you have *before* change comes about. Hope is believing in yourself *while* you have doubts. Hope comes from understanding how life works and seeing yourself as part of the system. Hope helps you persevere through marriage's trials and tribulations."[11]

You might say to yourself, *Things are difficult right now. It feels like we both want different things in the bedroom. But I believe we'll get there. I believe my husband's erectile dysfunction, premature orgasm, prostate surgery, or [fill in the blank] won't be the defining element in our relationship.* Or, *My wife's vaginismus, previous sexual abuse, current bout with hormones/menstruation/menopause is making things a little difficult right now, but we'll get through this together and come out on the other side closer and more in love with each other.*

During the writing of this chapter, I received an email from a husband whose prostate was removed due to cancer. This reality has had huge repercussions for what happens in the bedroom, including erectile dysfunction and even occasional incontinence. He confessed, "I often feel like I lost my man card, but my wife reminds me that we made the decision for total removal [of my prostate] for a longer life together as a husband and wife, parents, and grandparents (MiMi and PaPa). Our marriage is much more than sex. We continue to love each other, in sickness and in health." They haven't yet figured out how to fully recover and express their sexual intimacy, but their marriage is being buoyed by hope. They'll get there, in whatever way they can, as far as they can.

In a fallen world, hope is a particularly precious virtue. In marriage, hope is essential for sexual satisfaction throughout our lives.

The Path to Better

It's noble to want to become a better lover; it's divine to want to become a better *person*. This chapter teaches us that becoming a better person actually makes us a better lover. The Latin *virtus*, from which we get our English word *virtue*, carries the connotation of "strength" or "power."

Virtue strengthens us as people and as lovers. By all means, work on sexual techniques and understanding, but don't forget to work on your character as well. Take off the vices that destroy sexual desire and satisfaction; put on the virtues that make you desirable and generous. Sex between two virtuous people is the most intimate, enjoyable kind of sex any couple could ever experience. This is married sex.

FINAL WORDS

A Final Word from Gary

While writing this book, Debra and John became pregnant. I laughed so hard when Debra told me what had happened and why. Apparently, all the reading, research, and writing that led to this book resulted in Debra and John having more sex. Regardless of how many copies this book sells, if it has led to the creation of another human life, it has already been worth the time and energy spent on it.

But Debra and I write from two very different seasons of marriage. Barring a total miracle (in the neighborhood of Abraham and Sarah), Lisa and I will never conceive another child. But while I was writing this book, one of our adult children nearly died. A UTI and a kidney stone combined to cause more than a lot of pain; they unleashed an infection that seeped into our daughter's bloodstream and threatened to end her life.

I wrote in chapter 9 that marital intimacy can be an oasis in a troubling present, but in our case, taking turns spending entire days in the ICU and having Ivy League–trained doctors telling us, several days in a row, "This is what we're doing to keep your daughter alive today," cratered both of our libidos. Our "intimacy" was verbally sharing what we had learned that day about platelets, creatinine and potassium levels, white blood cell counts, and so many bodily functions that you rarely think about but that can determine life or death.

After the doctors began talking about recovery instead of survival, more days passed until Lisa and I could think about bodies as anything other than vulnerable arenas in which infections fight against a person's will to survive. We eventually made love, and Lisa reminded me of the last time we'd had sex before our daughter got sick.

"No," I said. "Really? That long ago?"

"Think about it," Lisa answered.

"I guess you're right."

There will be seasons when you can't get enough of each other, and if you're in that season and this book inspires you, enjoy it. Give yourself over to it: "Eat, friends, drink, and be drunk with love!" (Song of Songs 5:1 ESV). And there may be seasons when desire not only isn't noticed—it's not even missed. The reproductive system is the only system in our bodies not required for survival. If our circulation breaks down, if our respiration ceases, if digestion stops working, our very existence is imperiled. If a man has a vasectomy or a woman undergoes a hysterectomy, no one but their doctor would know. And life would go on.

Sexual intimacy may be the theme of Song of Songs, but our marriages are about so much more. Sexual desire and fulfillment in a lifelong marriage often resemble the tide. It goes in and out, comes back with force, and then can seemingly disappear for a while. Desire and pleasure are wonderful, but if they're made the central focus of sex, marriage may feel like an impediment to sexual pleasure rather than a protector of it.

When we recapture the truth that sex is about being a family unit (with or without kids), proclaiming that we are one, reminding ourselves of the covenant we have made, and often enjoying the "En Gedi" aspects of sex, we won't define any one encounter or even any one *season* by whether it "felt" better than it did when we were newlyweds.

"Good" sex doesn't always leave you tingling afterward. "Good" sex doesn't always result in two orgasms. "Good" sex doesn't always reach the pinnacles of pleasure. Sometimes good sex is simply a marker that things are back to normal and you can cuddle again without fear or dread.

I write this final word with an earnest prayer that every person reading this book will worship God for creating something so wonderful, will have a renewed desire to serve their spouse with something exceedingly powerful, and will explore the outer reaches of this delightful dance together with their spouse for many days to come.

A Final Word from Debra

As Gary mentioned, John and I conceived baby number four during the writing of this book. Before that, we had made peace with the thought that our family was complete, and we were ready to move forward. To say this baby was an unexpected surprise would be the understatement of a lifetime. John and I joke that all the sex conversations and "research" we did together for this book must have been the culprit. But the truth is, God had this planned all along. Throughout the writing of this book, we've been reminded that we, like you, are also on this journey to become better people just as much as better lovers. We're being stretched, transformed, renewed, and required to trust God more than we've ever trusted him before—certainly with our sex life, but more so, with our entire lives.

Throughout this book, our goal has been to encourage all of us to remember that a great sex life is not just something that happens along the way; it's something we have to work to create. A bigger picture is at play, one that God is at work on behind the scenes, and our sex lives are just a part of something even greater, something even more meaningful. I always say that *healthy people make healthy relationships*, but I think it's just as important to affirm, as Gary reminded us, that healthy people make healthy relationships, which make for healthy sex lives.

As our time together comes to an end, we encourage you to think through the next steps for becoming better people and better lovers.

Is anything in your life keeping you from enjoying sex to the fullest? Are you holding on to false beliefs, past shame, sins and struggles, bitterness and resentment, or anything else that may be inhibiting your sexual enjoyment? Are you allowing apathy, false sexpectations, or a lack of education or understanding to keep you in the status quo rather than pursuing God's best for your sex life? Does the next step for you mean an honest conversation with your spouse, an appointment with a medical doctor or licensed counselor, or even a shift in your busy schedule? What will you do when the last words of this book have been read to begin creating a better you, a better relationship, and a better sex life?

The best sex lives are not ones we stumble upon but ones we create. Our prayer for each of you is that you would not just read more about better sex in marriage but actually begin to work toward it. May God give you the courage, the passion, and the perspective to pursue a pleasureful sex life like never before. Here's to many more years of good sex! We're praying for you and cheering you on.

appendix
one

RESEARCH AND METHODOLOGY

Debra

Research for this book was gathered in two different ways. First and foremost, Gary and I thought it was important to include the stories and perspectives of many different couples. We didn't want to rely simply on our own limited personal perspectives and experiences, and we wanted to go above and beyond the stories of couples we've met with and counseled over the years.

Because of the sensitive nature of the content we discuss in this book, we decided it would be best to form a group of people online who were willing to share their stories and struggles. We started an interactive Facebook group limited to 110 members—people who are regular followers/readers of either my or Gary's work, representing Christian marriages from all across the country. The limited size allowed us to gather data quickly and conveniently and keep up with the interaction in a meaningful way. We relied on this group to gather personal stories and experiences, survey data, and information to help us shape the book throughout the writing process. We're grateful for the input we received from this special group, and we are confident you'll enjoy the honesty in their stories and perspectives scattered across the pages of this book.

The second way we gathered data was through an anonymous survey that was completed by more than 900 couples, representing more than 1,800 people from across the country. For further details on our survey methodology and for complete results of this survey, go to www.marriedsexbook.us.

appendix
two

HOW TO FIND A COUNSELOR

Debra

Finding a good counselor can be a daunting process for many people. In fact, one of the most common questions I receive is "How do I find a counselor?" To help you in this process, I put together this brief checklist to get you started:

- The most common route to finding a counselor (or pretty much anything these days) is to do an internet search. You want to make sure you are searching for a Christian licensed counselor. Many people who use the term *counselor* may have pastoral certification but are not licensed by the state. The term *licensed* is what you're looking for; these folks are trained professionals who have undergone a specific amount of training and education.
- Usually, a counselor's biography will list some of their areas of specialty, such as sex therapy, trauma, depression and anxiety, addictions, and so forth. Try to connect with a counselor who is gifted in your specific area of struggle.
- Feel free to give your selected counselor a call or send an email before scheduling your first session to ask them about the type

of therapy they typically use, the number of years they've been in practice, and the way they integrate the Christian faith into their clinical approach.

- Remember that when it comes to finding a good counselor, it's all about finding someone you feel comfortable with. The therapeutic relationship between you and your counselor is important, but it's fairly common not to hit it off right away. I always recommend trying three to six sessions before you attempt to find another counselor. If after a handful of sessions, you don't feel a connection or don't feel comfortable, by all means don't quit on therapy. No offense is taken if you don't connect; the only true offense is if you give up on your situation! Reach out to another counselor (and if necessary even another and another), and try again.
- Always remember that healing is not linear; it's cyclical. When we're dealing with challenges in our lives, we don't just get "better and better" each day. Sometimes we'll take a few steps forward and one step back. Sometimes we'll want to give up. But the key is to keep moving forward, because as we do, we get healthier and stronger and draw closer to achieving our goals. Healing is not only possible; it's *attainable* for those willing to put in the work.
- Gary and I have compiled a list of resources and referrals, and even the option of connecting with me for counseling and therapy. You can find this information at www.marriedsexbook.us.

ACKNOWLEDGMENTS

Gary

I've had a vision for a book like this for at least fifteen years, but I'm so glad it took this long for the book to come to fruition, in no small part because it has given me the chance to collaborate with Debra. I rarely co-write books, but in this case, working with a younger writer of different gender who has a different skill set proved so beneficial, particularly for this topic. This collaboration exceeded all my hopes, and I'm so thankful Debra agreed to do it. Her husband, John, was an active participant behind the scenes, and I'm thankful for his wisdom and insight as well.

Mike Salisbury and Curtis Yates, our agents for this book, did a fantastic job of early representation; they weren't going to let it happen unless it was given top consideration by our publisher. And I'm especially grateful for the Zondervan team that accepted the manuscript and put the right people in place to produce it, including Webster Younce, Paul Fisher, Andy Rogers, Carolyn McCready, Dirk Buursma, Alicia Kasen, Keith Finnegan, Stefanie Schroeder, Andrea Kelly, and Kait Lamphere.

For their willingness to contribute their stories, I am immensely grateful to the few dozen couples who made up our private Facebook group (Debra's idea). Their willingness to share their stories, answer questions, participate in digital dialogues, and offer personal anecdotes was invaluable. To Jocelyn and Danny, Julie and Doug, and Skye and Brad, thanks especially for your particular contributions.

Numerous people graciously reviewed this manuscript before we sent it to the editors, including Mary Kay Smith, Byron and Carla Weathersbee, Scott Kedersha, Rob Hardman, Danny and Jocelyn Boutwell, Doug and Julie Macrae, Dr. Steve Wilke, Laura Kates, and Kristen Beadles. I'm also grateful to Alli Sepulveda, my assistant at Second, and Andi Perkins, who manages my marketing.

From the bottom of my heart, I want to acknowledge the readers and book buyers (as well as the leadership and membership of Second Baptist Church) who make my continued writing possible. Your support of past books gives me the time to think about, do research for, and write new books. I'm more grateful than you could possibly know.

Finally, I'm especially grateful to my wife, Lisa. This is a particularly vulnerable topic to address in book form, but Lisa was enthusiastic about the need for it, courageous in her permission about what was shared, and gracious in her willingness to be married to a man who gets asked, "What's your next book about?" several times a week and who now, in polite company, must hear me say (as she stands by my side), "Well, actually . . ."

Debra

First and foremost, my deepest gratitude goes to Jesus. Where would I be without him? He's changed me from the inside out, and I want to spend the rest of my days making him known. He is the author of love, and he has given us the beautiful gift of sex and intimacy in marriage. He gets the first of my heart, and the first of my gratitude.

Second, I want to thank my husband, John, for his support and love on every step of my ministry journey. This book is no exception. Thank you for cheering me on, loving me well, and being my safest space. And thank you for all the good practice we got in too! But let's try not to have any more surprise babies. You are an exceptional man, father, and friend, and I'm so grateful for you.

Third, I want to acknowledge Gary and Lisa Thomas. The way you love, trust, and honor one another is inspiring. A book like this could only be coauthored with two strong marriages standing behind it. Thank you for not only believing in this message but living it out.

Fourth, a very special thanks to the men and women who participated in the surveys and especially the Facebook group. Your authenticity and willingness to share for the sake of this message were so valuable to this book! May God continue to bless your marriages and your love lives!

And lastly, I want to thank the entire team behind this book, from Zondervan and Yates & Yates all the way to Rachel Heisey for her cover inspiration. Thank you for believing in this message from day one and partnering with us to bring it into the world. May God do more with it than we could ever ask or imagine.

NOTES

Introduction

1. See Debra Fileta, *Choosing Marriage: Why It Has to Start with We > Me* (Eugene, OR: Harvest House, 2018), 159.

Chapter 1: The Song of All Songs

1. David Schnarch, *Resurrecting Sex: Solving Sexual Problems and Revolutionizing Your Relationship* (New York: Quill, 2003), 83.
2. Schnarch, *Resurrecting Sex*, 83.
3. Bruce Waltke, *The Book of Proverbs: Chapters 1–15*, New International Commentary on the Old Testament (Grand Rapids: Eerdmans, 2004), 320.
4. F. Delitzsch, "Proverbs," in *Commentary on the Old Testament*, ed. C. F. Keil and F. Delitzsch (Edinburgh: T&T Clark, 1872), 131, http://faculty.gordon.edu/hu/bi/ted_hildebrandt/otesources/20-proverbs/Text/Books/Delitzsch_Proverbs/Delitzsch_Proverbs_v1.htm.
5. Quoted in Waltke, *Book of Proverbs*, 322.
6. Waltke, *Book of Proverbs*, 322, italics in original.

Chapter 2: Sexpectations

1. Debra Fileta, *Choosing Marriage: Why It Has to Start with We > Me* (Eugene, OR: Harvest House, 2018), 156.
2. The authors want to thank Rob Hardman for giving us this line when he reviewed an early draft of this book.

Chapter 3: Your Body Is a Wonderland

1. See David Schnarch, *Resurrecting Sex: Solving Sexual Problems and Revolutionizing Your Relationship* (New York: Quill, 2003), 50.
2. See S. Marie Harvey, "Female Sexual Behavior: Fluctuations during the Menstrual Cycle," *Journal of Psychosomatic Research* 31, no. 1 (1987): 101–10, www.sciencedirect.com/science/article/abs/pii/0022399987901048.

Chapter 4: What Gets Him Going

1. Louann Brizendine, *The Male Brain: A Breakthrough Understanding of How Men and Boys Think* (New York: Three Rivers, 2010), 4.
2. See Donatella Marazziti et al., "Sex-Related Differences in Plasma Oxytocin Levels in Humans," *Clinical Practice and Epidemiology in Mental Health* 15 (March 2019): 58–63, https://clinical-practice-and-epidemiology-in-mental-health.com/VOLUME/15/PAGE/58/FULLTEXT; see also Heon-Jin Lee et al., "Oxytocin: The Great Facilitator of Life," *Progress in Neurobiology* 88, no. 2 (June 2010): 127–51, www.ncbi.nlm.nih.gov/pmc/articles/PMC2689929.
3. Earl Henslin, *This Is Your Brain in Love: New Scientific Breakthroughs for a More Passionate and Emotionally Healthy Marriage* (Nashville: Nelson, 2009), 9.
4. Shaunti Feldhahn, "When Your Husband Wants Sex . . . Again," January 10, 2018, https://shaunti.com/2018/01/husband-wants-sexagain.

Chapter 5: What Gets Her Going

1. See Kory Floyd et al., "Kissing in Marital and Cohabiting Relationships: Effects on Blood Lipids, Stress, and Relationship Satisfaction," *Western Journal of Communication* 73, no. 2 (April 2009): 113–33, www.tandfonline.com/doi/abs/10.1080/10570310902856071.
2. See, for example, Samantha A. Wagner et al., "Touch Me Just Enough: The Intersection of Adult Attachment, Intimate Touch, and Marital Satisfaction," *Journal of Social and Personal Relationships* 37, no. 6 (March 2020), https://journals.sagepub.com/doi/10.1177/0265407520910791.
3. Quoted in Ruth Buezis, *Awaken Love: The Truth about Sex That Will Transform Your Marriage* (Minneapolis: Awaken-Love, 2018), 167.

Chapter 6: What Gets *You* Going

1. See Daniel Amen, *Sex on the Brain: 12 Lessons to Enhance Your Love Life* (New York: Three Rivers, 2007), 8.
2. A 2014 Barna Group survey revealed that in the United States, 65 percent of non-Christian men and 64 percent of Christian men looked at pornography at least once a month; see Dan Armstrong, "The Real Answer to 'Do All Men Watch Porn?'" July 30, 2018, www.covenanteyes.com/2018/07/30/do-all-men-watch-porn.

Chapter 7: Choose Your Own Adventure

1. Douglas Rosenau's book *Celebration of Sex: A Guide to Enjoying God's Gift of Sexual Intimacy*, rev. ed. (Nashville: Nelson, 2002), offers clear descriptions with realistic line drawings. For an easy online resource, consider www.christianfriendlysexpositions.com.
2. Rosenau, *Celebration of Sex*, 141.

Chapter 8: The Five Senses of Sex

1. Dan B. Allender and Tremper Longman III, *God Loves Sex: An Honest Conversation about Sexual Desire and Holiness* (Grand Rapids: Baker, 2014), 45.
2. Allender and Longman, *God Loves Sex*, 45; they cite Bruce J. Ellis and Donald Symons, "Sex Differences in Sexual Fantasy: An Evolutionary Psychological Approach," *Journal of Sex Research* 27 (1990): 527–55.
3. See Yella Hewings-Martin, "The Female Orgasm: What Do Women Want?" *Medical News Today*, October 6, 2017, www.medicalnewstoday.com/articles/319671.
4. Daniel Amen, *Sex on the Brain: 12 Lessons to Enhance Your Love Life* (New York: Three Rivers, 2007), 81.
5. Cited in Amen, *Sex on the Brain*, 163.
6. Quoted in David Nield, "The Human Brain Can Locate the Sensation of Touch Even beyond the Body. Here's How," *Science Alert*, December 30, 2019, www.sciencealert.com/the-human-brain-can-locate-the-sensation-of-touch-even-beyond-the-body.
7. Quoted in Sydnee Lyons, "Listening to Music during Sex Has These Three Effects on Your Body and Brain," *Elite Daily*, March 27, 2018.
8. Quoted in Lyons, "Listening to Music."
9. Amen, *Sex on the Brain*, 157.

10. Cited in Amen, *Sex on the Brain*, 157–58.
11. Dr. Michael Fenster, "Food and Sex: Why We Are Hard-Wired for Food Pleasure," *Psychology Today*, February 27, 2017, www.psychologytoday.com/us/blog/you-are-what-you-eat/201702/food-and-sex.
12. Amen, *Sex on the Brain*, 58.
13. Cited in Amen, *Sex on the Brain*, 58; see also pp. 154–55.
14. Cited in Amen, *Sex on the Brain*, 155.
15. See Amen, *Sex on the Brain*, 155.
16. Ruth Buezis, *Awaken Love: The Truth about Sex That Will Transform Your Marriage* (Minneapolis: Awaken-Love, 2018), 221.
17. Dr. David Schnarch, *Resurrecting Sex: Solving Sexual Problems and Revolutionizing Your Relationship* (New York: Quill, 2003), 83.
18. See Schnarch, *Resurrecting Sex*, 32–33, 83–84.

Chapter 9: En Gedi Sex

1. See Esther Perel, *Mating in Captivity: Unlocking Erotic Intelligence* (New York: HarperCollins, 2006), 159.
2. Quoted in Perel, *Mating in Captivity*, 79.

Chapter 11: Problem Spots

1. Cited in Debra Fileta, *Choosing Marriage: Why It Has to Start with We > Me* (Eugene, OR: Harvest House, 2018), 160–61.
2. See Patrick Carnes, *Sexual Anorexia: Overcoming Sexual Self-Hatred* (Center City, MN: Hazelden, 1997).
3. Dr. David Schnarch, *Resurrecting Sex: Solving Sexual Problems and Revolutionizing Your Relationship* (New York: Quill, 2003).
4. Schnarch, *Resurrecting Sex*, 66.

Chapter 12: Shades of Gray

1. For a detailed discussion of masturbation, check out pages 141–63 in Dr. Les Parrott's book *Crazy Good Sex: Putting to Bed the Myths Men Have about Sex* (Grand Rapids: Zondervan, 2009). It's the most thorough discussion I've ever read on this issue from a Christian perspective.
2. Mark Laaser, "The Secret That Ruins Great Sex: Masturbation," True Love Dates, May 5, 2015, https://truelovedates.com/the-secret-that-ruins-great-sex-masturbation.

Chapter 13: Going Backward to Go Forward

1. Quoted in Debra Fileta, "Your Identity Impacts Relationships, with Christine Caine," *Love + Relationships* podcast, August 10, 2020, https://truelovedates.com/identity-christine-caine-podcast.
2. See Catherine Pittman and Elizabeth Karle, *Rewire Your Anxious Brain: How to Use the Neuroscience of Fear to End Anxiety, Panic, and Worry* (Oakland, CA: New Harbinger, 2015), 6.
3. Debra Fileta, *Are You Really OK? Getting Real about Who You Are, How You're Doing, and Why It Matters* (Eugene, OR: Harvest House, 2021).

Chapter 14: Above the Sheets

1. Debra Fileta, *Choosing Marriage: Why It Has to Start with We > Me* (Eugene, OR: Harvest House, 2018), 62.
2. For in-depth discussions about ways to strengthen the relational health of your marriage, I recommend Gary's book *Cherish* (Grand Rapids: Zondervan, 2017) and my book *Choosing Marriage.*
3. Debra Fileta, *Are You Really OK? Getting Real about Who You Are, How You're Doing, and Why It Matters* (Eugene, OR: Harvest House, 2021).

Chapter 15: Better People, Better Sex

1. Giuseppe Scimeca et al., "Anger and Sexual Behavior," in *Psychology of Anger: Symptoms, Causes, and Coping*, ed. James P. Welty (Hauppauge, NY: Nova Science, 2011), 231–41, www.researchgate.net/publication/248556281_Anger_and_Sexual_Behavior.
2. Scimeca, et al., "Anger and Sexual Behavior."
3. Alexander Strauch, *Leading with Love* (Littleton, CO: Lewis and Roth, 2006), 44.
4. Esther Perel, *Mating in Captivity: Unlocking Erotic Intelligence* (New York: HarperCollins, 2006), 96.
5. Tim Alan Gardner, *Sacred Sex: A Spiritual Celebration of Oneness in Marriage* (Colorado Springs, CO: WaterBrook, 2002), 191.
6. Gardner, *Sacred Sex*, 192.
7. David Schnarch, *Resurrecting Sex: Solving Sexual Problems and Revolutionizing Your Relationship* (New York: Quill, 2003), 278.
8. Schnarch, *Resurrecting Sex*, 278–79.

9. Schnarch, *Resurrecting Sex*, 276.
10. Schnarch, *Resurrecting Sex*, 277.
11. Schnarch, *Resurrecting Sex*, 279, italics in original.